Borg Backup 1.1.0 Reference Manual

A catalogue record for this book is available from the Hong Kong Public Libraries.

Published in Hong Kong by Samurai Media Limited.

Email: info@samuraimedia.org

ISBN 978-988-8407-32-3

Background Cover Image by https://www.flickr.com/people/webtreatsetc/

Contents

CHAPTER 1

Introduction

More screencasts: installation[6], advanced usage[7]

What is BorgBackup?

BorgBackup (short: Borg) is a deduplicating backup program. Optionally, it supports compression and authenticated encryption.

The main goal of Borg is to provide an efficient and secure way to backup data. The data deduplication technique used makes Borg suitable for daily backups since only changes are stored. The authenticated encryption technique makes it suitable for backups to not fully trusted targets.

See the installation manual[8] or, if you have already downloaded Borg, `docs/installation.rst` to get started with Borg.

Main features

Space efficient storage Deduplication based on content-defined chunking is used to reduce the number of bytes stored: each file is split into a number of variable length chunks and only chunks that have never been seen before are added to the repository.

A chunk is considered duplicate if its id_hash value is identical. A cryptographically strong hash or MAC function is used as id_hash, e.g. (hmac-)sha256.

To deduplicate, all the chunks in the same repository are considered, no matter whether they come from different machines, from previous backups, from the same backup or even from the same single file.

Compared to other deduplication approaches, this method does NOT depend on:

- file/directory names staying the same: So you can move your stuff around without killing the deduplication, even between machines sharing a repo.

---

[5] https://asciinema.org/a/133292?autoplay=1&speed=1
[6] https://asciinema.org/a/133291?autoplay=1&speed=1
[7] https://asciinema.org/a/133293?autoplay=1&speed=1
[8] https://borgbackup.readthedocs.org/en/stable/installation.html

---

- complete files or time stamps staying the same: If a big file changes a little, only a few new chunks need to be stored - this is great for VMs or raw disks.

- The absolute position of a data chunk inside a file: Stuff may get shifted and will still be found by the deduplication algorithm.

Speed

- performance critical code (chunking, compression, encryption) is implemented in C/Cython

- local caching of files/chunks index data

- quick detection of unmodified files

Data encryption All data can be protected using 256-bit AES encryption, data integrity and authenticity is verified using HMAC-SHA256. Data is encrypted clientside.

Compression All data can be compressed by lz4 (super fast, low compression), zlib (medium speed and compression) or lzma (low speed, high compression).

Off-site backups Borg can store data on any remote host accessible over SSH. If Borg is installed on the remote host, big performance gains can be achieved compared to using a network filesystem (sshfs, nfs, ...).

Backups mountable as filesystems Backup archives are mountable as userspace filesystems for easy interactive backup examination and restores (e.g. by using a regular file manager).

Easy installation on multiple platforms We offer single-file binaries that do not require installing anything - you can just run them on these platforms:

- Linux

- Mac OS X

- FreeBSD

- OpenBSD and NetBSD (no xattrs/ACLs support or binaries yet)

- Cygwin (not supported, no binaries yet)

- Linux Subsystem of Windows 10 (not supported)

Free and Open Source Software

- security and functionality can be audited independently

- licensed under the BSD (3-clause) license, see License[9] for the complete license

Easy to use

Initialize a new backup repository and create a backup archive:

```
$ borg init /path/to/repo
$ borg create /path/to/repo::Saturday1 ~/Documents
```

Now doing another backup, just to show off the great deduplication:

```
$ borg create -v --stats /path/to/repo::Saturday2 ~/Documents
------------------------------------------------------------------------
Archive name: Saturday2
Archive fingerprint: 622b7c53c...
Time (start): Sat, 2016-02-27 14:48:13
Time (end):   Sat, 2016-02-27 14:48:14
Duration: 0.88 seconds
Number of files: 163
------------------------------------------------------------------------
               Original size      Compressed size     Deduplicated size
```

---

[9] https://borgbackup.readthedocs.org/en/stable/authors.html#license

```
This archive:          6.85 MB              6.85 MB            30.79 kB  <-- !
All archives:         13.69 MB             13.71 MB             6.88 MB

                  Unique chunks        Total chunks
Chunk index:             167                  330
------------------------------------------------------------------------------
```

For a graphical frontend refer to our complementary project BorgWeb[10].

Helping, Donations and Bounties

Your help is always welcome! Spread the word, give feedback, help with documentation, testing or development.
You can also give monetary support to the project, see there for details:

https://borgbackup.readthedocs.io/en/stable/support.html#bounties-and-fundraisers

Links

- Main Web Site[11]
- Releases[12], PyPI packages[13] and ChangeLog[14]
- GitHub[15] and Issue Tracker[16].
- Web-Chat (IRC)[17] and Mailing List[18]
- License[19]
- Security contact[20]

Compatibility notes

EXPECT THAT WE WILL BREAK COMPATIBILITY REPEATEDLY WHEN MAJOR RELEASE NUMBER CHANGES (like when going from 0.x.y to 1.0.0 or from 1.x.y to 2.0.0).

NOT RELEASED DEVELOPMENT VERSIONS HAVE UNKNOWN COMPATIBILITY PROPERTIES.

THIS IS SOFTWARE IN DEVELOPMENT, DECIDE YOURSELF WHETHER IT FITS YOUR NEEDS.

Security issues should be reported to the Security contact[21] (or see `docs/suppport.rst` in the source distribution).

[22][23][24][25][26]

---

[10] https://borgweb.readthedocs.io/
[11] https://borgbackup.readthedocs.org/
[12] https://github.com/borgbackup/borg/releases
[13] https://pypi.python.org/pypi/borgbackup
[14] https://github.com/borgbackup/borg/blob/master/docs/changes.rst
[15] https://github.com/borgbackup/borg
[16] https://github.com/borgbackup/borg/issues
[17] http://webchat.freenode.net/?randomnick=1&channels=%23borgbackup&uio=MTY9dHJ1ZSY5PXRydWUa8
[18] https://mail.python.org/mailman/listinfo/borgbackup
[19] https://borgbackup.readthedocs.org/en/stable/authors.html#license
[20] https://borgbackup.readthedocs.io/en/latest/support.html#security-contact
[21] https://borgbackup.readthedocs.io/en/latest/support.html#security-contact
[22] https://borgbackup.readthedocs.org/en/stable/
[23] https://travis-ci.org/borgbackup/borg
[24] https://codecov.io/github/borgbackup/borg?branch=master
[25] https://bestpractices.coreinfrastructure.org/projects/271
[26] https://www.bountysource.com/teams/borgbackup

## CHAPTER 2

Installation

There are different ways to install Borg:

- *Distribution Package* - easy and fast if a package is available from your distribution.

- *Standalone Binary* - easy and fast, we provide a ready-to-use binary file that comes bundled with all dependencies.

- *From Source*, either:

  - *Using pip* - installing a source package with pip needs more installation steps and requires all dependencies with development headers and a compiler.

  - *Using git* - for developers and power users who want to have the latest code or use revision control (each release is tagged).

Distribution Package

Some distributions might offer a ready-to-use `borgbackup` package which can be installed with the package manager.

Important: Those packages may not be up to date with the latest Borg releases. Before submitting a bug report, check the package version and compare that to our latest release then review *Important notes* to see if the bug has been fixed. Report bugs to the package maintainer rather than directly to Borg if the package is out of date in the distribution.

Distribution	Source	Command
Arch Linux	[community][33]	`pacman -S borg`
Debian	Debian packages[34]	`apt install borgbackup`
Gentoo	ebuild[35]	`emerge borgbackup`
GNU Guix	GNU Guix[36]	`guix package --install borg`
Fedora/RHEL	Fedora official repository[37]	`dnf install borgbackup`
FreeBSD	FreeBSD ports[38]	`cd /usr/ports/ archivers/py-borgbackup && make install clean`
Mageia	cauldron[39]	`urpmi borgbackup`
NetBSD	pkgsrc[40]	`pkg_add py-borgbackup`
NixOS	.nix file[41]	N/A
OpenBSD	OpenBSD ports[42]	`pkg_add borgbackup`
OpenIndiana	OpenIndiana hipster repository[43]	`pkg install borg`
openSUSE	openSUSE official repository[44]	`zypper in borgbackup`
OS X	Brew cask[45]	`brew cask install borgbackup`
Raspbian	Raspbian testing[46]	`apt install borgbackup`
Ubuntu	Ubuntu packages[47], Ubuntu PPA[48]	`apt install borgbackup`

Please ask package maintainers to build a package or, if you can package / submit it yourself, please help us with that! See #105[49] on github to followup on packaging efforts.

Standalone Binary

Note: Releases are signed with an OpenPGP key, see *Security* for more instructions.

Borg binaries (generated with pyinstaller[50]) are available on the releases[51] page for the following platforms:

- **Linux**: glibc >= 2.13 (ok for most supported Linux releases). Older glibc releases are untested and may not work.

- **Mac OS X**: 10.10 (does not work with older OS X releases)

- **FreeBSD**: 10.2 (unknown whether it works for older releases)

To install such a binary, just drop it into a directory in your PATH, make borg readable and executable for its users and then you can run borg:

[33] https://www.archlinux.org/packages/?name=borg
[34] https://packages.debian.org/search?keywords=borgbackup&searchon=names&exact=1&suite=all&section=all
[35] https://packages.gentoo.org/packages/app-backup/borgbackup
[36] https://www.gnu.org/software/guix/package-list.html#borg
[37] https://apps.fedoraproject.org/packages/borgbackup
[38] http://www.freshports.org/archivers/py-borgbackup/
[39] http://madb.mageia.org/package/show/application/0/release/cauldron/name/borgbackup
[40] http://pkgsrc.se/sysutils/py-borgbackup
[41] https://github.com/NixOS/nixpkgs/blob/master/pkgs/tools/backup/borg/default.nix
[42] http://cvsweb.openbsd.org/cgi-bin/cvsweb/ports/sysutils/borgbackup/
[43] http://pkg.openindiana.org/hipster/en/search.shtml?token=borg&action=Search
[44] http://software.opensuse.org/package/borgbackup
[45] https://caskroom.github.io/
[46] http://archive.raspbian.org/raspbian/pool/main/b/borgbackup/
[47] http://packages.ubuntu.com/xenial/borgbackup
[48] https://launchpad.net/~costamagnagianfranco/+archive/ubuntu/borgbackup
[49] https://github.com/borgbackup/borg/issues/105
[50] http://www.pyinstaller.org
[51] https://github.com/borgbackup/borg/releases

```
sudo cp borg-linux64 /usr/local/bin/borg
sudo chown root:root /usr/local/bin/borg
sudo chmod 755 /usr/local/bin/borg
```

Optionally you can create a symlink to have `borgfs` available, which is an alias for `borg mount`:

```
ln -s /usr/local/bin/borg /usr/local/bin/borgfs
```

Note that the binary uses /tmp to unpack Borg with all dependencies. It will fail if /tmp has not enough free space or is mounted with the `noexec` option. You can change the temporary directory by setting the `TEMP` environment variable before running Borg.

If a new version is released, you will have to manually download it and replace the old version using the same steps as shown above.

From Source

Note: Some older Linux systems (like RHEL/CentOS 5) and Python interpreter binaries compiled to be able to run on such systems (like Python installed via Anaconda) might miss functions required by Borg.

This issue will be detected early and Borg will abort with a fatal error.

Dependencies

To install Borg from a source package (including pip), you have to install the following dependencies first:

- Python 3[52] >= 3.4.0, plus development headers. Even though Python 3 is not the default Python version on most systems, it is usually available as an optional install.
- OpenSSL[53] >= 1.0.0, plus development headers.
- libacl[54] (which depends on libattr[55]), both plus development headers.
- liblz4[56], plus development headers.
- some Python dependencies, pip will automatically install them for you
- optionally, the llfuse[57] Python package is required if you wish to mount an archive as a FUSE filesystem. See setup.py about the version requirements.
- optionally libb2[58]. If it is not found a bundled implementation is used instead.

If you have troubles finding the right package names, have a look at the distribution specific sections below or the Vagrantfile in the git repository, which contains installation scripts for a number of operating systems.

In the following, the steps needed to install the dependencies are listed for a selection of platforms. If your distribution is not covered by these instructions, try to use your package manager to install the dependencies. On FreeBSD, you may need to get a recent enough OpenSSL version from FreeBSD ports.

After you have installed the dependencies, you can proceed with steps outlined under *Using pip*.

---

[52] https://www.python.org/
[53] https://www.openssl.org/
[54] https://savannah.nongnu.org/projects/acl/
[55] https://savannah.nongnu.org/projects/attr/
[56] https://github.com/Cyan4973/lz4
[57] https://pypi.python.org/pypi/llfuse/
[58] https://github.com/BLAKE2/libb2

Debian / Ubuntu

Install the dependencies with development headers:

```
sudo apt-get install python3 python3-dev python3-pip python-virtualenv \
libssl-dev openssl \
libacl1-dev libacl1 \
liblz4-dev liblz4-1 \
build-essential
sudo apt-get install libfuse-dev fuse pkg-config    # optional, for FUSE support
```

In case you get complaints about permission denied on /etc/fuse.conf: on Ubuntu this means your user is not in the fuse group. Add yourself to that group, log out and log in again.

Fedora / Korora

Install the dependencies with development headers:

```
sudo dnf install python3 python3-devel python3-pip python3-virtualenv
sudo dnf install openssl-devel openssl
sudo dnf install libacl-devel libacl
sudo dnf install lz4-devel
sudo dnf install gcc gcc-c++
sudo dnf install redhat-rpm-config          # not needed in Korora
sudo dnf install fuse-devel fuse pkgconfig  # optional, for FUSE support
```

openSUSE Tumbleweed / Leap

Install the dependencies automatically using zypper:

```
sudo zypper source-install --build-deps-only borgbackup
```

Alternatively, you can enumerate all build dependencies in the command line:

```
sudo zypper install python3 python3-devel \
libacl-devel liblz4-devel openssl-devel \
python3-Cython python3-Sphinx python3-msgpack-python \
python3-pytest python3-setuptools python3-setuptools_scm \
python3-sphinx_rtd_theme python3-llfuse gcc gcc-c++
```

Mac OS X

Assuming you have installed homebrew[59], the following steps will install all the dependencies:

```
brew install python3 lz4 openssl
brew install pkg-config                         # optional, for FUSE support
pip3 install virtualenv
```

For FUSE support to mount the backup archives, you need at least version 3.0 of FUSE for OS X, which is available as a pre-release[60].

FreeBSD

Listed below are packages you will need to install Borg, its dependencies, and commands to make FUSE work for using the mount command.

---

[59] http://brew.sh/
[60] https://github.com/osxfuse/osxfuse/releases

```
pkg install -y python3 openssl liblz4 fusefs-libs pkgconf
pkg install -y git
python3.4 -m ensurepip # to install pip for Python3
To use the mount command:
echo 'fuse_load="YES"' >> /boot/loader.conf
echo 'vfs.usermount=1' >> /etc/sysctl.conf
kldload fuse
sysctl vfs.usermount=1
```

Windows 10's Linux Subsystem

Note: Running under Windows 10's Linux Subsystem is experimental and has not been tested much yet.

Just follow the Ubuntu Linux installation steps. You can omit the FUSE stuff, it won't work anyway.

Cygwin

Note: Running under Cygwin is experimental and has only been tested with Cygwin (x86-64) v2.5.2. Remote repositories are known broken, local repositories should work.

Use the Cygwin installer to install the dependencies:

```
python3 python3-devel python3-setuptools
binutils gcc-g++
libopenssl openssl-devel
liblz4_1 liblz4-devel
git make openssh
```

You can then install pip and virtualenv:

```
easy_install-3.4 pip
pip install virtualenv
```

Using pip

Virtualenv[61] can be used to build and install Borg without affecting the system Python or requiring root access. Using a virtual environment is optional, but recommended except for the most simple use cases.

Note: If you install into a virtual environment, you need to **activate** it first (source borg-env/bin/activate), before running borg. Alternatively, symlink borg-env/bin/borg into some directory that is in your PATH so you can just run borg.

This will use pip to install the latest release from PyPi:

```
virtualenv --python=python3 borg-env
source borg-env/bin/activate

# install Borg + Python dependencies into virtualenv
pip install borgbackup
# or alternatively (if you want FUSE support):
pip install borgbackup[fuse]
```

---

[61] https://pypi.python.org/pypi/virtualenv/

To upgrade Borg to a new version later, run the following after activating your virtual environment:

```
pip install -U borgbackup  # or ... borgbackup[fuse]
```

Using git

This uses latest, unreleased development code from git. While we try not to break master, there are no guarantees on anything.

```
# get borg from github
git clone https://github.com/borgbackup/borg.git

virtualenv --python=python3 borg-env
source borg-env/bin/activate   # always before using!

# install borg + dependencies into virtualenv
cd borg
pip install -r requirements.d/development.txt
pip install -r requirements.d/docs.txt  # optional, to build the docs
pip install -r requirements.d/fuse.txt  # optional, for FUSE support
pip install -e .  # in-place editable mode

# optional: run all the tests, on all supported Python versions
# requires fakeroot, available through your package manager
fakeroot -u tox
```

Note: As a developer or power user, you always want to use a virtual environment.

## CHAPTER 3

Quick Start

This chapter will get you started with Borg and covers various use cases.

A step by step example

1. Before a backup can be made a repository has to be initialized:

   ```
   $ borg init --encryption=repokey /path/to/repo
   ```

2. Backup the ~/src and ~/Documents directories into an archive called *Monday*:

   ```
   $ borg create /path/to/repo::Monday ~/src ~/Documents
   ```

3. The next day create a new archive called *Tuesday*:

   ```
   $ borg create --stats /path/to/repo::Tuesday ~/src ~/Documents
   ```

   This backup will be a lot quicker and a lot smaller since only new never before seen data is stored. The --stats option causes Borg to output statistics about the newly created archive such as the amount of unique data (not shared with other archives):

   ```
   ------------------------------------------------------------------------------
   Archive name: Tuesday
   Archive fingerprint:
    bd31004d58f51ea06ff735d2e5ac49376901b21d58035f8fb05dbf866566e3c2
   Time (start): Tue, 2016-02-16 18:15:11
   Time (end):   Tue, 2016-02-16 18:15:11

   Duration: 0.19 seconds
   Number of files: 127
   ------------------------------------------------------------------------------
                      Original size      Compressed size     Deduplicated size
   This archive:           4.16 MB              4.17 MB               26.78 kB
   All archives:           8.33 MB              8.34 MB                4.19 MB

                      Unique chunks        Total chunks
   Chunk index:                 132                 261
   ------------------------------------------------------------------------------
   ```

4. List all archives in the repository:

```
$ borg list /path/to/repo
Monday                              Mon, 2016-02-15 19:14:44
Tuesday                             Tue, 2016-02-16 19:15:11
```

5. List the contents of the *Monday* archive:

```
$ borg list /path/to/repo::Monday
drwxr-xr-x user    group          0 Mon, 2016-02-15 18:22:30 home/user/Documents
-rw-r--r-- user    group       7961 Mon, 2016-02-15 18:22:30 home/user/
⌐Documents/Important.doc
...
```

6. Restore the *Monday* archive by extracting the files relative to the current directory:

```
$ borg extract /path/to/repo::Monday
```

7. Recover disk space by manually deleting the *Monday* archive:

```
$ borg delete /path/to/repo::Monday
```

Note: Borg is quiet by default (it works on WARNING log level). You can use options like --progress or --list to get specific reports during command execution. You can also add the -v (or --verbose or --info) option to adjust the log level to INFO to get other informational messages.

Important note about free space

Before you start creating backups, please make sure that there is *always* a good amount of free space on the filesystem that has your backup repository (and also on ~/.cache). A few GB should suffice for most hard-drive sized repositories. See also *Indexes / Caches memory usage*.

Borg doesn't use space reserved for root on repository disks (even when run as root), on file systems which do not support this mechanism (e.g. XFS) we recommend to reserve some space in Borg itself just to be safe by adjusting the additional_free_space setting in the [repository] section of a repositories config file. A good starting point is 2G.

If Borg runs out of disk space, it tries to free as much space as it can while aborting the current operation safely, which allows to free more space by deleting/pruning archives. This mechanism is not bullet-proof in some circumstances[1].

If you *really* run out of disk space, it can be hard or impossible to free space, because Borg needs free space to operate - even to delete backup archives.

You can use some monitoring process or just include the free space information in your backup log files (you check them regularly anyway, right?).

Also helpful:

- create a big file as a "space reserve", that you can delete to free space

- if you use LVM: use a LV + a filesystem that you can resize later and have some unallocated PEs you can add to the LV.

- consider using quotas

---

[1] This failsafe can fail in these circumstances:

- The underlying file system doesn't support statvfs(2), or returns incorrect data, or the repository doesn't reside on a single file system
- Other tasks fill the disk simultaneously
- Hard quotas (which may not be reflected in statvfs(2))

- use *prune* regularly

Automating backups

The following example script is meant to be run daily by the `root` user on different local machines. It backs up a machine's important files (but not the complete operating system) to a repository `~/backup/main` on a remote server. Some files which aren't necessarily needed in this backup are excluded. See *borg help patterns* on how to add more exclude options.

After the backup this script also uses the *borg prune* subcommand to keep only a certain number of old archives and deletes the others in order to preserve disk space.

Before running, make sure that the repository is initialized as documented in *Remote repositories* and that the script has the correct permissions to be executable by the root user, but not executable or readable by anyone else, i.e. root:root 0700.

You can use this script as a starting point and modify it where it's necessary to fit your setup.

Do not forget to test your created backups to make sure everything you need is being backed up and that the `prune` command is keeping and deleting the correct backups.

```sh
#!/bin/sh

# Setting this, so the repo does not need to be given on the commandline:
export BORG_REPO=ssh://username@example.com:2022/~/backup/main

# Setting this, so you won't be asked for your repository passphrase:
export BORG_PASSPHRASE='XYZl0ngandsecurepa_55_phrasea&&123'
# or this to ask an external program to supply the passphrase:
export BORG_PASSCOMMAND='pass show backup'

# some helpers and error handling:
info() { printf "\n%s %s\n\n" "$( date )" "$*" >&2; }
trap 'echo $( date ) Backup interrupted >&2; exit 2' INT TERM

info "Starting backup"

# Backup the most important directories into an archive named after
# the machine this script is currently running on:

borg create                             \
    --verbose                           \
    --filter AME                        \
    --list                              \
    --stats                             \
    --show-rc                           \
    --compression lz4                   \
    --exclude-caches                    \
    --exclude '/home/*/.cache/*'        \
    --exclude '/var/cache/*'            \
    --exclude '/var/tmp/*'              \
                                        \
    ::'{hostname}-{now}'                \
    /etc                                \
    /home                               \
    /root                               \
    /var                                \

backup_exit=$?

info "Pruning repository"
```

```
# Use the `prune` subcommand to maintain 7 daily, 4 weekly and 6 monthly
# archives of THIS machine. The '{hostname}-' prefix is very important to
# limit prune's operation to this machine's archives and not apply to
# other machines' archives also:

borg prune                          \
    --list                          \
    --prefix '{hostname}-'          \
    --show-rc                       \
    --keep-daily    7               \
    --keep-weekly   4               \
    --keep-monthly  6               \

prune_exit=$?

# use highest exit code as global exit code
global_exit=$(( backup_exit > prune_exit ? backup_exit : prune_exit ))

if [ ${global_exit} -eq 1 ];
then
    info "Backup and/or Prune finished with a warning"
fi

if [ ${global_exit} -gt 1 ];
then
    info "Backup and/or Prune finished with an error"
fi

exit ${global_exit}
```

Pitfalls with shell variables and environment variables

This applies to all environment variables you want borg to see, not just BORG_PASSPHRASE. The short explanation is: always export your variable, and use single quotes if you're unsure of the details of your shell's expansion behavior. E.g.:

```
export BORG_PASSPHRASE='complicated & long'
```

This is because export exposes variables to subprocesses, which borg may be one of. More on export can be found in the "ENVIRONMENT" section of the bash(1) man page.

Beware of how sudo interacts with environment variables. For example, you may be surprised that the following export has no effect on your command:

```
export BORG_PASSPHRASE='complicated & long'
sudo ./yourborgwrapper.sh   # still prompts for password
```

For more information, refer to the sudo(8) man page and env_keep in the sudoers(5) man page.

Tip: To debug what your borg process is actually seeing, find its PID (ps aux|grep borg) and then look into /proc/<PID>/environ.

Backup compression

The default is lz4 (very fast, but low compression ratio), but other methods are supported for different situations.

If you have a fast repo storage and you want minimum CPU usage, no compression:

```
$ borg create --compression none /path/to/repo::arch ~
```

If you have a less fast repo storage and you want a bit more compression (N=0..9, 0 means no compression, 9 means high compression):

```
$ borg create --compression zlib,N /path/to/repo::arch ~
```

If you have a very slow repo storage and you want high compression (N=0..9, 0 means low compression, 9 means high compression):

```
$ borg create --compression lzma,N /path/to/repo::arch ~
```

You'll need to experiment a bit to find the best compression for your use case. Keep an eye on CPU load and throughput.

Repository encryption

Repository encryption can be enabled or disabled at repository creation time (the default is enabled, with *repokey* method):

```
$ borg init --encryption=none|repokey|keyfile PATH
```

When repository encryption is enabled all data is encrypted using 256-bit AES[62] encryption and the integrity and authenticity is verified using HMAC-SHA256[63].

All data is encrypted on the client before being written to the repository. This means that an attacker who manages to compromise the host containing an encrypted archive will not be able to access any of the data, even while the backup is being made.

Borg supports different methods to store the AES and HMAC keys.

repokey mode The key is stored inside the repository (in its "config" file). Use this mode if you trust in your good passphrase giving you enough protection. The repository server never sees the plaintext key.

keyfile mode The key is stored on your local disk (in ~/.config/borg/keys/). Use this mode if you want "passphrase and having-the-key" security.

In both modes, the key is stored in encrypted form and can be only decrypted by providing the correct passphrase.

For automated backups the passphrase can be specified using the *BORG_PASSPHRASE* environment variable.

Note: Be careful about how you set that environment, see *this note about password environments* for more information.

> **Warning:** The repository data is totally inaccessible without the key and the key passphrase.
>
> Make a backup copy of the key file (keyfile mode) or repo config file (repokey mode) and keep it at a safe place, so you still have the key in case it gets corrupted or lost. Also keep your passphrase at a safe place.
>
> You can make backups using *borg key export* subcommand.
>
> If you want to print a backup of your key to paper use the --paper option of this command and print the result, or this print template if you need a version with QR-Code.
>
> A backup inside of the backup that is encrypted with that key/passphrase won't help you with that, of course.

---

[62] https://en.wikipedia.org/wiki/Advanced_Encryption_Standard
[63] https://en.wikipedia.org/wiki/HMAC

Remote repositories

Borg can initialize and access repositories on remote hosts if the host is accessible using SSH. This is fastest and easiest when Borg is installed on the remote host, in which case the following syntax is used:

```
$ borg init user@hostname:/path/to/repo
```

Note: please see the usage chapter for a full documentation of repo URLs.

Remote operations over SSH can be automated with SSH keys. You can restrict the use of the SSH keypair by prepending a forced command to the SSH public key in the remote server's *authorized_keys* file. This example will start Borg in server mode and limit it to a specific filesystem path:

```
command="borg serve --restrict-to-path /path/to/repo",restrict ssh-rsa AAAAB3[...]
```

If it is not possible to install Borg on the remote host, it is still possible to use the remote host to store a repository by mounting the remote filesystem, for example, using sshfs:

```
$ sshfs user@hostname:/path/to /path/to
$ borg init /path/to/repo
$ fusermount -u /path/to
```

You can also use other remote filesystems in a similar way. Just be careful, not all filesystems out there are really stable and working good enough to be acceptable for backup usage.

## CHAPTER 4

Usage

General

Borg consists of a number of commands. Each command accepts a number of arguments and options and interprets various environment variables. The following sections will describe each command in detail.

Commands, options, parameters, paths and such are `set in fixed-width`. Option values are *underlined*. Borg has few options accepting a fixed set of values (e.g. `--encryption` of *borg init*).

Experimental features are marked with red stripes on the sides, like this paragraph.

Experimental features are not stable, which means that they may be changed in incompatible ways or even removed entirely without prior notice in following releases.

Repository URLs

Local filesystem (or locally mounted network filesystem):

`/path/to/repo` - filesystem path to repo directory, absolute path

`path/to/repo` - filesystem path to repo directory, relative path

Also, stuff like `~/path/to/repo` or `~other/path/to/repo` works (this is expanded by your shell).

Note: you may also prepend a `file://` to a filesystem path to get URL style.

Remote repositories accessed via ssh user@host:

`user@host:/path/to/repo` - remote repo, absolute path

`ssh://user@host:port/path/to/repo` - same, alternative syntax, port can be given

Remote repositories with relative paths can be given using this syntax:

`user@host:path/to/repo` - path relative to current directory

`user@host:~/path/to/repo` - path relative to user's home directory

`user@host:~other/path/to/repo` - path relative to other's home directory

Note: giving `user@host:./path/to/repo` or `user@host:/~/path/to/repo` or `user@host:/~other/path/to/repo` is also supported, but not required here.

Remote repositories with relative paths, alternative syntax with port:

`ssh://user@host:port/./path/to/repo` - path relative to current directory

`ssh://user@host:port/~/path/to/repo` - path relative to user's home directory

`ssh://user@host:port/~other/path/to/repo` - path relative to other's home directory

If you frequently need the same repo URL, it is a good idea to set the `BORG_REPO` environment variable to set a default for the repo URL:

```
export BORG_REPO='ssh://user@host:port/path/to/repo'
```

Then just leave away the repo URL if only a repo URL is needed and you want to use the default - it will be read from BORG_REPO then.

Use `::` syntax to give the repo URL when syntax requires giving a positional argument for the repo (e.g. `borg mount :: /mnt`).

Repository / Archive Locations

Many commands want either a repository (just give the repo URL, see above) or an archive location, which is a repo URL followed by `::archive_name`.

Archive names must not contain the / (slash) character. For simplicity, maybe also avoid blanks or other characters that have special meaning on the shell or in a filesystem (borg mount will use the archive name as directory name).

If you have set BORG_REPO (see above) and an archive location is needed, use `::archive_name` - the repo URL part is then read from BORG_REPO.

Type of log output

The log level of the builtin logging configuration defaults to WARNING. This is because we want Borg to be mostly silent and only output warnings, errors and critical messages, unless output has been requested by supplying an option that implies output (e.g. `--list` or `--progress`).

Log levels: DEBUG < INFO < WARNING < ERROR < CRITICAL

Use `--debug` to set DEBUG log level - to get debug, info, warning, error and critical level output.

Use `--info` (or `-v` or `--verbose`) to set INFO log level - to get info, warning, error and critical level output.

Use `--warning` (default) to set WARNING log level - to get warning, error and critical level output.

Use `--error` to set ERROR log level - to get error and critical level output.

Use `--critical` to set CRITICAL log level - to get critical level output.

While you can set misc. log levels, do not expect that every command will give different output on different log levels - it's just a possibility.

Warning: Options `--critical` and `--error` are provided for completeness, their usage is not recommended as you might miss important information.

Return codes

Borg can exit with the following return codes (rc):

Return code	Meaning
0	success (logged as INFO)
1	warning (operation reached its normal end, but there were warnings – you should check the log, logged as WARNING)
2	error (like a fatal error, a local or remote exception, the operation did not reach its normal end, logged as ERROR)
128+N	killed by signal N (e.g. 137 == kill -9)

If you use `--show-rc`, the return code is also logged at the indicated level as the last log entry.

Environment Variables

Borg uses some environment variables for automation:

General:

BORG_REPO When set, use the value to give the default repository location. If a command needs an archive parameter, you can abbreviate as `::archive`. If a command needs a repository parameter, you can either leave it away or abbreviate as `::`, if a positional parameter is required.

BORG_PASSPHRASE When set, use the value to answer the passphrase question for encrypted repositories. It is used when a passphrase is needed to access an encrypted repo as well as when a new passphrase should be initially set when initializing an encrypted repo. See also BORG_NEW_PASSPHRASE.

BORG_PASSCOMMAND When set, use the standard output of the command (trailing newlines are stripped) to answer the passphrase question for encrypted repositories. It is used when a passphrase is needed to access an encrypted repo as well as when a new passphrase should be initially set when initializing an encrypted repo. If BORG_PASSPHRASE is also set, it takes precedence. See also BORG_NEW_PASSPHRASE.

BORG_NEW_PASSPHRASE When set, use the value to answer the passphrase question when a **new** passphrase is asked for. This variable is checked first. If it is not set, BORG_PASSPHRASE and BORG_PASSCOMMAND will also be checked. Main usecase for this is to fully automate `borg change-passphrase`.

BORG_DISPLAY_PASSPHRASE When set, use the value to answer the "display the passphrase for verification" question when defining a new passphrase for encrypted repositories.

BORG_HOSTNAME_IS_UNIQUE=no Borg assumes that it can derive a unique hostname / identity (see `borg debug info`). If this is not the case or you do not want Borg to automatically remove stale locks, set this to *no*.

BORG_LOGGING_CONF When set, use the given filename as INI[64]-style logging configuration.

BORG_RSH When set, use this command instead of `ssh`. This can be used to specify ssh options, such as a custom identity file `ssh -i /path/to/private/key`. See `man ssh` for other options.

BORG_REMOTE_PATH When set, use the given path as borg executable on the remote (defaults to "borg" if unset). Using `--remote-path PATH` commandline option overrides the environment variable.

BORG_FILES_CACHE_TTL When set to a numeric value, this determines the maximum "time to live" for the files cache entries (default: 20). The files cache is used to quickly determine whether a file is unchanged. The FAQ explains this more detailed in: *It always chunks all my files, even unchanged ones!*

TMPDIR where temporary files are stored (might need a lot of temporary space for some operations)

Some automatic "answerers" (if set, they automatically answer confirmation questions):

---

[64] https://docs.python.org/3.4/library/logging.config.html#configuration-file-format

BORG_UNKNOWN_UNENCRYPTED_REPO_ACCESS_IS_OK=no (or =yes) For "Warning: Attempting to access a previously unknown unencrypted repository"

BORG_RELOCATED_REPO_ACCESS_IS_OK=no (or =yes) For "Warning: The repository at location ... was previously located at ..."

BORG_CHECK_I_KNOW_WHAT_I_AM_DOING=NO (or =YES) For "Warning: 'check –repair' is an experimental feature that might result in data loss."

BORG_DELETE_I_KNOW_WHAT_I_AM_DOING=NO (or =YES) For "You requested to completely DELETE the repository *including* all archives it contains:"

BORG_RECREATE_I_KNOW_WHAT_I_AM_DOING=NO (or =YES) For "recreate is an experimental feature."

Note: answers are case sensitive. setting an invalid answer value might either give the default answer or ask you interactively, depending on whether retries are allowed (they by default are allowed). So please test your scripts interactively before making them a non-interactive script.

Directories and files:

BORG_KEYS_DIR Default to '~/.config/borg/keys'. This directory contains keys for encrypted repositories.

BORG_KEY_FILE When set, use the given filename as repository key file.

BORG_SECURITY_DIR Default to '~/.config/borg/security'. This directory contains information borg uses to track its usage of NONCES ("numbers used once" - usually in encryption context) and other security relevant data.

BORG_CACHE_DIR Default to '~/.cache/borg'. This directory contains the local cache and might need a lot of space for dealing with big repositories).

Building:

BORG_OPENSSL_PREFIX Adds given OpenSSL header file directory to the default locations (setup.py).

BORG_LZ4_PREFIX Adds given LZ4 header file directory to the default locations (setup.py).

BORG_LIBB2_PREFIX Adds given prefix directory to the default locations. If a 'include/blake2.h' is found Borg will be linked against the system libb2 instead of a bundled implementation. (setup.py)

Please note:

- be very careful when using the "yes" sayers, the warnings with prompt exist for your / your data's security/safety

- also be very careful when putting your passphrase into a script, make sure it has appropriate file permissions (e.g. mode 600, root:root).

File systems

We strongly recommend against using Borg (or any other database-like software) on non-journaling file systems like FAT, since it is not possible to assume any consistency in case of power failures (or a sudden disconnect of an external drive or similar failures).

While Borg uses a data store that is resilient against these failures when used on journaling file systems, it is not possible to guarantee this with some hardware – independent of the software used. We don't know a list of affected hardware.

If you are suspicious whether your Borg repository is still consistent and readable after one of the failures mentioned above occurred, run `borg check --verify-data` to make sure it is consistent.

Requirements for Borg repository file systems

- Long file names

- At least three directory levels with short names

- Typically, file sizes up to a few hundred MB. Large repositories may require large files (>2 GB).

- Up to 1000 files per directory (10000 for repositories initialized with Borg 1.0)

- mkdir(2) should be atomic, since it is used for locking

- Hardlinks are needed for *borg upgrade* `--inplace`

Units

To display quantities, Borg takes care of respecting the usual conventions of scale. Disk sizes are displayed in decimal[65], using powers of ten (so kB means 1000 bytes). For memory usage, binary prefixes[66] are used, and are indicated using the IEC binary prefixes[67], using powers of two (so KiB means 1024 bytes).

Date and Time

We format date and time conforming to ISO-8601, that is: YYYY-MM-DD and HH:MM:SS (24h clock).

For more information about that, see: https://xkcd.com/1179/

Unless otherwise noted, we display local date and time. Internally, we store and process date and time as UTC.

Resource Usage

Borg might use a lot of resources depending on the size of the data set it is dealing with.

If one uses Borg in a client/server way (with a ssh: repository), the resource usage occurs in part on the client and in another part on the server.

If one uses Borg as a single process (with a filesystem repo), all the resource usage occurs in that one process, so just add up client + server to get the approximate resource usage.

CPU client: borg create: does chunking, hashing, compression, crypto (high CPU usage) chunks cache sync: quite heavy on CPU, doing lots of hashtable operations. borg extract: crypto, decompression (medium to high CPU usage) borg check: similar to extract, but depends on options given. borg prune / borg delete archive: low to medium CPU usage borg delete repo: done on the server It won't go beyond 100% of 1 core as the code is currently single-threaded. Especially higher zlib and lzma compression levels use significant amounts of CPU cycles. Crypto might be cheap on the CPU (if hardware accelerated) or expensive (if not).

CPU server: It usually doesn't need much CPU, it just deals with the key/value store (repository) and uses the repository index for that.

borg check: the repository check computes the checksums of all chunks (medium CPU usage) borg delete repo: low CPU usage

CPU (only for client/server operation): When using borg in a client/server way with a ssh:-type repo, the ssh processes used for the transport layer will need some CPU on the client and on the server due to the crypto they are doing - esp. if you are pumping big amounts of data.

Memory (RAM) client: The chunks index and the files index are read into memory for performance reasons. Might need big amounts of memory (see below). Compression, esp. lzma compression with high levels might need substantial amounts of memory.

---

[65] https://en.wikipedia.org/wiki/Decimal
[66] https://en.wikipedia.org/wiki/Binary_prefix
[67] https://en.wikipedia.org/wiki/IEC_80000-13#Prefixes_for_binary_multiples

Memory (RAM) server: The server process will load the repository index into memory. Might need considerable amounts of memory, but less than on the client (see below).

Chunks index (client only): Proportional to the amount of data chunks in your repo. Lots of chunks in your repo imply a big chunks index. It is possible to tweak the chunker params (see create options).

Files index (client only): Proportional to the amount of files in your last backups. Can be switched off (see create options), but next backup might be much slower if you do. The speed benefit of using the files cache is proportional to file size.

Repository index (server only): Proportional to the amount of data chunks in your repo. Lots of chunks in your repo imply a big repository index. It is possible to tweak the chunker params (see create options) to influence the amount of chunks being created.

Temporary files (client): Reading data and metadata from a FUSE mounted repository will consume up to the size of all deduplicated, small chunks in the repository. Big chunks won't be locally cached.

Temporary files (server): None.

Cache files (client only): Contains the chunks index and files index (plus a collection of single- archive chunk indexes which might need huge amounts of disk space, depending on archive count and size - see FAQ about how to reduce).

Network (only for client/server operation): If your repository is remote, all deduplicated (and optionally compressed/ encrypted) data of course has to go over the connection (`ssh://` repo url). If you use a locally mounted network filesystem, additionally some copy operations used for transaction support also go over the connection. If you backup multiple sources to one target repository, additional traffic happens for cache resynchronization.

Support for file metadata

Besides regular file and directory structures, Borg can preserve

- symlinks (stored as symlink, the symlink is not followed)
- special files:
    - character and block device files (restored via mknod)
    - FIFOs ("named pipes")
    - special file *contents* can be backed up in `--read-special` mode. By default the metadata to create them with mknod(2), mkfifo(2) etc. is stored.
- hardlinked regular files, devices, FIFOs (considering all items in the same archive)
- timestamps in nanosecond precision: mtime, atime, ctime
- permissions:
    - IDs of owning user and owning group
    - names of owning user and owning group (if the IDs can be resolved)
    - Unix Mode/Permissions (u/g/o permissions, suid, sgid, sticky)

On some platforms additional features are supported:

Platform	ACLs[71]	xattr[72]	Flags[73]
Linux	Yes	Yes	Yes[1]
Mac OS X	Yes	Yes	
FreeBSD	Yes	Yes	Yes (all)
OpenBSD	n/a	n/a	
NetBSD	n/a	No[2]	
Solaris 11	No[3]		n/a
OpenIndiana			
Windows (cygwin)	No[4]	No	No

Other Unix-like operating systems may work as well, but have not been tested at all.

Note that most of the platform-dependent features also depend on the file system. For example, ntfs-3g on Linux isn't able to convey NTFS ACLs.

In case you are interested in more details (like formulas), please see *Internals*. For details on the available JSON output, refer to *All about JSON: How to develop frontends*.

Common options

All Borg commands share these options:

-h, --help   show this help message and exit

--critical   work on log level CRITICAL

--error   work on log level ERROR

--warning   work on log level WARNING (default)

--info, -v, --verbose   work on log level INFO

--debug   enable debug output, work on log level DEBUG

--debug-topic TOPIC   enable TOPIC debugging (can be specified multiple times). The logger path is borg.debug.<TOPIC> if TOPIC is not fully qualified.

-p, --progress   show progress information

--log-json   Output one JSON object per log line instead of formatted text.

--lock-wait SECONDS   wait at most SECONDS for acquiring a repository/cache lock (default: 1).

--show-version   show/log the borg version

--show-rc   show/log the return code (rc)

--no-files-cache   do not load/update the file metadata cache used to detect unchanged files

--umask M   set umask to M (local and remote, default: 0077)

--remote-path PATH   use PATH as borg executable on the remote (default: "borg")

--remote-ratelimit RATE   set remote network upload rate limit in kiByte/s (default: 0=unlimited)

--consider-part-files   treat part files like normal files (e.g. to list/extract them)

--debug-profile FILE   Write execution profile in Borg format into FILE. For local use a Python-compatible file can be generated by suffixing FILE with ".pyprof".

---

[71] The native access control list mechanism of the OS. This normally limits access to non-native ACLs. For example, NTFS ACLs aren't completely accessible on Linux with ntfs-3g.

[72] extended attributes; key-value pairs attached to a file, mainly used by the OS. This includes resource forks on Mac OS X.

[73] aka *BSD flags*. The Linux set of flags[1] is portable across platforms. The BSDs define additional flags.

[1] Only "nodump", "immutable", "compressed" and "append" are supported. Feature request #618 for more flags.

[2] Feature request #1332

[3] Feature request #1337

[4] Cygwin tries to map NTFS ACLs to permissions with varying degress of success.

borg init

```
borg [common options] init [options] [REPOSITORY]
```

REPOSITORY repository to create

optional arguments

> **-e MODE, --encryption MODE** select encryption key mode **(required)**
>
> **--append-only** create an append-only mode repository
>
> **--storage-quota QUOTA** Set storage quota of the new repository (e.g. 5G, 1.5T). Default: no quota.

Common options

Description

This command initializes an empty repository. A repository is a filesystem directory containing the deduplicated data from zero or more archives.

Encryption can be enabled at repository init time. It cannot be changed later.

It is not recommended to work without encryption. Repository encryption protects you e.g. against the case that an attacker has access to your backup repository.

But be careful with the key / the passphrase:

If you want "passphrase-only" security, use one of the repokey modes. The key will be stored inside the repository (in its "config" file). In above mentioned attack scenario, the attacker will have the key (but not the passphrase).

If you want "passphrase and having-the-key" security, use one of the keyfile modes. The key will be stored in your home directory (in .config/borg/keys). In the attack scenario, the attacker who has just access to your repo won't have the key (and also not the passphrase).

Make a backup copy of the key file (keyfile mode) or repo config file (repokey mode) and keep it at a safe place, so you still have the key in case it gets corrupted or lost. Also keep the passphrase at a safe place. The backup that is encrypted with that key won't help you with that, of course.

Make sure you use a good passphrase. Not too short, not too simple. The real encryption / decryption key is encrypted with / locked by your passphrase. If an attacker gets your key, he can't unlock and use it without knowing the passphrase.

Be careful with special or non-ascii characters in your passphrase:

- Borg processes the passphrase as unicode (and encodes it as utf-8), so it does not have problems dealing with even the strangest characters.

- BUT: that does not necessarily apply to your OS / VM / keyboard configuration.

So better use a long passphrase made from simple ascii chars than one that includes non-ascii stuff or characters that are hard/impossible to enter on a different keyboard layout.

You can change your passphrase for existing repos at any time, it won't affect the encryption/decryption key or other secrets.

Encryption modes

Hash/MAC	Not encrypted no auth	Not encrypted, but authenticated	Encrypted (AEAD w/ AES) and authenticated
SHA-256	none	*authenticated*	repokey keyfile
BLAKE2b	n/a	*authenticated-blake2*	*repokey-blake2 keyfile-blake2*

Marked modes are new in Borg 1.1 and are not backwards-compatible with Borg 1.0.x.

On modern Intel/AMD CPUs (except very cheap ones), AES is usually hardware-accelerated. BLAKE2b is faster than SHA256 on Intel/AMD 64-bit CPUs (except AMD Ryzen and future CPUs with SHA extensions), which makes *authenticated-blake2* faster than *none* and *authenticated*.

On modern ARM CPUs, NEON provides hardware acceleration for SHA256 making it faster than BLAKE2b-256 there. NEON accelerates AES as well.

Hardware acceleration is always used automatically when available.

repokey and *keyfile* use AES-CTR-256 for encryption and HMAC-SHA256 for authentication in an encrypt-then-MAC (EtM) construction. The chunk ID hash is HMAC-SHA256 as well (with a separate key). These modes are compatible with Borg 1.0.x.

repokey-blake2 and *keyfile-blake2* are also authenticated encryption modes, but use BLAKE2b-256 instead of HMAC-SHA256 for authentication. The chunk ID hash is a keyed BLAKE2b-256 hash. These modes are new and *not* compatible with Borg 1.0.x.

authenticated mode uses no encryption, but authenticates repository contents through the same HMAC-SHA256 hash as the *repokey* and *keyfile* modes (it uses it as the chunk ID hash). The key is stored like *repokey*. This mode is new and *not* compatible with Borg 1.0.x.

authenticated-blake2 is like *authenticated*, but uses the keyed BLAKE2b-256 hash from the other blake2 modes. This mode is new and *not* compatible with Borg 1.0.x.

none mode uses no encryption and no authentication. It uses SHA256 as chunk ID hash. Not recommended, rather consider using an authenticated or authenticated/encrypted mode. This mode has possible denial-of-service issues when running `borg create` on contents controlled by an attacker. Use it only for new repositories where no encryption is wanted **and** when compatibility with 1.0.x is important. If compatibility with 1.0.x is not important, use *authenticated-blake2* or *authenticated* instead. This mode is compatible with Borg 1.0.x.

Examples

```
# Local repository, repokey encryption, BLAKE2b (often faster, since Borg 1.1)
$ borg init --encryption=repokey-blake2 /path/to/repo

# Local repository (no encryption)
$ borg init --encryption=none /path/to/repo

# Remote repository (accesses a remote borg via ssh)
$ borg init --encryption=repokey-blake2 user@hostname:backup

# Remote repository (store the key your home dir)
$ borg init --encryption=keyfile user@hostname:backup
```

borg create

```
borg [common options] create [options] ARCHIVE [PATH...]
```

ARCHIVE name of archive to create (must be also a valid directory name)

PATH paths to archive

optional arguments

-n, --dry-run	do not create a backup archive
-s, --stats	print statistics for the created archive
--list	output verbose list of items (files, dirs, ...)

--filter STATUSCHARS only display items with the given status characters (see description)

--json output stats as JSON. Implies `--stats`.

--no-cache-sync experimental: do not synchronize the cache. Implies not using the files cache.

Common options

Exclusion options

-e PATTERN, --exclude PATTERN exclude paths matching PATTERN

--exclude-from EXCLUDEFILE read exclude patterns from EXCLUDEFILE, one per line

--pattern PATTERN experimental: include/exclude paths matching PATTERN

--patterns-from PATTERNFILE experimental: read include/exclude patterns from PATTERNFILE, one per line

--exclude-caches exclude directories that contain a CACHEDIR.TAG file (http://www.brynosaurus.com/cachedir/spec.html)

--exclude-if-present NAME exclude directories that are tagged by containing a filesystem object with the given NAME

--keep-exclude-tags, --keep-tag-files if tag objects are specified with `--exclude-if-present`, don't omit the tag objects themselves from the backup archive

Filesystem options

-x, --one-file-system stay in the same file system and do not store mount points of other file systems

--numeric-owner only store numeric user and group identifiers

--noatime do not store atime into archive

--noctime do not store ctime into archive

--ignore-inode ignore inode data in the file metadata cache used to detect unchanged files.

--files-cache MODE operate files cache in MODE. default: ctime,size,inode

--read-special open and read block and char device files as well as FIFOs as if they were regular files. Also follows symlinks pointing to these kinds of files.

Archive options

--comment COMMENT add a comment text to the archive

--timestamp TIMESTAMP manually specify the archive creation date/time (UTC, yyyy-mm-ddThh:mm:ss format). Alternatively, give a reference file/directory.

-c SECONDS, --checkpoint-interval SECONDS write checkpoint every SECONDS seconds (Default: 1800)

--chunker-params PARAMS specify the chunker parameters (CHUNK_MIN_EXP, CHUNK_MAX_EXP, HASH_MASK_BITS, HASH_WINDOW_SIZE). default: 19,23,21,4095

-C COMPRESSION, --compression COMPRESSION select compression algorithm, see the output of the "borg help compression" command for details.

Description

This command creates a backup archive containing all files found while recursively traversing all paths specified. Paths are added to the archive as they are given, that means if relative paths are desired, the command has to be run from the correct directory.

When giving '-' as path, borg will read data from standard input and create a file 'stdin' in the created archive from that data.

The archive will consume almost no disk space for files or parts of files that have already been stored in other archives.

The archive name needs to be unique. It must not end in '.checkpoint' or '.checkpoint.N' (with N being a number), because these names are used for checkpoints and treated in special ways.

In the archive name, you may use the following placeholders: {now}, {utcnow}, {fqdn}, {hostname}, {user} and some others.

Backup speed is increased by not reprocessing files that are already part of existing archives and weren't modified. The detection of unmodified files is done by comparing multiple file metadata values with previous values kept in the files cache.

This comparison can operate in different modes as given by `--files-cache`:

- ctime,size,inode (default)
- mtime,size,inode (default behaviour of borg versions older than 1.1.0rc4)
- ctime,size (ignore the inode number)
- mtime,size (ignore the inode number)
- rechunk,ctime (all files are considered modified - rechunk, cache ctime)
- rechunk,mtime (all files are considered modified - rechunk, cache mtime)
- disabled (disable the files cache, all files considered modified - rechunk)

inode number: better safety, but often unstable on network filesystems

Normally, detecting file modifications will take inode information into consideration to improve the reliability of file change detection. This is problematic for files located on sshfs and similar network file systems which do not provide stable inode numbers, such files will always be considered modified. You can use modes without *inode* in this case to improve performance, but reliability of change detection might be reduced.

ctime vs. mtime: safety vs. speed

- ctime is a rather safe way to detect changes to a file (metadata and contents) as it can not be set from userspace. But, a metadata-only change will already update the ctime, so there might be some unnecessary chunking/hashing even without content changes. Some filesystems do not support ctime (change time).
- mtime usually works and only updates if file contents were changed. But mtime can be arbitrarily set from userspace, e.g. to set mtime back to the same value it had before a content change happened. This can be used maliciously as well as well-meant, but in both cases mtime based cache modes can be problematic.

The mount points of filesystems or filesystem snapshots should be the same for every creation of a new archive to ensure fast operation. This is because the file cache that is used to determine changed files quickly uses absolute filenames. If this is not possible, consider creating a bind mount to a stable location.

The `--progress` option shows (from left to right) Original, Compressed and Deduplicated (O, C and D, respectively), then the Number of files (N) processed so far, followed by the currently processed path.

See the output of the "borg help patterns" command for more help on exclude patterns. See the output of the "borg help placeholders" command for more help on placeholders.

The `--exclude` patterns are not like tar. In tar `--exclude` .bundler/gems will exclude foo/.bundler/gems. In borg it will not, you need to use `--exclude` '*/.bundler/gems' to get the same effect. See `borg help patterns` for more information.

In addition to using `--exclude` patterns, it is possible to use `--exclude-if-present` to specify the name of a filesystem object (e.g. a file or folder name) which, when contained within another folder, will prevent the containing folder from being backed up. By default, the containing folder and all of its contents will be omitted from the backup. If, however, you wish to only include the objects specified by `--exclude-if-present` in your backup, and not include any other contents of the containing folder, this can be enabled through using the `--keep-exclude-tags` option.

Borg respects the nodump flag. Files flagged nodump will be marked as excluded (x) in `--list` output.

Item flags

`--list` outputs a list of all files, directories and other file system items it considered (no matter whether they had content changes or not). For each item, it prefixes a single-letter flag that indicates type and/or status of the item.

If you are interested only in a subset of that output, you can give e.g. `--filter=AME` and it will only show regular files with A, M or E status (see below).

A uppercase character represents the status of a regular file relative to the "files" cache (not relative to the repo – this is an issue if the files cache is not used). Metadata is stored in any case and for 'A' and 'M' also new data chunks are stored. For 'U' all data chunks refer to already existing chunks.

- 'A' = regular file, added (see also *I am seeing 'A' (added) status for an unchanged file!?* in the FAQ)
- 'M' = regular file, modified
- 'U' = regular file, unchanged
- 'E' = regular file, an error happened while accessing/reading *this* file

A lowercase character means a file type other than a regular file, borg usually just stores their metadata:

- 'd' = directory
- 'b' = block device
- 'c' = char device
- 'h' = regular file, hardlink (to already seen inodes)
- 's' = symlink
- 'f' = fifo

Other flags used include:

- 'i' = backup data was read from standard input (stdin)
- '-' = dry run, item was *not* backed up
- 'x' = excluded, item was *not* backed up
- '?' = missing status code (if you see this, please file a bug report!)

Examples

```
# Backup ~/Documents into an archive named "my-documents"
$ borg create /path/to/repo::my-documents ~/Documents

# same, but list all files as we process them
$ borg create --list /path/to/repo::my-documents ~/Documents

# Backup ~/Documents and ~/src but exclude pyc files
$ borg create /path/to/repo::my-files \
    ~/Documents                       \
    ~/src                             \
    --exclude '*.pyc'
```

```
# Backup home directories excluding image thumbnails (i.e. only
# /home/<one directory>/.thumbnails is excluded, not /home/*/*/.thumbnails etc.)
$ borg create /path/to/repo::my-files /home \
    --exclude 'sh:/home/*/.thumbnails'

# Backup the root filesystem into an archive named "root-YYYY-MM-DD"
# use zlib compression (good, but slow) - default is lz4 (fast, low compression␣
↪ratio)
$ borg create -C zlib,6 /path/to/repo::root-{now:%Y-%m-%d} / --one-file-system

# Backup a remote host locally ("pull" style) using sshfs
$ mkdir sshfs-mount
$ sshfs root@example.com:/ sshfs-mount
$ cd sshfs-mount
$ borg create /path/to/repo::example.com-root-{now:%Y-%m-%d} .
$ cd ..
$ fusermount -u sshfs-mount

# Make a big effort in fine granular deduplication (big chunk management
# overhead, needs a lot of RAM and disk space, see formula in internals
# docs - same parameters as borg < 1.0 or attic):
$ borg create --chunker-params 10,23,16,4095 /path/to/repo::small /smallstuff

# Backup a raw device (must not be active/in use/mounted at that time)
$ dd if=/dev/sdx bs=10M | borg create /path/to/repo::my-sdx -

# No compression (none)
$ borg create --compression none /path/to/repo::arch ~

# Super fast, low compression (lz4, default)
$ borg create /path/to/repo::arch ~

# Less fast, higher compression (zlib, N = 0..9)
$ borg create --compression zlib,N /path/to/repo::arch ~

# Even slower, even higher compression (lzma, N = 0..9)
$ borg create --compression lzma,N /path/to/repo::arch ~

# Only compress compressible data with lzma,N (N = 0..9)
$ borg create --compression auto,lzma,N /path/to/repo::arch ~

# Use short hostname, user name and current time in archive name
$ borg create /path/to/repo::{hostname}-{user}-{now} ~
# Similar, use the same datetime format as borg 1.1 will have as default
$ borg create /path/to/repo::{hostname}-{user}-{now:%Y-%m-%dT%H:%M:%S} ~
# As above, but add nanoseconds
$ borg create /path/to/repo::{hostname}-{user}-{now:%Y-%m-%dT%H:%M:%S.%f} ~

# Backing up relative paths by moving into the correct directory first
$ cd /home/user/Documents
# The root directory of the archive will be "projectA"
$ borg create /path/to/repo::daily-projectA-{now:%Y-%m-%d} projectA
```

borg extract

```
borg [common options] extract [options] ARCHIVE [PATH...]
```

ARCHIVE archive to extract

PATH paths to extract; patterns are supported

optional arguments

--list	output verbose list of items (files, dirs, ...)
-n, --dry-run	do not actually change any files
--numeric-owner	only obey numeric user and group identifiers
--stdout	write all extracted data to stdout
--sparse	create holes in output sparse file from all-zero chunks

Common options

Exclusion options

-e PATTERN, --exclude PATTERN	exclude paths matching PATTERN
--exclude-from EXCLUDEFILE	read exclude patterns from EXCLUDEFILE, one per line
--pattern PATTERN	experimental: include/exclude paths matching PATTERN
--patterns-from PATTERNFILE	experimental: read include/exclude patterns from PAT-TERNFILE, one per line
--strip-components NUMBER	Remove the specified number of leading path elements. Paths with fewer elements will be silently skipped.

Description

This command extracts the contents of an archive. By default the entire archive is extracted but a subset of files and directories can be selected by passing a list of PATHs as arguments. The file selection can further be restricted by using the --exclude option.

See the output of the "borg help patterns" command for more help on exclude patterns.

By using --dry-run, you can do all extraction steps except actually writing the output data: reading metadata and data chunks from the repo, checking the hash/hmac, decrypting, decompressing.

--progress can be slower than no progress display, since it makes one additional pass over the archive metadata.

Note: Currently, extract always writes into the current working directory ("."), so make sure you cd to the right place before calling borg extract.

Examples

```
# Extract entire archive
$ borg extract /path/to/repo::my-files

# Extract entire archive and list files while processing
$ borg extract --list /path/to/repo::my-files

# Verify whether an archive could be successfully extracted, but do not write
↪files to disk
$ borg extract --dry-run /path/to/repo::my-files

# Extract the "src" directory
$ borg extract /path/to/repo::my-files home/USERNAME/src
```

```
# Extract the "src" directory but exclude object files
$ borg extract /path/to/repo::my-files home/USERNAME/src --exclude '*.o'

# Restore a raw device (must not be active/in use/mounted at that time)
$ borg extract --stdout /path/to/repo::my-sdx | dd of=/dev/sdx bs=10M
```

borg check

```
borg [common options] check [options] [REPOSITORY_OR_ARCHIVE]
```

REPOSITORY_OR_ARCHIVE repository or archive to check consistency of

optional arguments

--repository-only	only perform repository checks
--archives-only	only perform archives checks
--verify-data	perform cryptographic archive data integrity verification (conflicts with `--repository-only`)
--repair	attempt to repair any inconsistencies found
--save-space	work slower, but using less space

Common options

Archive filters

-P PREFIX, --prefix PREFIX	only consider archive names starting with this prefix.
-a GLOB, --glob-archives GLOB	only consider archive names matching the glob. sh: rules apply, see "borg help patterns". `--prefix` and `--glob-archives` are mutually exclusive.
--sort-by KEYS	Comma-separated list of sorting keys; valid keys are: timestamp, name, id; default is: timestamp
--first N	consider first N archives after other filters were applied
--last N	consider last N archives after other filters were applied

Description

The check command verifies the consistency of a repository and the corresponding archives.

First, the underlying repository data files are checked:

- For all segments the segment magic (header) is checked
- For all objects stored in the segments, all metadata (e.g. crc and size) and all data is read. The read data is checked by size and CRC. Bit rot and other types of accidental damage can be detected this way.
- If we are in repair mode and a integrity error is detected for a segment, we try to recover as many objects from the segment as possible.
- In repair mode, it makes sure that the index is consistent with the data stored in the segments.
- If you use a remote repo server via ssh:, the repo check is executed on the repo server without causing significant network traffic.
- The repository check can be skipped using the `--archives-only` option.

Second, the consistency and correctness of the archive metadata is verified:

- Is the repo manifest present? If not, it is rebuilt from archive metadata chunks (this requires reading and decrypting of all metadata and data).

- Check if archive metadata chunk is present. if not, remove archive from manifest.

- For all files (items) in the archive, for all chunks referenced by these files, check if chunk is present. If a chunk is not present and we are in repair mode, replace it with a same-size replacement chunk of zeros. If a previously lost chunk reappears (e.g. via a later backup) and we are in repair mode, the all-zero replacement chunk will be replaced by the correct chunk. This requires reading of archive and file metadata, but not data.

- If we are in repair mode and we checked all the archives: delete orphaned chunks from the repo.

- if you use a remote repo server via ssh:, the archive check is executed on the client machine (because if encryption is enabled, the checks will require decryption and this is always done client-side, because key access will be required).

- The archive checks can be time consuming, they can be skipped using the `--repository-only` option.

The `--verify-data` option will perform a full integrity verification (as opposed to checking the CRC32 of the segment) of data, which means reading the data from the repository, decrypting and decompressing it. This is a cryptographic verification, which will detect (accidental) corruption. For encrypted repositories it is tamper-resistant as well, unless the attacker has access to the keys.

It is also very slow.

borg rename

```
borg [common options] rename [options] ARCHIVE NEWNAME
```

ARCHIVE archive to rename

NEWNAME the new archive name to use

Common options

Description

This command renames an archive in the repository.

This results in a different archive ID.

Examples

```
$ borg create /path/to/repo::archivename ~
$ borg list /path/to/repo
archivename                          Mon, 2016-02-15 19:50:19

$ borg rename /path/to/repo::archivename newname
$ borg list /path/to/repo
newname                              Mon, 2016-02-15 19:50:19
```

borg list

```
borg [common options] list [options] [REPOSITORY_OR_ARCHIVE] [PATH...]
```

REPOSITORY_OR_ARCHIVE repository/archive to list contents of

PATH paths to list; patterns are supported

optional arguments

--short	only print file/directory names, nothing else
--format FORMAT, --list-format FORMAT	specify format for file listing (default: "{mode} {user:6} {group:6} {size:8d} {mtime} {path}{extra}{NL}")
--json	Only valid for listing repository contents. Format output as JSON. The form of `--format` is ignored, but keys used in it are added to the JSON output. Some keys are always present. Note: JSON can only represent text. A "barchive" key is therefore not available.
--json-lines	Only valid for listing archive contents. Format output as JSON Lines. The form of `--format` is ignored, but keys used in it are added to the JSON output. Some keys are always present. Note: JSON can only represent text. A "bpath" key is therefore not available.

Common options

Archive filters

-P PREFIX, --prefix PREFIX	only consider archive names starting with this prefix.
-a GLOB, --glob-archives GLOB	only consider archive names matching the glob. sh: rules apply, see "borg help patterns". `--prefix` and `--glob-archives` are mutually exclusive.
--sort-by KEYS	Comma-separated list of sorting keys; valid keys are: timestamp, name, id; default is: timestamp
--first N	consider first N archives after other filters were applied
--last N	consider last N archives after other filters were applied

Exclusion options

-e PATTERN, --exclude PATTERN	exclude paths matching PATTERN
--exclude-from EXCLUDEFILE	read exclude patterns from EXCLUDEFILE, one per line
--pattern PATTERN	experimental: include/exclude paths matching PATTERN
--patterns-from PATTERNFILE	experimental: read include/exclude patterns from PATTERNFILE, one per line
--exclude-caches	exclude directories that contain a CACHEDIR.TAG file (http://www.brynosaurus.com/cachedir/spec.html)
--exclude-if-present NAME	exclude directories that are tagged by containing a filesystem object with the given NAME
--keep-exclude-tags, --keep-tag-files	if tag objects are specified with `--exclude-if-present`, don't omit the tag objects themselves from the backup archive

Description

This command lists the contents of a repository or an archive.

See the "borg help patterns" command for more help on exclude patterns.

The following keys are available for `--format`:

- NEWLINE: OS dependent line separator
- NL: alias of NEWLINE

- NUL: NUL character for creating print0 / xargs -0 like output, see barchive/bpath
- SPACE
- TAB
- CR
- LF

Keys for listing repository archives:

- name: archive name interpreted as text (might be missing non-text characters, see barchive)
- archive: archive name interpreted as text (might be missing non-text characters, see barchive)
- barchive: verbatim archive name, can contain any character except NUL
- comment: archive comment interpreted as text (might be missing non-text characters, see bcomment)
- bcomment: verbatim archive comment, can contain any character except NUL
- id: internal ID of the archive
- time: time (start) of creation of the archive
- start: time (start) of creation of the archive
- end: time (end) of creation of the archive

Keys for listing archive files:

- type
- mode
- uid
- gid
- user
- group
- path: path interpreted as text (might be missing non-text characters, see bpath)
- bpath: verbatim POSIX path, can contain any character except NUL
- source: link target for links (identical to linktarget)
- linktarget
- flags
- size
- csize: compressed size
- dsize: deduplicated size
- dcsize: deduplicated compressed size
- num_chunks: number of chunks in this file
- unique_chunks: number of unique chunks in this file
- mtime
- ctime
- atime
- isomtime
- isoctime
- isoatime

- md5
- sha1
- sha224
- sha256
- sha384
- sha512
- archiveid
- archivename
- extra: prepends {source} with " -> " for soft links and " link to " for hard links
- health: either "healthy" (file ok) or "broken" (if file has all-zero replacement chunks)

Examples

```
$ borg list /path/to/repo
Monday                          Mon, 2016-02-15 19:15:11
repo                            Mon, 2016-02-15 19:26:54
root-2016-02-15                 Mon, 2016-02-15 19:36:29
newname                         Mon, 2016-02-15 19:50:19
...

$ borg list /path/to/repo::root-2016-02-15
drwxr-xr-x root   root           0 Mon, 2016-02-15 17:44:27 .
drwxrwxr-x root   root           0 Mon, 2016-02-15 19:04:49 bin
-rwxr-xr-x root   root     1029624 Thu, 2014-11-13 00:08:51 bin/bash
lrwxrwxrwx root   root           0 Fri, 2015-03-27 20:24:26 bin/bzcmp -> bzdiff
-rwxr-xr-x root   root        2140 Fri, 2015-03-27 20:24:22 bin/bzdiff
...

$ borg list /path/to/repo::archiveA --list-format="{mode} {user:6} {group:6}
↪{size:8d} {isomtime} {path}{extra}{NEWLINE}"
drwxrwxr-x user   user           0 Sun, 2015-02-01 11:00:00 .
drwxrwxr-x user   user           0 Sun, 2015-02-01 11:00:00 code
drwxrwxr-x user   user           0 Sun, 2015-02-01 11:00:00 code/myproject
-rw-rw-r-- user   user     1416192 Sun, 2015-02-01 11:00:00 code/myproject/file.ext
...
```

borg diff

```
borg [common options] diff [options] REPO_ARCHIVE1 ARCHIVE2 [PATH...]
```

REPO_ARCHIVE1 repository location and ARCHIVE1 name

ARCHIVE2 ARCHIVE2 name (no repository location allowed)

PATH paths of items inside the archives to compare; patterns are supported

optional arguments

> **--numeric-owner** only consider numeric user and group identifiers
>
> **--same-chunker-params** Override check of chunker parameters.
>
> **--sort** Sort the output lines by file path.

Common options

Exclusion options

-e PATTERN, --exclude PATTERN exclude paths matching PATTERN

--exclude-from EXCLUDEFILE read exclude patterns from EXCLUDEFILE, one per line

--pattern PATTERN experimental: include/exclude paths matching PATTERN

--patterns-from PATTERNFILE experimental: read include/exclude patterns from PAT-TERNFILE, one per line

--exclude-caches exclude directories that contain a CACHEDIR.TAG file (http://www.brynosaurus.com/cachedir/spec.html)

--exclude-if-present NAME exclude directories that are tagged by containing a filesystem object with the given NAME

--keep-exclude-tags, --keep-tag-files if tag objects are specified with `--exclude-if-present`, don't omit the tag objects themselves from the backup archive

Description

This command finds differences (file contents, user/group/mode) between archives.

A repository location and an archive name must be specified for REPO_ARCHIVE1. ARCHIVE2 is just another archive name in same repository (no repository location allowed).

For archives created with Borg 1.1 or newer diff automatically detects whether the archives are created with the same chunker params. If so, only chunk IDs are compared, which is very fast.

For archives prior to Borg 1.1 chunk contents are compared by default. If you did not create the archives with different chunker params, pass `--same-chunker-params`. Note that the chunker params changed from Borg 0.xx to 1.0.

See the output of the "borg help patterns" command for more help on exclude patterns.

Examples

```
$ borg init -e=none testrepo
$ mkdir testdir
$ cd testdir
$ echo asdf > file1
$ dd if=/dev/urandom bs=1M count=4 > file2
$ touch file3
$ borg create ../testrepo::archive1 .

$ chmod a+x file1
$ echo "something" >> file2
$ borg create ../testrepo::archive2 .

$ rm file3
$ touch file4
$ borg create ../testrepo::archive3 .

$ cd ..
$ borg diff testrepo::archive1 archive2
[-rw-r--r-- -> -rwxr-xr-x] file1
   +135 B    -252 B file2

$ borg diff testrepo::archive2 archive3
added           0 B file4
```

```
removed           0 B file3

$ borg diff testrepo::archive1 archive3
[-rw-r--r-- -> -rwxr-xr-x] file1
   +135 B    -252 B file2
added             0 B file4
removed           0 B file3
```

borg delete

```
borg [common options] delete [options] [TARGET] [ARCHIVE...]
```

TARGET archive or repository to delete

ARCHIVE archives to delete

optional arguments

       -s, --stats   print statistics for the deleted archive

       --cache-only   delete only the local cache for the given repository

       --force   force deletion of corrupted archives, use `--force --force` in case `--force` does not work.

       --save-space   work slower, but using less space

Common options

Archive filters

       -P PREFIX, --prefix PREFIX   only consider archive names starting with this prefix.

       -a GLOB, --glob-archives GLOB   only consider archive names matching the glob. sh: rules apply, see "borg help patterns". `--prefix` and `--glob-archives` are mutually exclusive.

       --sort-by KEYS   Comma-separated list of sorting keys; valid keys are: timestamp, name, id; default is: timestamp

       --first N   consider first N archives after other filters were applied

       --last N   consider last N archives after other filters were applied

Description

This command deletes an archive from the repository or the complete repository. Disk space is reclaimed accordingly. If you delete the complete repository, the local cache for it (if any) is also deleted.

Examples

```
# delete a single backup archive:
$ borg delete /path/to/repo::Monday

# delete the whole repository and the related local cache:
$ borg delete /path/to/repo
You requested to completely DELETE the repository *including* all archives it
  contains:
repo                            Mon, 2016-02-15 19:26:54
```

```
root-2016-02-15                          Mon, 2016-02-15 19:36:29
newname                                  Mon, 2016-02-15 19:50:19
Type 'YES' if you understand this and want to continue: YES
```

borg prune

```
borg [common options] prune [options] [REPOSITORY]
```

REPOSITORY repository to prune

optional arguments

-n, --dry-run	do not change repository
--force	force pruning of corrupted archives
-s, --stats	print statistics for the deleted archive
--list	output verbose list of archives it keeps/prunes
--keep-within INTERVAL	keep all archives within this time interval
--keep-last, --keep-secondly	number of secondly archives to keep
--keep-minutely	number of minutely archives to keep
-H, --keep-hourly	number of hourly archives to keep
-d, --keep-daily	number of daily archives to keep
-w, --keep-weekly	number of weekly archives to keep
-m, --keep-monthly	number of monthly archives to keep
-y, --keep-yearly	number of yearly archives to keep
--save-space	work slower, but using less space

Common options

Archive filters

-P PREFIX, --prefix PREFIX only consider archive names starting with this prefix.

-a GLOB, --glob-archives GLOB only consider archive names matching the glob. sh: rules apply, see "borg help patterns". `--prefix` and `--glob-archives` are mutually exclusive.

Description

The prune command prunes a repository by deleting all archives not matching any of the specified retention options. This command is normally used by automated backup scripts wanting to keep a certain number of historic backups.

Also, prune automatically removes checkpoint archives (incomplete archives left behind by interrupted backup runs) except if the checkpoint is the latest archive (and thus still needed). Checkpoint archives are not considered when comparing archive counts against the retention limits (`--keep-X`).

If a prefix is set with -P, then only archives that start with the prefix are considered for deletion and only those archives count towards the totals specified by the rules. Otherwise, *all* archives in the repository are candidates for deletion! There is no automatic distinction between archives representing different contents. These need to be distinguished by specifying matching prefixes.

If you have multiple sequences of archives with different data sets (e.g. from different machines) in one shared repository, use one prune call per data set that matches only the respective archives using the -P option.

The `--keep-within` option takes an argument of the form "<int><char>", where char is "H", "d", "w", "m", "y". For example, `--keep-within 2d` means to keep all archives that were created within the past 48 hours. "1m" is taken to mean "31d". The archives kept with this option do not count towards the totals specified by any other options.

A good procedure is to thin out more and more the older your backups get. As an example, `--keep-daily 7` means to keep the latest backup on each day, up to 7 most recent days with backups (days without backups do not count). The rules are applied from secondly to yearly, and backups selected by previous rules do not count towards those of later rules. The time that each backup starts is used for pruning purposes. Dates and times are interpreted in the local timezone, and weeks go from Monday to Sunday. Specifying a negative number of archives to keep means that there is no limit.

The `--keep-last` N option is doing the same as `--keep-secondly` N (and it will keep the last N archives under the assumption that you do not create more than one backup archive in the same second).

Examples

Be careful, prune is a potentially dangerous command, it will remove backup archives.

The default of prune is to apply to **all archives in the repository** unless you restrict its operation to a subset of the archives using `--prefix`. When using `--prefix`, be careful to choose a good prefix - e.g. do not use a prefix "foo" if you do not also want to match "foobar".

It is strongly recommended to always run `prune -v --list --dry-run ...` first so you will see what it would do without it actually doing anything.

```
# Keep 7 end of day and 4 additional end of week archives.
# Do a dry-run without actually deleting anything.
$ borg prune -v --list --dry-run --keep-daily=7 --keep-weekly=4 /path/to/repo

# Same as above but only apply to archive names starting with the hostname
# of the machine followed by a "-" character:
$ borg prune -v --list --keep-daily=7 --keep-weekly=4 --prefix='{hostname}-' /path/
↪to/repo

# Keep 7 end of day, 4 additional end of week archives,
# and an end of month archive for every month:
$ borg prune -v --list --keep-daily=7 --keep-weekly=4 --keep-monthly=-1 /path/to/
↪repo

# Keep all backups in the last 10 days, 4 additional end of week archives,
# and an end of month archive for every month:
$ borg prune -v --list --keep-within=10d --keep-weekly=4 --keep-monthly=-1 /path/
↪to/repo
```

There is also a visualized prune example in `docs/misc/prune-example.txt`:

```
borg prune visualized
=====================

Assume it is 2016-01-01, today's backup has not yet been made and you have
created at least one backup on each day in 2015 except on 2015-12-19 (no
backup made on that day).

This is what borg prune --keep-daily 14 --keep-monthly 6 would keep.

Backups kept by the --keep-daily rule are marked by a "d" to the right,
backups kept by the --keep-monthly rule are marked by a "m" to the right.
```

```
Calendar view
-------------

                               2015
            January                 February                  March
     Mo Tu We Th Fr Sa Su   Mo Tu We Th Fr Sa Su   Mo Tu We Th Fr Sa Su
                 1  2  3  4                     1                      1
      5  6  7  8  9 10 11    2  3  4  5  6  7  8    2  3  4  5  6  7  8
     12 13 14 15 16 17 18    9 10 11 12 13 14 15    9 10 11 12 13 14 15
     19 20 21 22 23 24 25   16 17 18 19 20 21 22   16 17 18 19 20 21 22
     26 27 28 29 30 31      23 24 25 26 27 28      23 24 25 26 27 28 29
                                                   30 31

             April                    May                     June
     Mo Tu We Th Fr Sa Su   Mo Tu We Th Fr Sa Su   Mo Tu We Th Fr Sa Su
                 1  2  3  4                1  2  3    1  2  3  4  5  6  7
      6  7  8  9 10 11 12    4  5  6  7  8  9 10     8  9 10 11 12 13 14
     13 14 15 16 17 18 19   11 12 13 14 15 16 17   15 16 17 18 19 20 21
     20 21 22 23 24 25 26   18 19 20 21 22 23 24   22 23 24 25 26 27 28
     27 28 29 30            25 26 27 28 29 30 31   29 30m

             July                   August                 September
     Mo Tu We Th Fr Sa Su   Mo Tu We Th Fr Sa Su   Mo Tu We Th Fr Sa Su
                 1  2  3  4                1  2      1  2  3  4  5  6
      6  7  8  9 10 11 12    3  4  5  6  7  8  9     7  8  9 10 11 12 13
     13 14 15 16 17 18 19   10 11 12 13 14 15 16   14 15 16 17 18 19 20
     20 21 22 23 24 25 26   17 18 19 20 21 22 23   21 22 23 24 25 26 27
     27 28 29 30 31m        24 25 26 27 28 29 30   28 29 30m
                            31m

            October                 November                December
     Mo Tu We Th Fr Sa Su   Mo Tu We Th Fr Sa Su   Mo Tu We Th Fr Sa Su
                 1  2  3  4                     1    1  2  3  4  5  6
      5  6  7  8  9 10 11    2  3  4  5  6  7  8     7  8  9 10 11 12 13
     12 13 14 15 16 17 18    9 10 11 12 13 14 15   14 15 16 17d18d19 20d
     19 20 21 22 23 24 25   16 17 18 19 20 21 22   21d22d23d24d25d26d27d
     26 27 28 29 30 31m     23 24 25 26 27 28 29   28d29d30d31d
                            30m

List view
---------

--keep-daily 14     --keep-monthly 6
-------------------------------------------------
 1. 2015-12-31          (2015-12-31 kept by daily rule)
 2. 2015-12-30       1. 2015-11-30
 3. 2015-12-29       2. 2015-10-31
 4. 2015-12-28       3. 2015-09-30
 5. 2015-12-27       4. 2015-08-31
 6. 2015-12-26       5. 2015-07-31
 7. 2015-12-25       6. 2015-06-30
 8. 2015-12-24
 9. 2015-12-23
10. 2015-12-22
11. 2015-12-21
12. 2015-12-20
    (no backup made on 2015-12-19)
13. 2015-12-18
14. 2015-12-17


Notes
```

```
-----

2015-12-31 is kept due to the --keep-daily 14 rule (because it is applied
first), not due to the --keep-monthly rule.

Because of that, the --keep-monthly 6 rule keeps Nov, Oct, Sep, Aug, Jul and
Jun. December is not considered for this rule, because that backup was already
kept because of the daily rule.

2015-12-17 is kept to satisfy the --keep-daily 14 rule - because no backup was
made on 2015-12-19. If a backup had been made on that day, it would not keep
the one from 2015-12-17.

We did not include yearly, weekly, hourly, minutely or secondly rules to keep
this example simple. They all work in basically the same way.

The weekly rule is easy to understand roughly, but hard to understand in all
details. If interested, read "ISO 8601:2000 standard week-based year".
```

borg info

```
borg [common options] info [options] [REPOSITORY_OR_ARCHIVE]
```

REPOSITORY_OR_ARCHIVE archive or repository to display information about

optional arguments

> **--json**   format output as JSON

Common options

Archive filters

> **-P PREFIX, --prefix PREFIX**   only consider archive names starting with this prefix.
>
> **-a GLOB, --glob-archives GLOB**   only consider archive names matching the glob. sh: rules apply, see "borg help patterns". `--prefix` and `--glob-archives` are mutually exclusive.
>
> **--sort-by KEYS**   Comma-separated list of sorting keys; valid keys are: timestamp, name, id; default is: timestamp
>
> **--first N**   consider first N archives after other filters were applied
>
> **--last N**   consider last N archives after other filters were applied

Description

This command displays detailed information about the specified archive or repository.

Please note that the deduplicated sizes of the individual archives do not add up to the deduplicated size of the repository ("all archives"), because the two are meaning different things:

This archive / deduplicated size = amount of data stored ONLY for this archive = unique chunks of this archive. All archives / deduplicated size = amount of data stored in the repo = all chunks in the repository.

Borg archives can only contain a limited amount of file metadata. The size of an archive relative to this limit depends on a number of factors, mainly the number of files, the lengths of paths and other metadata stored for files. This is shown as *utilization of maximum supported archive size*.

Examples

```
$ borg info /path/to/repo::2017-06-29T11:00-srv
Archive name: 2017-06-29T11:00-srv
Archive fingerprint:␣
↪b2f1beac2bd553b34e06358afa45a3c1689320d39163890c5bbbd49125f00fe5
Comment:
Hostname: myhostname
Username: root
Time (start): Thu, 2017-06-29 11:03:07
Time (end): Thu, 2017-06-29 11:03:13
Duration: 5.66 seconds
Number of files: 17037
Command line: /usr/sbin/borg create /path/to/repo::2017-06-29T11:00-srv /srv
Utilization of max. archive size: 0%
------------------------------------------------------------------------------
                      Original size      Compressed size    Deduplicated size
This archive:              12.53 GB             12.49 GB              1.62 kB
All archives:             121.82 TB            112.41 TB            215.42 GB

                      Unique chunks        Total chunks
Chunk index:                1015213           626934122

$ borg info /path/to/repo --last 1
Archive name: 2017-06-29T11:00-srv
Archive fingerprint:␣
↪b2f1beac2bd553b34e06358afa45a3c1689320d39163890c5bbbd49125f00fe5
Comment:
Hostname: myhostname
Username: root
Time (start): Thu, 2017-06-29 11:03:07
Time (end): Thu, 2017-06-29 11:03:13
Duration: 5.66 seconds
Number of files: 17037
Command line: /usr/sbin/borg create /path/to/repo::2017-06-29T11:00-srv /srv
Utilization of max. archive size: 0%
------------------------------------------------------------------------------
                      Original size      Compressed size    Deduplicated size
This archive:              12.53 GB             12.49 GB              1.62 kB
All archives:             121.82 TB            112.41 TB            215.42 GB

                      Unique chunks        Total chunks
Chunk index:                1015213           626934122

$ borg info /path/to/repo
Repository ID: d857ce5788c51272c61535062e89eac4e8ef5a884ffbe976e0af9d8765dedfa5
Location: /path/to/repo
Encrypted: Yes (repokey)
Cache: /root/.cache/borg/
↪d857ce5788c51272c61535062e89eac4e8ef5a884ffbe976e0af9d8765dedfa5
Security dir: /root/.config/borg/security/
↪d857ce5788c51272c61535062e89eac4e8ef5a884ffbe976e0af9d8765dedfa5
------------------------------------------------------------------------------
                      Original size      Compressed size    Deduplicated size
All archives:             121.82 TB            112.41 TB            215.42 GB

                      Unique chunks        Total chunks
Chunk index:                1015213           626934122
```

borg mount

```
borg [common options] mount [options] REPOSITORY_OR_ARCHIVE MOUNTPOINT
```

REPOSITORY_OR_ARCHIVE repository/archive to mount

MOUNTPOINT where to mount filesystem

optional arguments

> **-f, --foreground**   stay in foreground, do not daemonize
>
> **-o**   Extra mount options

Common options

Archive filters

> **-P PREFIX, --prefix PREFIX** only consider archive names starting with this prefix.
>
> **-a GLOB, --glob-archives GLOB** only consider archive names matching the glob. sh: rules apply, see "borg help patterns". `--prefix` and `--glob-archives` are mutually exclusive.
>
> **--sort-by KEYS**   Comma-separated list of sorting keys; valid keys are: timestamp, name, id; default is: timestamp
>
> **--first N**   consider first N archives after other filters were applied
>
> **--last N**   consider last N archives after other filters were applied

Description

This command mounts an archive as a FUSE filesystem. This can be useful for browsing an archive or restoring individual files. Unless the `--foreground` option is given the command will run in the background until the filesystem is `umounted`.

The command `borgfs` provides a wrapper for `borg mount`. This can also be used in fstab entries: `/path/to/repo /mnt/point fuse.borgfs defaults,noauto 0 0`

To allow a regular user to use fstab entries, add the `user` option: `/path/to/repo /mnt/point fuse.borgfs defaults,noauto,user 0 0`

For mount options, see the fuse(8) manual page. Additional mount options supported by borg:

- versions: when used with a repository mount, this gives a merged, versioned view of the files in the archives. EXPERIMENTAL, layout may change in future.
- allow_damaged_files: by default damaged files (where missing chunks were replaced with runs of zeros by borg check `--repair`) are not readable and return EIO (I/O error). Set this option to read such files.

The BORG_MOUNT_DATA_CACHE_ENTRIES environment variable is meant for advanced users to tweak the performance. It sets the number of cached data chunks; additional memory usage can be up to ~8 MiB times this number. The default is the number of CPU cores.

When the daemonized process receives a signal or crashes, it does not unmount. Unmounting in these cases could cause an active rsync or similar process to unintentionally delete data.

When running in the foreground ^C/SIGINT unmounts cleanly, but other signals or crashes do not.

borg umount

```
borg [common options] umount [options] MOUNTPOINT
```

MOUNTPOINT mountpoint of the filesystem to umount

Common options

Description

This command un-mounts a FUSE filesystem that was mounted with `borg mount`.

This is a convenience wrapper that just calls the platform-specific shell command - usually this is either umount or fusermount -u.

Examples

```
# Mounting the repository shows all archives.
# Archives are loaded lazily, expect some delay when navigating to an archive
# for the first time.
$ borg mount /path/to/repo /tmp/mymountpoint
$ ls /tmp/mymountpoint
root-2016-02-14 root-2016-02-15
$ borg umount /tmp/mymountpoint

# Mounting a specific archive is possible as well.
$ borg mount /path/to/repo::root-2016-02-15 /tmp/mymountpoint
$ ls /tmp/mymountpoint
bin  boot  etc     home  lib  lib64  lost+found  media  mnt  opt
root  sbin  srv  tmp  usr  var
$ borg umount /tmp/mymountpoint

# The experimental "versions view" merges all archives in the repository
# and provides a versioned view on files.
$ borg mount -o versions /path/to/repo /tmp/mymountpoint
$ ls -l /tmp/mymountpoint/home/user/doc.txt/
total 24
-rw-rw-r-- 1 user group 12357 Aug 26 21:19 doc.cda00bc9.txt
-rw-rw-r-- 1 user group 12204 Aug 26 21:04 doc.fa760f28.txt
$ borg umount /tmp/mymountpoint

# Archive filters are supported.
# These are especially handy for the "versions view",
# which does not support lazy processing of archives.
$ borg mount -o versions --glob-archives '*-my-home' --last 10 /path/to/repo /tmp/
↪mymountpoint
```

borgfs

```
$ echo '/mnt/backup /tmp/myrepo fuse.borgfs defaults,noauto 0 0' >> /etc/fstab
$ echo '/mnt/backup::root-2016-02-15 /tmp/myarchive fuse.borgfs defaults,noauto 0 0
↪' >> /etc/fstab
$ mount /tmp/myrepo
$ mount /tmp/myarchive
$ ls /tmp/myrepo
root-2016-02-01 root-2016-02-2015
```

```
$ ls /tmp/myarchive
bin  boot  etc       home  lib  lib64  lost+found  media  mnt  opt  root  sbin  srv
↪  tmp  usr  var
```

Note: `borgfs` will be automatically provided if you used a distribution package, `pip` or `setup.py` to install Borg. Users of the standalone binary will have to manually create a symlink (see *Standalone Binary*).

borg key change-passphrase

```
borg [common options] key change-passphrase [options] [REPOSITORY]
```

REPOSITORY

Common options

Description

The key files used for repository encryption are optionally passphrase protected. This command can be used to change this passphrase.

Please note that this command only changes the passphrase, but not any secret protected by it (like e.g. encryption/MAC keys or chunker seed). Thus, changing the passphrase after passphrase and borg key got compromised does not protect future (nor past) backups to the same repository.

Examples

```
# Create a key file protected repository
$ borg init --encryption=keyfile -v /path/to/repo
Initializing repository at "/path/to/repo"
Enter new passphrase:
Enter same passphrase again:
Remember your passphrase. Your data will be inaccessible without it.
Key in "/root/.config/borg/keys/mnt_backup" created.
Keep this key safe. Your data will be inaccessible without it.
Synchronizing chunks cache...
Archives: 0, w/ cached Idx: 0, w/ outdated Idx: 0, w/o cached Idx: 0.
Done.

# Change key file passphrase
$ borg key change-passphrase -v /path/to/repo
Enter passphrase for key /root/.config/borg/keys/mnt_backup:
Enter new passphrase:
Enter same passphrase again:
Remember your passphrase. Your data will be inaccessible without it.
Key updated
```

Fully automated using environment variables:

```
$ BORG_NEW_PASSPHRASE=old borg init -e=repokey repo
# now "old" is the current passphrase.
$ BORG_PASSPHRASE=old BORG_NEW_PASSPHRASE=new borg key change-passphrase repo
# now "new" is the current passphrase.
```

borg key export

```
borg [common options] key export [options] [REPOSITORY] [PATH]
```

REPOSITORY

PATH where to store the backup

optional arguments

       --paper   Create an export suitable for printing and later type-in

       --qr-html   Create an html file suitable for printing and later type-in or qr scan

Common options

Description

If repository encryption is used, the repository is inaccessible without the key. This command allows to backup this essential key.

There are two backup formats. The normal backup format is suitable for digital storage as a file. The `--paper` backup format is optimized for printing and typing in while importing, with per line checks to reduce problems with manual input.

For repositories using keyfile encryption the key is saved locally on the system that is capable of doing backups. To guard against loss of this key, the key needs to be backed up independently of the main data backup.

For repositories using the repokey encryption the key is saved in the repository in the config file. A backup is thus not strictly needed, but guards against the repository becoming inaccessible if the file is damaged for some reason.

borg key import

```
borg [common options] key import [options] [REPOSITORY] [PATH]
```

REPOSITORY

PATH path to the backup ('-' to read from stdin)

optional arguments

       --paper   interactively import from a backup done with `--paper`

Common options

Description

This command allows to restore a key previously backed up with the export command.

If the `--paper` option is given, the import will be an interactive process in which each line is checked for plausibility before proceeding to the next line. For this format PATH must not be given.

borg upgrade

```
borg [common options] upgrade [options] [REPOSITORY]
```

REPOSITORY path to the repository to be upgraded

optional arguments

-n, --dry-run	do not change repository
--inplace	rewrite repository in place, with no chance of going back to older versions of the repository.
--force	Force upgrade
--tam	Enable manifest authentication (in key and cache) (Borg 1.0.9 and later).
--disable-tam	Disable manifest authentication (in key and cache).

Common options

Description

Upgrade an existing, local Borg repository.

When you do not need borg upgrade

Not every change requires that you run `borg upgrade`.

You do **not** need to run it when:

- moving your repository to a different place
- upgrading to another point release (like 1.0.x to 1.0.y), except when noted otherwise in the changelog
- upgrading from 1.0.x to 1.1.x, except when noted otherwise in the changelog

Borg 1.x.y upgrades

Use `borg upgrade --tam REPO` to require manifest authentication introduced with Borg 1.0.9 to address security issues. This means that modifying the repository after doing this with a version prior to 1.0.9 will raise a validation error, so only perform this upgrade after updating all clients using the repository to 1.0.9 or newer.

This upgrade should be done on each client for safety reasons.

If a repository is accidentally modified with a pre-1.0.9 client after this upgrade, use `borg upgrade --tam --force REPO` to remedy it.

If you routinely do this you might not want to enable this upgrade (which will leave you exposed to the security issue). You can reverse the upgrade by issuing `borg upgrade --disable-tam REPO`.

See https://borgbackup.readthedocs.io/en/stable/changes.html#pre-1-0-9-manifest-spoofing-vulnerability for details.

Attic and Borg 0.xx to Borg 1.x

This currently supports converting an Attic repository to Borg and also helps with converting Borg 0.xx to 1.0.

Currently, only LOCAL repositories can be upgraded (issue #465).

Please note that `borg create` (since 1.0.0) uses bigger chunks by default than old borg or attic did, so the new chunks won't deduplicate with the old chunks in the upgraded repository. See `--chunker-params` option of `borg create` and `borg recreate`.

`borg upgrade` will change the magic strings in the repository's segments to match the new Borg magic strings. The keyfiles found in $ATTIC_KEYS_DIR or ~/.attic/keys/ will also be converted and copied to $BORG_KEYS_DIR or ~/.config/borg/keys.

The cache files are converted, from $ATTIC_CACHE_DIR or ~/.cache/attic to $BORG_CACHE_DIR or ~/.cache/borg, but the cache layout between Borg and Attic changed, so it is possible the first backup after the conversion takes longer than expected due to the cache resync.

Upgrade should be able to resume if interrupted, although it will still iterate over all segments. If you want to start from scratch, use *borg delete* over the copied repository to make sure the cache files are also removed:

> borg delete borg

Unless `--inplace` is specified, the upgrade process first creates a backup copy of the repository, in REPOSITORY.before-upgrade-DATETIME, using hardlinks. This takes longer than in place upgrades, but is much safer and gives progress information (as opposed to `cp -al`). Once you are satisfied with the conversion, you can safely destroy the backup copy.

WARNING: Running the upgrade in place will make the current copy unusable with older version, with no way of going back to previous versions. This can PERMANENTLY DAMAGE YOUR REPOSITORY! Attic CAN NOT READ BORG REPOSITORIES, as the magic strings have changed. You have been warned.

Examples

```
# Upgrade the borg repository to the most recent version.
$ borg upgrade -v /path/to/repo
making a hardlink copy in /path/to/repo.before-upgrade-2016-02-15-20:51:55
opening attic repository with borg and converting
no key file found for repository
converting repo index /path/to/repo/index.0
converting 1 segments...
converting borg 0.xx to borg current
no key file found for repository
```

Upgrading a passphrase encrypted attic repo

attic offered a "passphrase" encryption mode, but this was removed in borg 1.0 and replaced by the "repokey" mode (which stores the passphrase-protected encryption key into the repository config).

Thus, to upgrade a "passphrase" attic repo to a "repokey" borg repo, 2 steps are needed, in this order:

- borg upgrade repo
- borg key migrate-to-repokey repo

borg recreate

```
borg [common options] recreate [options] [REPOSITORY_OR_ARCHIVE] [PATH...]
```

REPOSITORY_OR_ARCHIVE repository/archive to recreate

PATH paths to recreate; patterns are supported

optional arguments

--list	output verbose list of items (files, dirs, ...)
--filter STATUSCHARS	only display items with the given status characters (listed in borg create –help)
-n, --dry-run	do not change anything
-s, --stats	print statistics at end

Common options

Exclusion options

-e PATTERN, --exclude PATTERN	exclude paths matching PATTERN
--exclude-from EXCLUDEFILE	read exclude patterns from EXCLUDEFILE, one per line
--pattern PATTERN	experimental: include/exclude paths matching PATTERN
--patterns-from PATTERNFILE	experimental: read include/exclude patterns from PATTERNFILE, one per line
--exclude-caches	exclude directories that contain a CACHEDIR.TAG file (http://www.brynosaurus.com/cachedir/spec.html)
--exclude-if-present NAME	exclude directories that are tagged by containing a filesystem object with the given NAME
--keep-exclude-tags, --keep-tag-files	if tag objects are specified with `--exclude-if-present`, don't omit the tag objects themselves from the backup archive

Archive options

--target TARGET	create a new archive with the name ARCHIVE, do not replace existing archive (only applies for a single archive)
-c SECONDS, --checkpoint-interval SECONDS	write checkpoint every SECONDS seconds (Default: 1800)
--comment COMMENT	add a comment text to the archive
--timestamp TIMESTAMP	manually specify the archive creation date/time (UTC, yyyy-mm-ddThh:mm:ss format). alternatively, give a reference file/directory.
-C COMPRESSION, --compression COMPRESSION	select compression algorithm, see the output of the "borg help compression" command for details.
--recompress	recompress data chunks according to `--compression` if *if-different*. When *always*, chunks that are already compressed that way are not skipped, but compressed again. Only the algorithm is considered for *if-different*, not the compression level (if any).
--chunker-params PARAMS	specify the chunker parameters (CHUNK_MIN_EXP, CHUNK_MAX_EXP, HASH_MASK_BITS, HASH_WINDOW_SIZE) or *default* to use the current defaults. default: 19,23,21,4095

Description

Recreate the contents of existing archives.

This is an *experimental* feature. Do *not* use this on your only backup.

`--exclude`, `--exclude-from`, `--exclude-if-present`, `--keep-exclude-tags`, and PATH have the exact same semantics as in "borg create". If PATHs are specified the resulting archive will only contain files from these PATHs.

Note that all paths in an archive are relative, therefore absolute patterns/paths will *not* match (`--exclude`, `--exclude-from`, PATHs).

`--recompress` allows to change the compression of existing data in archives. Due to how Borg stores compressed size information this might display incorrect information for archives that were not recreated at the same time. There is no risk of data loss by this.

`--chunker-params` will re-chunk all files in the archive, this can be used to have upgraded Borg 0.xx or Attic archives deduplicate with Borg 1.x archives.

USE WITH CAUTION. Depending on the PATHs and patterns given, recreate can be used to permanently delete files from archives. When in doubt, use `--dry-run --verbose --list` to see how patterns/PATHS are interpreted.

The archive being recreated is only removed after the operation completes. The archive that is built during the operation exists at the same time at "<ARCHIVE>.recreate". The new archive will have a different archive ID.

With `--target` the original archive is not replaced, instead a new archive is created.

When rechunking space usage can be substantial, expect at least the entire deduplicated size of the archives using the previous chunker params. When recompressing expect approx. (throughput / checkpoint-interval) in space usage, assuming all chunks are recompressed.

Examples

```
# Make old (Attic / Borg 0.xx) archives deduplicate with Borg 1.x archives.
# Archives created with Borg 1.1+ and the default chunker params are skipped
# (archive ID stays the same).
$ borg recreate /mnt/backup --chunker-params default --progress

# Create a backup with little but fast compression
$ borg create /mnt/backup::archive /some/files --compression lz4
# Then compress it - this might take longer, but the backup has already completed,
# so no inconsistencies from a long-running backup job.
$ borg recreate /mnt/backup::archive --recompress --compression zlib,9

# Remove unwanted files from all archives in a repository.
# Note the relative path for the --exclude option - archives only contain relative␣
→paths.
$ borg recreate /mnt/backup --exclude home/icke/Pictures/drunk_photos

# Change archive comment
$ borg create --comment "This is a comment" /mnt/backup::archivename ~
$ borg info /mnt/backup::archivename
Name: archivename
Fingerprint: ...
Comment: This is a comment
...
$ borg recreate --comment "This is a better comment" /mnt/backup::archivename
$ borg info /mnt/backup::archivename
Name: archivename
Fingerprint: ...
Comment: This is a better comment
...
```

borg export-tar

```
borg [common options] export-tar [options] ARCHIVE FILE [PATH...]
```

ARCHIVE archive to export

FILE output tar file. "-" to write to stdout instead.

PATH paths to extract; patterns are supported

optional arguments

> **--tar-filter** filter program to pipe data through
>
> **--list** output verbose list of items (files, dirs, ...)

Common options

Exclusion options

> **-e PATTERN, --exclude PATTERN** exclude paths matching PATTERN
>
> **--exclude-from EXCLUDEFILE** read exclude patterns from EXCLUDEFILE, one per line
>
> **--pattern PATTERN** experimental: include/exclude paths matching PATTERN
>
> **--patterns-from PATTERNFILE** experimental: read include/exclude patterns from PATTERNFILE, one per line
>
> **--strip-components NUMBER** Remove the specified number of leading path elements. Paths with fewer elements will be silently skipped.

Description

This command creates a tarball from an archive.

When giving '-' as the output FILE, Borg will write a tar stream to standard output.

By default (`--tar-filter=auto`) Borg will detect whether the FILE should be compressed based on its file extension and pipe the tarball through an appropriate filter before writing it to FILE:

- .tar.gz: gzip
- .tar.bz2: bzip2
- .tar.xz: xz

Alternatively a `--tar-filter` program may be explicitly specified. It should read the uncompressed tar stream from stdin and write a compressed/filtered tar stream to stdout.

The generated tarball uses the GNU tar format.

export-tar is a lossy conversion: BSD flags, ACLs, extended attributes (xattrs), atime and ctime are not exported. Timestamp resolution is limited to whole seconds, not the nanosecond resolution otherwise supported by Borg.

A `--sparse` option (as found in borg extract) is not supported.

By default the entire archive is extracted but a subset of files and directories can be selected by passing a list of PATHs as arguments. The file selection can further be restricted by using the `--exclude` option.

See the output of the "borg help patterns" command for more help on exclude patterns.

`--progress` can be slower than no progress display, since it makes one additional pass over the archive metadata.

Examples

```
# export as uncompressed tar
$ borg export-tar /path/to/repo::Monday Monday.tar

# exclude some types, compress using gzip
$ borg export-tar /path/to/repo::Monday Monday.tar.gz --exclude '*.so'

# use higher compression level with gzip
$ borg export-tar testrepo::linux --tar-filter="gzip -9" Monday.tar.gz

# export a gzipped tar, but instead of storing it on disk,
# upload it to a remote site using curl.
$ borg export-tar ... --tar-filter="gzip" - | curl --data-binary @- https://
↪somewhere/to/POST

# remote extraction via "tarpipe"
$ borg export-tar /path/to/repo::Monday - | ssh somewhere "cd extracted; tar x"
```

borg serve

```
borg [common options] serve [options]
```

optional arguments

--restrict-to-path PATH restrict repository access to PATH. Can be specified multiple times to allow the client access to several directories. Access to all sub-directories is granted implicitly; PATH doesn't need to directly point to a repository.

--restrict-to-repository PATH restrict repository access. Only the repository located at PATH (no sub-directories are considered) is accessible. Can be specified multiple times to allow the client access to several repositories. Unlike --restrict-to-path sub-directories are not accessible; PATH needs to directly point at a repository location. PATH may be an empty directory or the last element of PATH may not exist, in which case the client may initialize a repository there.

--append-only only allow appending to repository segment files

--storage-quota QUOTA Override storage quota of the repository (e.g. 5G, 1.5T). When a new repository is initialized, sets the storage quota on the new repository as well. Default: no quota.

Common options

Description

This command starts a repository server process. This command is usually not used manually.

Examples

borg serve has special support for ssh forced commands (see authorized_keys example below): it will detect that you use such a forced command and extract the value of the --restrict-to-path option(s).

It will then parse the original command that came from the client, makes sure that it is also `borg serve` and enforce path restriction(s) as given by the forced command. That way, other options given by the client (like `--info` or `--umask`) are preserved (and are not fixed by the forced command).

Environment variables (such as BORG_HOSTNAME_IS_UNIQUE) contained in the original command sent by the client are *not* interpreted, but ignored. If BORG_XXX environment variables should be set on the `borg serve` side, then these must be set in system-specific locations like `/etc/environment` or in the forced command itself (example below).

```
# Allow an SSH keypair to only run borg, and only have access to /path/to/repo.
# Use key options to disable unneeded and potentially dangerous SSH functionality.
# This will help to secure an automated remote backup system.
$ cat ~/.ssh/authorized_keys
command="borg serve --restrict-to-path /path/to/repo",restrict ssh-rsa AAAAB3[...]

# Set a BORG_XXX environment variable on the "borg serve" side
$ cat ~/.ssh/authorized_keys
command="export BORG_XXX=value; borg serve [...]",restrict ssh-rsa [...]
```

Note: The examples above use the `restrict` directive. This does automatically block potential dangerous ssh features, even when they are added in a future update. Thus, this option should be preferred.

If you're using openssh-server < 7.2, however, you have to explicitly specify the ssh features to restrict and cannot simply use the restrict option as it has been introduced in v7.2. We recommend to use `no-port-forwarding`, `no-X11-forwarding`, `no-pty`, `no-agent-forwarding`, `no-user-rc` in this case.

---

borg with-lock

```
borg [common options] with-lock [options] REPOSITORY COMMAND [ARGS...]
```

REPOSITORY repository to lock

COMMAND command to run

ARGS command arguments

Common options

Description

This command runs a user-specified command while the repository lock is held.

It will first try to acquire the lock (make sure that no other operation is running in the repo), then execute the given command as a subprocess and wait for its termination, release the lock and return the user command's return code as borg's return code.

Note: If you copy a repository with the lock held, the lock will be present in the copy. Thus, before using borg on the copy from a different host, you need to use "borg break-lock" on the copied repository, because Borg is cautious and does not automatically remove stale locks made by a different host.

---

borg break-lock

```
borg [common options] break-lock [options] [REPOSITORY]
```

REPOSITORY repository for which to break the locks

Common options

Description

This command breaks the repository and cache locks. Please use carefully and only while no borg process (on any machine) is trying to access the Cache or the Repository.

borg benchmark crud

```
borg [common options] benchmark crud [options] REPO PATH
```

REPO repo to use for benchmark (must exist)

PATH path were to create benchmark input data

Common options

Description

This command benchmarks borg CRUD (create, read, update, delete) operations.

It creates input data below the given PATH and backups this data into the given REPO. The REPO must already exist (it could be a fresh empty repo or an existing repo, the command will create / read / update / delete some archives named borg-test-data* there.

Make sure you have free space there, you'll need about 1GB each (+ overhead).

If your repository is encrypted and borg needs a passphrase to unlock the key, use:

BORG_PASSPHRASE=mysecret borg benchmark crud REPO PATH

Measurements are done with different input file sizes and counts. The file contents are very artificial (either all zero or all random), thus the measurement results do not necessarily reflect performance with real data. Also, due to the kind of content used, no compression is used in these benchmarks.

C- == borg create (1st archive creation, no compression, do not use files cache) C-Z- == all-zero files. full dedup, this is primarily measuring reader/chunker/hasher. C-R- == random files. no dedup, measuring throughput through all processing stages.

R- == borg extract (extract archive, dry-run, do everything, but do not write files to disk) R-Z- == all zero files. Measuring heavily duplicated files. R-R- == random files. No duplication here, measuring throughput through all processing

stages, except writing to disk.

U- == borg create (2nd archive creation of unchanged input files, measure files cache speed) The throughput value is kind of virtual here, it does not actually read the file. U-Z- == needs to check the 2 all-zero chunks' existence in the repo. U-R- == needs to check existence of a lot of different chunks in the repo.

D- == borg delete archive (delete last remaining archive, measure deletion + compaction) D-Z- == few chunks to delete / few segments to compact/remove. D-R- == many chunks to delete / many segments to compact/remove.

Please note that there might be quite some variance in these measurements. Try multiple measurements and having a otherwise idle machine (and network, if you use it).

Miscellaneous Help

borg help patterns

File patterns support these styles: fnmatch, shell, regular expressions, path prefixes and path full-matches. By default, fnmatch is used for `--exclude` patterns and shell-style is used for the experimental `--pattern` option.

If followed by a colon (':') the first two characters of a pattern are used as a style selector. Explicit style selection is necessary when a non-default style is desired or when the desired pattern starts with two alphanumeric characters followed by a colon (i.e. *aa:something/*).

Fnmatch[74], selector *fm:* This is the default style for `--exclude` and `--exclude-from`. These patterns use a variant of shell pattern syntax, with '*' matching any number of characters, '?' matching any single character, '[...]' matching any single character specified, including ranges, and '[!...]' matching any character not specified. For the purpose of these patterns, the path separator ('' for Windows and '/' on other systems) is not treated specially. Wrap meta-characters in brackets for a literal match (i.e. *[?]* to match the literal character *?*). For a path to match a pattern, it must completely match from start to end, or must match from the start to just before a path separator. Except for the root path, paths will never end in the path separator when matching is attempted. Thus, if a given pattern ends in a path separator, a '*' is appended before matching is attempted.

Shell-style patterns, selector *sh:* This is the default style for `--pattern` and `--patterns-from`. Like fnmatch patterns these are similar to shell patterns. The difference is that the pattern may include **/ for matching zero or more directory levels, * for matching zero or more arbitrary characters with the exception of any path separator.

Regular expressions, selector *re:* Regular expressions similar to those found in Perl are supported. Unlike shell patterns regular expressions are not required to match the complete path and any substring match is sufficient. It is strongly recommended to anchor patterns to the start ('^'), to the end ('$') or both. Path separators ('' for Windows and '/' on other systems) in paths are always normalized to a forward slash ('/') before applying a pattern. The regular expression syntax is described in the Python documentation for the re module[75].

Path prefix, selector *pp:* This pattern style is useful to match whole sub-directories. The pattern *pp:/data/bar* matches */data/bar* and everything therein.

Path full-match, selector *pf:* This pattern style is useful to match whole paths. This is kind of a pseudo pattern as it can not have any variable or unspecified parts - the full, precise path must be given. *pf:/data/foo.txt* matches */data/foo.txt* only.

Implementation note: this is implemented via very time-efficient O(1) hashtable lookups (this means you can have huge amounts of such patterns without impacting performance much). Due to that, this kind of pattern does not respect any context or order. If you use such a pattern to include a file, it will always be included (if the directory recursion encounters it). Other include/exclude patterns that would normally match will be ignored. Same logic applies for exclude.

Note: *re:*, *sh:* and *fm:* patterns are all implemented on top of the Python SRE engine. It is very easy to formulate patterns for each of these types which requires an inordinate amount of time to match paths. If untrusted users

---

[74] https://docs.python.org/3/library/fnmatch.html
[75] https://docs.python.org/3/library/re.html

are able to supply patterns, ensure they cannot supply *re:* patterns. Further, ensure that *sh:* and *fm:* patterns only contain a handful of wildcards at most.

Exclusions can be passed via the command line option `--exclude`. When used from within a shell the patterns should be quoted to protect them from expansion.

The `--exclude-from` option permits loading exclusion patterns from a text file with one pattern per line. Lines empty or starting with the number sign ('#') after removing whitespace on both ends are ignored. The optional style selector prefix is also supported for patterns loaded from a file. Due to whitespace removal paths with whitespace at the beginning or end can only be excluded using regular expressions.

Examples:

```
# Exclude '/home/user/file.o' but not '/home/user/file.odt':
$ borg create -e '*.o' backup /

# Exclude '/home/user/junk' and '/home/user/subdir/junk' but
# not '/home/user/importantjunk' or '/etc/junk':
$ borg create -e '/home/*/junk' backup /

# Exclude the contents of '/home/user/cache' but not the directory itself:
$ borg create -e /home/user/cache/ backup /

# The file '/home/user/cache/important' is *not* backed up:
$ borg create -e /home/user/cache/ backup / /home/user/cache/important

# The contents of directories in '/home' are not backed up when their name
# ends in '.tmp'
$ borg create --exclude 're:^/home/[^/]+\.tmp/' backup /

# Load exclusions from file
$ cat >exclude.txt <<EOF
# Comment line
/home/*/junk
*.tmp
fm:aa:something/*
re:^/home/[^/]\.tmp/
sh:/home/*/.thumbnails
EOF
$ borg create --exclude-from exclude.txt backup /
```

A more general and easier to use way to define filename matching patterns exists with the experimental `--pattern` and `--patterns-from` options. Using these, you may specify the backup roots (starting points) and patterns for inclusion/exclusion. A root path starts with the prefix *R*, followed by a path (a plain path, not a file pattern). An include rule starts with the prefix +, an exclude rule starts with the prefix -, both followed by a pattern. Inclusion patterns are useful to include paths that are contained in an excluded path. The first matching pattern is used so if an include pattern matches before an exclude pattern, the file is backed up.

Note that the default pattern style for `--pattern` and `--patterns-from` is shell style (*sh:*), so those patterns behave similar to rsync include/exclude patterns. The pattern style can be set via the *P* prefix.

Patterns (`--pattern`) and excludes (`--exclude`) from the command line are considered first (in the order of appearance). Then patterns from `--patterns-from` are added. Exclusion patterns from `--exclude-from` files are appended last.

An example `--patterns-from` file could look like that:

```
# "sh:" pattern style is the default, so the following line is not needed:
P sh
R /
# can be rebuild
- /home/*/.cache
# they're downloads for a reason
```

```
- /home/*/Downloads
# susan is a nice person
# include susans home
+ /home/susan
# don't backup the other home directories
- /home/*
```

borg help placeholders

Repository (or Archive) URLs, `--prefix` and `--remote-path` values support these placeholders:

{hostname} The (short) hostname of the machine.

{fqdn} The full name of the machine.

{now} The current local date and time, by default in ISO-8601 format. You can also supply your own format string[76], e.g. {now:%Y-%m-%d_%H:%M:%S}

{utcnow} The current UTC date and time, by default in ISO-8601 format. You can also supply your own format string[77], e.g. {utcnow:%Y-%m-%d_%H:%M:%S}

{user} The user name (or UID, if no name is available) of the user running borg.

{pid} The current process ID.

{borgversion} The version of borg, e.g.: 1.0.8rc1

{borgmajor} The version of borg, only the major version, e.g.: 1

{borgminor} The version of borg, only major and minor version, e.g.: 1.0

{borgpatch} The version of borg, only major, minor and patch version, e.g.: 1.0.8

If literal curly braces need to be used, double them for escaping:

```
borg create /path/to/repo::{{literal_text}}
```

Examples:

```
borg create /path/to/repo::{hostname}-{user}-{utcnow} ...
borg create /path/to/repo::{hostname}-{now:%Y-%m-%d_%H:%M:%S} ...
borg prune --prefix '{hostname}-' ...
```

Note: systemd uses a difficult, non-standard syntax for command lines in unit files (refer to the *systemd.unit(5)* manual page).

When invoking borg from unit files, pay particular attention to escaping, especially when using the now/utcnow placeholders, since systemd performs its own %-based variable replacement even in quoted text. To avoid interference from systemd, double all percent signs (`{hostname}-{now:%Y-%m-%d_%H:%M:%S}` becomes `{hostname}-{now:%%Y-%%m-%%d_%%H:%%M:%%S}`).

borg help compression

It is no problem to mix different compression methods in one repo, deduplication is done on the source data chunks (not on the compressed or encrypted data).

If some specific chunk was once compressed and stored into the repo, creating another backup that also uses this chunk will not change the stored chunk. So if you use different compression specs for the backups, whichever stores a chunk first determines its compression. See also borg recreate.

---

[76] https://docs.python.org/3.4/library/datetime.html#strftime-and-strptime-behavior
[77] https://docs.python.org/3.4/library/datetime.html#strftime-and-strptime-behavior

---

Compression is lz4 by default. If you want something else, you have to specify what you want.

Valid compression specifiers are:

none Do not compress.

lz4 Use lz4 compression. High speed, low compression. (default)

zlib[,L] Use zlib ("gz") compression. Medium speed, medium compression. If you do not explicitly give the compression level L (ranging from 0 to 9), it will use level 6. Giving level 0 (means "no compression", but still has zlib protocol overhead) is usually pointless, you better use "none" compression.

lzma[,L] Use lzma ("xz") compression. Low speed, high compression. If you do not explicitly give the compression level L (ranging from 0 to 9), it will use level 6. Giving levels above 6 is pointless and counterproductive because it does not compress better due to the buffer size used by borg - but it wastes lots of CPU cycles and RAM.

auto,C[,L] Use a built-in heuristic to decide per chunk whether to compress or not. The heuristic tries with lz4 whether the data is compressible. For incompressible data, it will not use compression (uses "none"). For compressible data, it uses the given C[,L] compression - with C[,L] being any valid compression specifier.

Examples:

```
borg create --compression lz4 REPO::ARCHIVE data
borg create --compression zlib REPO::ARCHIVE data
borg create --compression zlib,1 REPO::ARCHIVE data
borg create --compression auto,lzma,6 REPO::ARCHIVE data
borg create --compression auto,lzma ...
```

Debugging Facilities

There is a `borg debug` command that has some subcommands which are all **not intended for normal use** and **potentially very dangerous** if used incorrectly.

For example, `borg debug put-obj` and `borg debug delete-obj` will only do what their name suggests: put objects into repo / delete objects from repo.

Please note:

- they will not update the chunks cache (chunks index) about the object
- they will not update the manifest (so no automatic chunks index resync is triggered)
- they will not check whether the object is in use (e.g. before delete-obj)
- they will not update any metadata which may point to the object

They exist to improve debugging capabilities without direct system access, e.g. in case you ever run into some severe malfunction. Use them only if you know what you are doing or if a trusted Borg developer tells you what to do.

Borg has a `--debug-topic TOPIC` option to enable specific debugging messages. Topics are generally not documented.

A `--debug-profile FILE` option exists which writes a profile of the main program's execution to a file. The format of these files is not directly compatible with the Python profiling tools, since these use the "marshal" format, which is not intended to be secure (quoting the Python docs: "Never unmarshal data received from an untrusted or unauthenticated source.").

The `borg debug profile-convert` command can be used to take a Borg profile and convert it to a profile file that is compatible with the Python tools.

Additionally, if the filename specified for `--debug-profile` ends with ".pyprof" a Python compatible profile is generated. This is only intended for local use by developers.

Additional Notes

Here are misc. notes about topics that are maybe not covered in enough detail in the usage section.

--chunker-params

The chunker params influence how input files are cut into pieces (chunks) which are then considered for deduplication. They also have a big impact on resource usage (RAM and disk space) as the amount of resources needed is (also) determined by the total amount of chunks in the repository (see *Indexes / Caches memory usage* for details).

`--chunker-params=10,23,16,4095` results in a fine-grained deduplication| and creates a big amount of chunks and thus uses a lot of resources to manage them. This is good for relatively small data volumes and if the machine has a good amount of free RAM and disk space.

`--chunker-params=19,23,21,4095` (default) results in a coarse-grained deduplication and creates a much smaller amount of chunks and thus uses less resources. This is good for relatively big data volumes and if the machine has a relatively low amount of free RAM and disk space.

If you already have made some archives in a repository and you then change chunker params, this of course impacts deduplication as the chunks will be cut differently.

In the worst case (all files are big and were touched in between backups), this will store all content into the repository again.

Usually, it is not that bad though:

- usually most files are not touched, so it will just re-use the old chunks it already has in the repo
- files smaller than the (both old and new) minimum chunksize result in only one chunk anyway, so the resulting chunks are same and deduplication will apply

If you switch chunker params to save resources for an existing repo that already has some backup archives, you will see an increasing effect over time, when more and more files have been touched and stored again using the bigger chunksize **and** all references to the smaller older chunks have been removed (by deleting / pruning archives).

If you want to see an immediate big effect on resource usage, you better start a new repository when changing chunker params.

For more details, see *Chunks*.

--noatime / --noctime

You can use these `borg create` options to not store the respective timestamp into the archive, in case you do not really need it.

Besides saving a little space for the not archived timestamp, it might also affect metadata stream deduplication: if only this timestamp changes between backups and is stored into the metadata stream, the metadata stream chunks won't deduplicate just because of that.

--umask

If you use `--umask`, make sure that all repository-modifying borg commands (create, delete, prune) that access the repository in question use the same `--umask` value.

If multiple machines access the same repository, this should hold true for all of them.

--read-special

The --read-special option is special - you do not want to use it for normal full-filesystem backups, but rather after carefully picking some targets for it.

The option --read-special triggers special treatment for block and char device files as well as FIFOs. Instead of storing them as such a device (or FIFO), they will get opened, their content will be read and in the backup archive they will show up like a regular file.

Symlinks will also get special treatment if (and only if) they point to such a special file: instead of storing them as a symlink, the target special file will get processed as described above.

One intended use case of this is backing up the contents of one or multiple block devices, like e.g. LVM snapshots or inactive LVs or disk partitions.

You need to be careful about what you include when using --read-special, e.g. if you include /dev/zero, your backup will never terminate.

Restoring such files' content is currently only supported one at a time via --stdout option (and you have to redirect stdout to where ever it shall go, maybe directly into an existing device file of your choice or indirectly via dd).

To some extent, mounting a backup archive with the backups of special files via borg mount and then loop-mounting the image files from inside the mount point will work. If you plan to access a lot of data in there, it likely will scale and perform better if you do not work via the FUSE mount.

Example

Imagine you have made some snapshots of logical volumes (LVs) you want to backup.

Note: For some scenarios, this is a good method to get "crash-like" consistency (I call it crash-like because it is the same as you would get if you just hit the reset button or your machine would abrubtly and completely crash). This is better than no consistency at all and a good method for some use cases, but likely not good enough if you have databases running.

Then you create a backup archive of all these snapshots. The backup process will see a "frozen" state of the logical volumes, while the processes working in the original volumes continue changing the data stored there.

You also add the output of lvdisplay to your backup, so you can see the LV sizes in case you ever need to recreate and restore them.

After the backup has completed, you remove the snapshots again.

```
$ # create snapshots here
$ lvdisplay > lvdisplay.txt
$ borg create --read-special /path/to/repo::arch lvdisplay.txt /dev/vg0/*-snapshot
$ # remove snapshots here
```

Now, let's see how to restore some LVs from such a backup.

```
$ borg extract /path/to/repo::arch lvdisplay.txt
$ # create empty LVs with correct sizes here (look into lvdisplay.txt).
$ # we assume that you created an empty root and home LV and overwrite it now:
$ borg extract --stdout /path/to/repo::arch dev/vg0/root-snapshot > /dev/vg0/root
$ borg extract --stdout /path/to/repo::arch dev/vg0/home-snapshot > /dev/vg0/home
```

Append-only mode

A repository can be made "append-only", which means that Borg will never overwrite or delete committed data (append-only refers to the segment files, but borg will also reject to delete the repository completely). This is

---

useful for scenarios where a backup client machine backups remotely to a backup server using `borg serve`, since a hacked client machine cannot delete backups on the server permanently.

To activate append-only mode, edit the repository `config` file and add a line `append_only=1` to the `[repository]` section (or edit the line if it exists).

In append-only mode Borg will create a transaction log in the `transactions` file, where each line is a transaction and a UTC timestamp.

In addition, `borg serve` can act as if a repository is in append-only mode with its option `--append-only`. This can be very useful for fine-tuning access control in `.ssh/authorized_keys`

```
command="borg serve --append-only ..." ssh-rsa <key used for not-always-trustable
 backup clients>
command="borg serve ..." ssh-rsa <key used for backup management>
```

Running `borg init` via a `borg serve --append-only` server will *not* create an append-only repository. Running `borg init --append-only` creates an append-only repository regardless of server settings.

Example

Suppose an attacker remotely deleted all backups, but your repository was in append-only mode. A transaction log in this situation might look like this:

```
transaction 1, UTC time 2016-03-31T15:53:27.383532
transaction 5, UTC time 2016-03-31T15:53:52.588922
transaction 11, UTC time 2016-03-31T15:54:23.887256
transaction 12, UTC time 2016-03-31T15:55:54.022540
transaction 13, UTC time 2016-03-31T15:55:55.472564
```

From your security logs you conclude the attacker gained access at 15:54:00 and all the backups where deleted or replaced by compromised backups. From the log you know that transactions 11 and later are compromised. Note that the transaction ID is the name of the *last* file in the transaction. For example, transaction 11 spans files 6 to 11.

In a real attack you'll likely want to keep the compromised repository intact to analyze what the attacker tried to achieve. It's also a good idea to make this copy just in case something goes wrong during the recovery. Since recovery is done by deleting some files, a hard link copy (`cp -al`) is sufficient.

The first step to reset the repository to transaction 5, the last uncompromised transaction, is to remove the `hints.N` and `index.N` files in the repository (these two files are always expendable). In this example N is 13.

Then remove or move all segment files from the segment directories in `data/` starting with file 6:

```
rm data/**/{6..13}
```

That's all to it.

Drawbacks

As data is only appended, and nothing removed, commands like `prune` or `delete` won't free disk space, they merely tag data as deleted in a new transaction.

Be aware that as soon as you write to the repo in non-append-only mode (e.g. prune, delete or create archives from an admin machine), it will remove the deleted objects permanently (including the ones that were already marked as deleted, but not removed, in append-only mode).

Note that you can go back-and-forth between normal and append-only operation by editing the configuration file, it's not a "one way trip".

Further considerations

Append-only mode is not respected by tools other than Borg. `rm` still works on the repository. Make sure that backup client machines only get to access the repository via `borg serve`.

Ensure that no remote access is possible if the repository is temporarily set to normal mode for e.g. regular pruning.

Further protections can be implemented, but are outside of Borg's scope. For example, file system snapshots or wrapping `borg serve` to set special permissions or ACLs on new data files.

SSH batch mode

When running Borg using an automated script, `ssh` might still ask for a password, even if there is an SSH key for the target server. Use this to make scripts more robust:

```
export BORG_RSH='ssh -oBatchMode=yes'
```

CHAPTER 5

Deployment

This chapter details deployment strategies for the following scenarios.

Central repository server with Ansible or Salt

This section will give an example how to setup a borg repository server for multiple clients.

Machines

There are multiple machines used in this section and will further be named by their respective fully qualified domain name (fqdn).

- The backup server: *backup01.srv.local*
- The clients:
  - John Doe's desktop: *johndoe.clnt.local*
  - Webserver 01: *web01.srv.local*
  - Application server 01: *app01.srv.local*

User and group

The repository server needs to have only one UNIX user for all the clients. Recommended user and group with additional settings:

- User: *backup*
- Group: *backup*
- Shell: */bin/bash* (or other capable to run the *borg serve* command)
- Home: */home/backup*

Most clients shall initiate a backup from the root user to catch all users, groups and permissions (e.g. when backing up */home*).

Folders

The following folder tree layout is suggested on the repository server:

- User home directory, /home/backup
- Repositories path (storage pool): /home/backup/repos
- Clients restricted paths (*/home/backup/repos/<client fqdn>*):
  - johndoe.clnt.local: */home/backup/repos/johndoe.clnt.local*
  - web01.srv.local: */home/backup/repos/web01.srv.local*
  - app01.srv.local: */home/backup/repos/app01.srv.local*

Restrictions

Borg is instructed to restrict clients into their own paths: `borg serve --restrict-to-path /home/backup/repos/<client fqdn>`

The client will be able to access any file or subdirectory inside of `/home/backup/repos/<client fqdn>` but no other directories. You can allow a client to access several separate directories by passing multiple `--restrict-to-path` flags, for instance: `borg serve --restrict-to-path /home/backup/repos/<client fqdn> --restrict-to-path /home/backup/repos/<other client fqdn>`, which could make sense if multiple machines belong to one person which should then have access to all the backups of their machines.

There is only one ssh key per client allowed. Keys are added for `johndoe.clnt.local`, `web01.srv.local` and `app01.srv.local`. But they will access the backup under only one UNIX user account as: `backup@backup01.srv.local`. Every key in `$HOME/.ssh/authorized_keys` has a forced command and restrictions applied as shown below:

```
command="cd /home/backup/repos/<client fqdn>;
        borg serve --restrict-to-path /home/backup/repos/<client fqdn>",
        restrict <keytype> <key> <host>
```

Note: The text shown above needs to be written on a single line!

The options which are added to the key will perform the following:

1. Change working directory
2. Run `borg serve` restricted to the client base path
3. Restrict ssh and do not allow stuff which imposes a security risk

Due to the `cd` command we use, the server automatically changes the current working directory. Then client doesn't need to have knowledge of the absolute or relative remote repository path and can directly access the repositories at `<user>@<host>:<repo>`.

Note: The setup above ignores all client given commandline parameters which are normally appended to the *borg serve* command.

Client

The client needs to initialize the *pictures* repository like this:

borg init backup@backup01.srv.local:pictures

Or with the full path (should actually never be used, as only for demonstrational purposes). The server should automatically change the current working directory to the *<client fqdn>* folder.

> borg init backup@backup01.srv.local:/home/backup/repos/johndoe.clnt.local/pictures

When *johndoe.clnt.local* tries to access a not restricted path the following error is raised. John Doe tries to backup into the Web 01 path:

> borg init backup@backup01.srv.local:/home/backup/repos/web01.srv.local/pictures

```
~~~ SNIP ~~~
Remote: borg.remote.PathNotAllowed: /home/backup/repos/web01.srv.local/pictures
~~~ SNIP ~~~
Repository path not allowed
```

Ansible

Ansible takes care of all the system-specific commands to add the user, create the folder. Even when the configuration is changed the repository server configuration is satisfied and reproducible.

Automate setting up an repository server with the user, group, folders and permissions a Ansible playbook could be used. Keep in mind the playbook uses the Arch Linux pacman[78] package manager to install and keep borg up-to-date.

```
- hosts: backup01.srv.local
  vars:
    user: backup
    group: backup
    home: /home/backup
    pool: "{{ home }}/repos"
    auth_users:
      - host: johndoe.clnt.local
        key: "{{ lookup('file', '/path/to/keys/johndoe.clnt.local.pub') }}"
      - host: web01.clnt.local
        key: "{{ lookup('file', '/path/to/keys/web01.clnt.local.pub') }}"
      - host: app01.clnt.local
        key: "{{ lookup('file', '/path/to/keys/app01.clnt.local.pub') }}"
  tasks:
  - pacman: name=borg state=latest update_cache=yes
  - group: name="{{ group }}" state=present
  - user: name="{{ user }}" shell=/bin/bash home="{{ home }}" createhome=yes group=
 "{{ group }}" groups= state=present
  - file: path="{{ home }}" owner="{{ user }}" group="{{ group }}" mode=0700
 state=directory
  - file: path="{{ home }}/.ssh" owner="{{ user }}" group="{{ group }}" mode=0700
 state=directory
  - file: path="{{ pool }}" owner="{{ user }}" group="{{ group }}" mode=0700
 state=directory
  - authorized_key: user="{{ user }}"
                    key="{{ item.key }}"
                    key_options='command="cd {{ pool }}/{{ item.host }};borg serve
 --restrict-to-path {{ pool }}/{{ item.host }}",restrict'
    with_items: "{{ auth_users }}"
  - file: path="{{ home }}/.ssh/authorized_keys" owner="{{ user }}" group="{{
 group }}" mode=0600 state=file
  - file: path="{{ pool }}/{{ item.host }}" owner="{{ user }}" group="{{ group }}"
 mode=0700 state=directory
    with_items: "{{ auth_users }}"
```

---

[78] https://www.archlinux.org/pacman/pacman.8.html

Salt

This is a configuration similar to the one above, configured to be deployed with Salt running on a Debian system.

```
Install borg backup from pip:
  pkg.installed:
    - pkgs:
      - python3
      - python3-dev
      - python3-pip
      - python-virtualenv
      - libssl-dev
      - openssl
      - libacl1-dev
      - libacl1
      - liblz4-dev
      - liblz4-1
      - build-essential
      - libfuse-dev
      - fuse
      - pkg-config
  pip.installed:
    - pkgs: ["borgbackup"]
    - bin_env: /usr/bin/pip3

Setup backup user:
  user.present:
    - name: backup
    - fullname: Backup User
    - home: /home/backup
    - shell: /bin/bash
# CAUTION!
# If you change the ssh command= option below, it won't necessarily get pushed to
↪the backup
# server correctly unless you delete the ~/.ssh/authorized_keys file and re-create
↪it!
{% for host in backupclients %}
Give backup access to {{host}}:
  ssh_auth.present:
    - user: backup
    - source: salt://conf/ssh-pubkeys/{{host}}-backup.id_ecdsa.pub
    - options:
      - command="cd /home/backup/repos/{{host}}; borg serve --restrict-to-path /
↪home/backup/repos/{{host}}"
      - restrict
{% endfor %}
```

Enhancements

As this section only describes a simple and effective setup it could be further enhanced when supporting (a limited set) of client supplied commands. A wrapper for starting *borg serve* could be written. Or borg itself could be enhanced to autodetect it runs under SSH by checking the *SSH_ORIGINAL_COMMAND* environment variable. This is left open for future improvements.

When extending ssh autodetection in borg no external wrapper script is necessary and no other interpreter or application has to be deployed.

See also

- SSH Daemon manpage[79]
- Ansible[80]
- Salt[81]

Hosting repositories

This sections shows how to securely provide repository storage for users. Optionally, each user can have a storage quota.

Repositories are accessed through SSH. Each user of the service should have her own login which is only able to access the user's files. Technically it would be possible to have multiple users share one login, however, separating them is better. Separate logins increase isolation and are thus an additional layer of security and safety for both the provider and the users.

For example, if a user manages to breach `borg serve` then she can only damage her own data (assuming that the system does not have further vulnerabilities).

Use the standard directory structure of the operating system. Each user is assigned a home directory and repositories of the user reside in her home directory.

The following `~user/.ssh/authorized_keys` file is the most important piece for a correct deployment. It allows the user to login via their public key (which must be provided by the user), and restricts SSH access to safe operations only.

```
command="borg serve --restrict-to-repository /home/<user>/repository",restrict
<key type> <key> <key host>
```

Note: The text shown above needs to be written on a **single** line!

> **Warning:** If this file should be automatically updated (e.g. by a web console), pay **utmost attention** to sanitizing user input. Strip all whitespace around the user-supplied key, ensure that it **only** contains ASCII with no control characters and that it consists of three parts separated by a single space. Ensure that no newlines are contained within the key.

The *restrict* keyword enables all restrictions, i.e. disables port, agent and X11 forwarding, as well as disabling PTY allocation and execution of ~/.ssh/rc. If any future restriction capabilities are added to authorized_keys files they will be included in this set.

The *command* keyword forces execution of the specified command line upon login. This must be `borg serve`. The *–restrict-to-repository* option permits access to exactly **one** repository. It can be given multiple times to permit access to more than one repository.

The repository may not exist yet; it can be initialized by the user, which allows for encryption.

Storage quotas can be enabled by adding the `--storage-quota` option to the `borg serve` command line:

```
restrict,command="borg serve --storage-quota 20G ..." ...
```

The storage quotas of repositories are completely independent. If a client is able to access multiple repositories, each repository can be filled to the specified quota.

---

[79] http://www.openbsd.org/cgi-bin/man.cgi/OpenBSD-current/man8/sshd.8
[80] https://docs.ansible.com
[81] https://docs.saltstack.com/

If storage quotas are used, ensure that all deployed Borg releases support storage quotas.

Refer to *Storage quotas* for more details on storage quotas.

Refer to the sshd(8)[82] man page for more details on SSH options.

Automated backups to a local hard drive

This guide shows how to automate backups to a hard drive directly connected to your computer. If a backup hard drive is connected, backups are automatically started, and the drive shut-down and disconnected when they are done.

This guide is written for a Linux-based operating system and makes use of systemd and udev.

Overview

An udev rule is created to trigger on the addition of block devices. The rule contains a tag that triggers systemd to start a oneshot service. The oneshot service executes a script in the standard systemd service environment, which automatically captures stdout/stderr and logs it to the journal.

The script mounts the added block device, if it is a registered backup drive, and creates backups on it. When done, it optionally unmounts the file system and spins the drive down, so that it may be physically disconnected.

Configuring the system

First, create the /etc/backups directory (as root). All configuration goes into this directory.

Then, create etc/backups/40-backup.rules with the following content (all on one line):

```
ACTION=="add", SUBSYSTEM=="bdi", DEVPATH=="/devices/virtual/bdi/*",
TAG+="systemd", ENV{SYSTEMD_WANTS}="automatic-backup.service"
```

Finding a more precise udev rule

If you always connect the drive(s) to the same physical hardware path, e.g. the same eSATA port, then you can make a more precise udev rule.

Execute udevadm monitor and connect a drive to the port you intend to use. You should see a flurry of events, find those regarding the *block* subsystem. Pick the event whose device path ends in something similar to a device file name, typically 'sdX/sdXY'. Use the event's device path and replace *sdX/sdXY* after the */block/* part in the path with a star (*). For example: *DEV-PATH=="/devices/pci0000:00/0000:00:11.0/ata3/host2/target2:0:0/2:0:0:0/block/*"*.

Reboot a few times to ensure that the hardware path does not change: on some motherboards components of it can be random. In these cases you cannot use a more accurate rule, or need to insert additional stars for matching the path.

The "systemd" tag in conjunction with the SYSTEMD_WANTS environment variable has systemd launch the "automatic-backup" service, which we will create next, as the /etc/backups/automatic-backup. service file:

```
[Service]
Type=oneshot
ExecStart=/etc/backups/run.sh
```

---

[82] http://www.openbsd.org/cgi-bin/man.cgi/OpenBSD-current/man8/sshd.8

Now, create the main backup script, /etc/backups/run.sh. Below is a template, modify it to suit your needs (e.g. more backup sets, dumping databases etc.).

```bash
#!/bin/bash -ue

# The udev rule is not terribly accurate and may trigger our service before
# the kernel has finished probing partitions. Sleep for a bit to ensure
# the kernel is done.
#
# This can be avoided by using a more precise udev rule, e.g. matching
# a specific hardware path and partition.
sleep 5


#
# Script configuration
#

# The backup partition is mounted there
MOUNTPOINT=/mnt/backup

# This is the location of the Borg repository
TARGET=$MOUNTPOINT/borg-backups/backup.borg

# Archive name schema
DATE=$(date --iso-8601)-$(hostname)

# This is the file that will later contain UUIDs of registered backup drives
DISKS=/etc/backups/backup.disks

# Find whether the connected block device is a backup drive
for uuid in $(lsblk --noheadings --list --output uuid)
do
        if grep --quiet --fixed-strings $uuid $DISKS; then
                break
        fi
        uuid=
done

if [ ! $uuid ]; then
        echo "No backup disk found, exiting"
        exit 0
fi

echo "Disk $uuid is a backup disk"
partition_path=/dev/disk/by-uuid/$uuid
# Mount file system if not already done. This assumes that if something is already
# mounted at $MOUNTPOINT, it is the backup drive. It won't find the drive if
# it was mounted somewhere else.
(mount | grep $MOUNTPOINT) || mount $partition_path $MOUNTPOINT
drive=$(lsblk --inverse --noheadings --list --paths --output name $partition_path_
↪| head --lines 1)
echo "Drive path: $drive"


#
# Create backups
#

# Options for borg create
BORG_OPTS="--stats --one-file-system --compression lz4 --checkpoint-interval 86400"

# Set BORG_PASSPHRASE or BORG_PASSCOMMAND somewhere around here, using export,
# if encryption is used.
```

```
# No one can answer if Borg asks these questions, it is better to just fail quickly
# instead of hanging.
export BORG_RELOCATED_REPO_ACCESS_IS_OK=no
export BORG_UNKNOWN_UNENCRYPTED_REPO_ACCESS_IS_OK=no

# Log Borg version
borg --version

echo "Starting backup for $DATE"

# This is just an example, change it however you see fit
borg create $BORG_OPTS \
  --exclude /root/.cache \
  --exclude /var/cache \
  --exclude /var/lib/docker/devicemapper \
  $TARGET::$DATE-$$-system \
  / /boot

# /home is often a separate partition / file system.
# Even if it isn't (add --exclude /home above), it probably makes sense
# to have /home in a separate archive.
borg create $BORG_OPTS \
  --exclude 'sh:/home/*/.cache' \
  $TARGET::$DATE-$$-home \
  /home/

echo "Completed backup for $DATE"

# Just to be completely paranoid
sync

if [ -f /etc/backups/autoeject ]; then
        umount $MOUNTPOINT
        hdparm -Y $drive
fi

if [ -f /etc/backups/backup-suspend ]; then
        systemctl suspend
fi
```

Create the /etc/backups/autoeject file to have the script automatically eject the drive after creating the backup. Rename the file to something else (e.g. /etc/backup/autoeject-no) when you want to do something with the drive after creating backups (e.g running check).

Create the /etc/backups/backup-suspend file if the machine should suspend after completing the backup. Don't forget to physically disconnect the device before resuming, otherwise you'll enter a cycle. You can also add an option to power down instead.

Create an empty /etc/backups/backup.disks file, you'll register your backup drives there.

The last part is to actually enable the udev rules and services:

```
ln -s /etc/backups/40-backup.rules /etc/udev/rules.d/40-backup.rules
ln -s /etc/backups/automatic-backup.service /etc/systemd/system/automatic-backup.
↪service
systemctl daemon-reload
udevadm control --reload
```

Adding backup hard drives

Connect your backup hard drive. Format it, if not done already. Find the UUID of the file system that backups should be stored on:

```
lsblk -o+uuid,label
```

Note the UUID into the `/etc/backup/backup.disks` file.

Mount the drive to /mnt/backup.

Initialize a Borg repository at the location indicated by `TARGET`:

```
borg init --encryption ... /mnt/backup/borg-backups/backup.borg
```

Unmount and reconnect the drive, or manually start the `automatic-backup` service to start the first backup:

```
systemctl start --no-block automatic-backup
```

See backup logs using journalctl:

```
journalctl -fu automatic-backup [-n number-of-lines]
```

Security considerations

The script as shown above will mount any file system with an UUID listed in `/etc/backup/backup.disks`. The UUID check is a safety / annoyance-reduction mechanism to keep the script from blowing up whenever a random USB thumb drive is connected. It is not meant as a security mechanism. Mounting file systems and reading repository data exposes additional attack surfaces (kernel file system drivers, possibly user space services and Borg itself). On the other hand, someone standing right next to your computer can attempt a lot of attacks, most of which are easier to do than e.g. exploiting file systems (installing a physical key logger, DMA attacks, stealing the machine, ...).

Borg ensures that backups are not created on random drives that "just happen" to contain a Borg repository. If an unknown unencrypted repository is encountered, then the script aborts (BORG_UNKNOWN_UNENCRYPTED_REPO_ACCESS_IS_OK=no).

Backups are only created on hard drives that contain a Borg repository that is either known (by ID) to your machine or you are using encryption and the passphrase of the repository has to match the passphrase supplied to Borg.

Frequently asked questions

Usage & Limitations

Can I backup VM disk images?

Yes, the deduplication[83] technique used by Borg makes sure only the modified parts of the file are stored. Also, we have optional simple sparse file support for extract.

If you use non-snapshotting backup tools like Borg to back up virtual machines, then the VMs should be turned off for the duration of the backup. Backing up live VMs can (and will) result in corrupted or inconsistent backup contents: a VM image is just a regular file to Borg with the same issues as regular files when it comes to concurrent reading and writing from the same file.

For backing up live VMs use file system snapshots on the VM host, which establishes crash-consistency for the VM images. This means that with most file systems (that are journaling) the FS will always be fine in the backup (but may need a journal replay to become accessible).

Usually this does not mean that file *contents* on the VM are consistent, since file contents are normally not journaled. Notable exceptions are ext4 in data=journal mode, ZFS and btrfs (unless nodatacow is used).

Applications designed with crash-consistency in mind (most relational databases like PostgreSQL, SQLite etc. but also for example Borg repositories) should always be able to recover to a consistent state from a backup created with crash-consistent snapshots (even on ext4 with data=writeback or XFS).

Hypervisor snapshots capturing most of the VM's state can also be used for backups and can be a better alternative to pure file system based snapshots of the VM's disk, since no state is lost. Depending on the application this can be the easiest and most reliable way to create application-consistent backups.

Other applications may require a lot of work to reach application-consistency: It's a broad and complex issue that cannot be explained in entirety here.

Borg doesn't intend to address these issues due to their huge complexity and platform/software dependency. Combining Borg with the mechanisms provided by the platform (snapshots, hypervisor features) will be the best approach to start tackling them.

---

[83] https://en.wikipedia.org/wiki/Data_deduplication

Can I backup from multiple servers into a single repository?

Yes, but in order for the deduplication used by Borg to work, it needs to keep a local cache containing checksums of all file chunks already stored in the repository. This cache is stored in `~/.cache/borg/`. If Borg detects that a repository has been modified since the local cache was updated it will need to rebuild the cache. This rebuild can be quite time consuming.

So, yes it's possible. But it will be most efficient if a single repository is only modified from one place. Also keep in mind that Borg will keep an exclusive lock on the repository while creating or deleting archives, which may make *simultaneous* backups fail.

Can I copy or synchronize my repo to another location?

Yes, you could just copy all the files. Make sure you do that while no backup is running (use *borg with-lock ...*). So what you get here is this:

- client machine —borg create—> repo1
- repo1 —copy—> repo2

There is no special borg command to do the copying, just use cp or rsync if you want to do that.

But think about whether that is really what you want. If something goes wrong in repo1, you will have the same issue in repo2 after the copy.

If you want to have 2 independent backups, it is better to do it like this:

- client machine —borg create—> repo1
- client machine —borg create—> repo2

Which file types, attributes, etc. are *not* preserved?

- UNIX domain sockets (because it does not make sense - they are meaningless without the running process that created them and the process needs to recreate them in any case). So, don't panic if your backup misses a UDS!

- The precise on-disk (or rather: not-on-disk) representation of the holes in a sparse file. Archive creation has no special support for sparse files, holes are backed up as (deduplicated and compressed) runs of zero bytes. Archive extraction has optional support to extract all-zero chunks as holes in a sparse file.

- Some filesystem specific attributes, like btrfs NOCOW, see *Support for file metadata*.

Are there other known limitations?

- A single archive can only reference a limited volume of file/dir metadata, usually corresponding to tens or hundreds of millions of files/dirs. When trying to go beyond that limit, you will get a fatal IntegrityError exception telling that the (archive) object is too big. An easy workaround is to create multiple archives with less items each. See also the *Note about archive limitations* and #1452[84].

  borg info shows how large (relative to the maximum size) existing archives are.

If a backup stops mid-way, does the already-backed-up data stay there?

Yes, Borg supports resuming backups.

During a backup a special checkpoint archive named `<archive-name>.checkpoint` is saved every check-point interval (the default value for this is 30 minutes) containing all the data backed-up until that point.

---

[84] https://github.com/borgbackup/borg/issues/1452

This checkpoint archive is a valid archive, but it is only a partial backup (not all files that you wanted to backup are contained in it). Having it in the repo until a successful, full backup is completed is useful because it references all the transmitted chunks up to the checkpoint. This means that in case of an interruption, you only need to retransfer the data since the last checkpoint.

If a backup was interrupted, you do not need to do any special considerations, just invoke `borg create` as you always do. You may use the same archive name as in previous attempt or a different one (e.g. if you always include the current datetime), it does not matter.

Borg always does full single-pass backups, so it will start again from the beginning - but it will be much faster, because some of the data was already stored into the repo (and is still referenced by the checkpoint archive), so it does not need to get transmitted and stored again.

Once your backup has finished successfully, you can delete all `<archive-name>.checkpoint` archives. If you run `borg prune`, it will also care for deleting unneeded checkpoints.

Note: the checkpointing mechanism creates hidden, partial files in an archive, so that checkpoints even work while a big file is being processed. They are named `<filename>.borg_part_<N>` and all operations usually ignore these files, but you can make them considered by giving the option `--consider-part-files`. You usually only need that option if you are really desperate (e.g. if you have no completed backup of that file and you'ld rather get a partial file extracted than nothing). You do **not** want to give that option under any normal circumstances.

How can I backup huge file(s) over a unstable connection?

This is not a problem anymore.

For more details, see *If a backup stops mid-way, does the already-backed-up data stay there?*.

How can I restore huge file(s) over an unstable connection?

If you cannot manage to extract the whole big file in one go, you can extract all the part files and manually concatenate them together.

For more details, see *If a backup stops mid-way, does the already-backed-up data stay there?*.

Can Borg add redundancy to the backup data to deal with hardware malfunction?

No, it can't. While that at first sounds like a good idea to defend against some defect HDD sectors or SSD flash blocks, dealing with this in a reliable way needs a lot of low-level storage layout information and control which we do not have (and also can't get, even if we wanted).

So, if you need that, consider RAID or a filesystem that offers redundant storage or just make backups to different locations / different hardware.

See also #225[85].

Can Borg verify data integrity of a backup archive?

Yes, if you want to detect accidental data damage (like bit rot), use the `check` operation. It will notice corruption using CRCs and hashes. If you want to be able to detect malicious tampering also, use an encrypted repo. It will then be able to check using CRCs and HMACs.

---

[85] https://github.com/borgbackup/borg/issues/225

Can I use Borg on SMR hard drives?

SMR (shingled magnetic recording) hard drives are very different from regular hard drives. Applications have to behave in certain ways or performance will be heavily degraded.

Borg 1.1 ships with default settings suitable for SMR drives, and has been successfully tested on *Seagate Archive v2* drives using the ext4 file system.

Some Linux kernel versions between 3.19 and 4.5 had various bugs handling device-managed SMR drives, leading to IO errors, unresponsive drives and unreliable operation in general.

For more details, refer to #2252[86].

I get an IntegrityError or similar - what now?

A single error does not necessarily indicate bad hardware or a Borg bug. All hardware exhibits a bit error rate (BER). Hard drives are typically specified as exhibiting less than one error every 12 to 120 TB (one bit error in 10e14 to 10e15 bits). The specification is often called *unrecoverable read error rate* (URE rate).

Apart from these very rare errors there are two main causes of errors:

1. Defective hardware: described below.

2. Bugs in software (Borg, operating system, libraries): Ensure software is up to date. Check whether the issue is caused by any fixed bugs described in *Important notes*.

Finding defective hardware

Note: Hardware diagnostics are operating system dependent and do not apply universally. The commands shown apply for popular Unix-like systems. Refer to your operating system's manual.

Checking hard drives Find the drive containing the repository and use *findmnt*, *mount* or *lsblk* to learn the device path (typically */dev/...*) of the drive. Then, smartmontools can retrieve self-diagnostics of the drive in question:

```
# smartctl -a /dev/sdSomething
```

The *Offline_Uncorrectable*, *Current_Pending_Sector* and *Reported_Uncorrect* attributes indicate data corruption. A high *UDMA_CRC_Error_Count* usually indicates a bad cable.

I/O errors logged by the system (refer to the system journal or dmesg) can point to issues as well. I/O errors only affecting the file system easily go unnoticed, since they are not reported to applications (e.g. Borg), while these errors can still corrupt data.

Drives can corrupt some sectors in one event, while remaining reliable otherwise. Conversely, drives can fail completely with no advance warning. If in doubt, copy all data from the drive in question to another drive – just in case it fails completely.

If any of these are suspicious, a self-test is recommended:

```
# smartctl -t long /dev/sdSomething
```

Running `fsck` if not done already might yield further insights.

Checking memory Intermittent issues, such as `borg check` finding errors inconsistently between runs, are frequently caused by bad memory.

Run memtest86+ (or an equivalent memory tester) to verify that the memory subsystem is operating correctly.

---

[86] https://github.com/borgbackup/borg/issues/2252

Chapter 6. Frequently asked questions

Checking processors Processors rarely cause errors. If they do, they are usually overclocked or otherwise operated outside their specifications. We do not recommend to operate hardware outside its specifications for productive use.

Tools to verify correct processor operation include Prime95 (mprime), linpack, and the Intel Processor Diagnostic Tool[87] (applies only to Intel processors).

Repairing a damaged repository

With any defective hardware found and replaced, the damage done to the repository needs to be ascertained and fixed.

borg check provides diagnostics and `--repair` options for repositories with issues. We recommend to first run without `--repair` to assess the situation. If the found issues and proposed repairs seem right, re-run "check" with `--repair` enabled.

Security

How can I specify the encryption passphrase programmatically?

There are several ways to specify a passphrase without human intervention:

Setting BORG_PASSPHRASE The passphrase can be specified using the `BORG_PASSPHRASE` enviroment variable. This is often the simplest option, but can be insecure if the script that sets it is world-readable.

Note: Be careful how you set the environment; using the `env` command, a `system()` call or using inline shell scripts (e.g. `BORG_PASSPHRASE=hunter12 borg ...`) might expose the credentials in the process list directly and they will be readable to all users on a system. Using `export` in a shell script file should be safe, however, as the environment of a process is accessible only to that user[88].

Using BORG_PASSCOMMAND with a properly permissioned file Another option is to create a file with a password in it in your home directory and use permissions to keep anyone else from reading it. For example, first create a key:

```
head -c 1024 /dev/urandom | base64 > ~/.borg-passphrase
chmod 400 ~/.borg-passphrase
```

Then in an automated script one can put:

```
export BORG_PASSCOMMAND="cat ~/.borg-passphrase"
```

and Borg will automatically use that passphrase.

Using keyfile-based encryption with a blank passphrase It is possible to encrypt your repository in `keyfile` mode instead of the default `repokey` mode and use a blank passphrase for the key file. See *Repository encryption* for more details.

Using BORG_PASSCOMMAND with macOS Keychain macOS has a native manager for secrets (such as passphrases) which is safer than just using a file as it is encrypted at rest and unlocked manually (fortunately, the login keyring automatically unlocks when you login). With the built-in `security` command, you can access it from the command line, making it useful for BORG_PASSCOMMAND.

First generate a passphrase and use `security` to save it to your login (default) keychain:

```
security add-generic-password -D secret -U -a $USER -s borg-passphrase -w
↪$(head -c 1024 /dev/urandom | base64)
```

---

[87] https://downloadcenter.intel.com/download/19792/Intel-Processor-Diagnostic-Tool
[88] https://security.stackexchange.com/questions/14000/environment-variable-accessibility-in-linux/14009#14009

In your backup script retrieve it in the `BORG_PASSCOMMAND`:

```
export BORG_PASSCOMMAND="security find-generic-password -a $USER -s borg-
↪passphrase -w"
```

Using `BORG_PASSCOMMAND` with GNOME Keyring GNOME also has a keyring daemon that can be used to store a Borg passphrase. First ensure `libsecret-tools`, `gnome-keyring` and `libpam-gnome-keyring` are installed. If `libpam-gnome-keyring` wasn't already installed, ensure it runs on login:

```
sudo sh -c "echo session optional pam_gnome_keyring.so auto_start >> /etc/pam.
↪d/login"
sudo sh -c "echo password optional pam_gnome_keyring.so >> /etc/pam.d/passwd"
# you may need to relogin afterwards to activate the login keyring
```

Then add a secret to the login keyring:

```
head -c 1024 /dev/urandom | base64 | secret-tool store borg-repository repo-
↪name --label="Borg Passphrase"
```

If a dialog box pops up prompting you to pick a password for a new keychain, use your login password. If there is a checkbox for automatically unlocking on login, check it to allow backups without any user intervention whatsoever.

Once the secret is saved, retrieve it in a backup script using `BORG_PASSCOMMAND`:

```
export BORG_PASSCOMMAND="secret-tool lookup borg-repository repo-name"
```

Note: For this to automatically unlock the keychain it must be run in the `dbus` session of an unlocked terminal; for example, running a backup script as a `cron` job might not work unless you also `export DISPLAY=:0` so `secret-tool` can pick up your open session. It gets even more complicated[89] when you are running the tool as a different user (e.g. running a backup as root with the password stored in the user keyring).

Using `BORG_PASSCOMMAND` with KWallet KDE also has a keychain feature in the form of KWallet. The command-line tool `kwalletcli` can be used to store and retrieve secrets. Ensure `kwalletcli` is installed, generate a passphrase, and store it in your "wallet":

```
head -c 1024 /dev/urandom | base64 | kwalletcli -Pe borg-passphrase -f
↪Passwords
```

Once the secret is saved, retrieve it in a backup script using `BORG_PASSCOMMAND`:

```
export BORG_PASSCOMMAND="kwalletcli -e borg-passphrase -f Passwords"
```

When backing up to remote encrypted repos, is encryption done locally?

Yes, file and directory metadata and data is locally encrypted, before leaving the local machine. We do not mean the transport layer encryption by that, but the data/metadata itself. Transport layer encryption (e.g. when ssh is used as a transport) applies additionally.

When backing up to remote servers, do I have to trust the remote server?

Yes and No.

---

[89] https://github.com/borgbackup/borg/pull/2837#discussion_r127641330

No, as far as data confidentiality is concerned - if you use encryption, all your files/dirs data and metadata are stored in their encrypted form into the repository.

Yes, as an attacker with access to the remote server could delete (or otherwise make unavailable) all your backups.

How can I protect against a hacked backup client?

Assume you backup your backup client machine C to the backup server S and C gets hacked. In a simple push setup, the attacker could then use borg on C to delete all backups residing on S.

These are your options to protect against that:

- Do not allow to permanently delete data from the repo, see *Append-only mode*.
- Use a pull-mode setup using `ssh -R`, see #900[90].
- Mount C's filesystem on another machine and then create a backup of it.
- Do not give C filesystem-level access to S.

How can I protect against a hacked backup server?

Just in case you got the impression that pull-mode backups are way more safe than push-mode, you also need to consider the case that your backup server S gets hacked. In case S has access to a lot of clients C, that might bring you into even bigger trouble than a hacked backup client in the previous FAQ entry.

These are your options to protect against that:

- Use the standard push-mode setup (see also previous FAQ entry).
- Mount (the repo part of) S's filesystem on C.
- Do not give S file-system level access to C.
- Have your backup server at a well protected place (maybe not reachable from the internet), configure it safely, apply security updates, monitor it, ...

How can I protect against theft, sabotage, lightning, fire, ...?

In general: if your only backup medium is nearby the backupped machine and always connected, you can easily get into trouble: they likely share the same fate if something goes really wrong.

Thus:

- have multiple backup media
- have media disconnected from network, power, computer
- have media at another place
- have a relatively recent backup on your media

How do I report a security issue with Borg?

Send a private email to the *security contact* if you think you have discovered a security issue. Please disclose security issues responsibly.

---

[90] https://github.com/borgbackup/borg/issues/900

Common issues

Why do I get "connection closed by remote" after a while?

When doing a backup to a remote server (using a ssh: repo URL), it sometimes stops after a while (some minutes, hours, ... - not immediately) with "connection closed by remote" error message. Why?

That's a good question and we are trying to find a good answer in #636[91].

Why am I seeing idle borg serve processes on the repo server?

Maybe the ssh connection between client and server broke down and that was not yet noticed on the server. Try these settings:

```
# /etc/ssh/sshd_config on borg repo server - kill connection to client
# after ClientAliveCountMax * ClientAliveInterval seconds with no response
ClientAliveInterval 20
ClientAliveCountMax 3
```

If you have multiple borg create ... ; borg create ... commands in a already serialized way in a single script, you need to give them --lock-wait N (with N being a bit more than the time the server needs to terminate broken down connections and release the lock).

The borg cache eats way too much disk space, what can I do?

There is a temporary (but maybe long lived) hack to avoid using lots of disk space for chunks.archive.d (see #235[92] for details):

```
# this assumes you are working with the same user as the backup.
# you can get the REPOID from the "config" file inside the repository.
cd ~/.cache/borg/<REPOID>
rm -rf chunks.archive.d ; touch chunks.archive.d
```

This deletes all the cached archive chunk indexes and replaces the directory that kept them with a file, so borg won't be able to store anything "in" there in future.

This has some pros and cons, though:

- much less disk space needs for ~/.cache/borg.

- chunk cache resyncs will be slower as it will have to transfer chunk usage metadata for all archives from the repository (which might be slow if your repo connection is slow) and it will also have to build the hashtables from that data. chunk cache resyncs happen e.g. if your repo was written to by another machine (if you share same backup repo between multiple machines) or if your local chunks cache was lost somehow.

The long term plan to improve this is called "borgception", see #474[93].

Can I backup my root partition (/) with Borg?

Backing up your entire root partition works just fine, but remember to exclude directories that make no sense to backup, such as /dev, /proc, /sys, /tmp and /run, and to use --one-file-system if you only want to backup the root partition (and not any mounted devices e.g.).

---

[91] https://github.com/borgbackup/borg/issues/636
[92] https://github.com/borgbackup/borg/issues/235
[93] https://github.com/borgbackup/borg/issues/474

If it crashes with a UnicodeError, what can I do?

Check if your encoding is set correctly. For most POSIX-like systems, try:

```
export LANG=en_US.UTF-8  # or similar, important is correct charset
```

I can't extract non-ascii filenames by giving them on the commandline!?

This might be due to different ways to represent some characters in unicode or due to other non-ascii encoding issues.

If you run into that, try this:

- avoid the non-ascii characters on the commandline by e.g. extracting the parent directory (or even everything)
- mount the repo using FUSE and use some file manager

I am seeing 'A' (added) status for an unchanged file!?

The files cache is used to determine whether Borg already "knows" / has backed up a file and if so, to skip the file from chunking. It does intentionally *not* contain files that have a modification time (mtime) same as the newest mtime in the created archive.

So, if you see an 'A' status for unchanged file(s), they are likely the files with the most recent mtime in that archive.

This is expected: it is to avoid data loss with files that are backed up from a snapshot and that are immediately changed after the snapshot (but within mtime granularity time, so the mtime would not change). Without the code that removes these files from the files cache, the change that happened right after the snapshot would not be contained in the next backup as Borg would think the file is unchanged.

This does not affect deduplication, the file will be chunked, but as the chunks will often be the same and already stored in the repo (except in the above mentioned rare condition), it will just re-use them as usual and not store new data chunks.

If you want to avoid unnecessary chunking, just create or touch a small or empty file in your backup source file set (so that one has the latest mtime, not your 50GB VM disk image) and, if you do snapshots, do the snapshot after that.

Since only the files cache is used in the display of files status, those files are reported as being added when, really, chunks are already used.

It always chunks all my files, even unchanged ones!

Borg maintains a files cache where it remembers the mtime, size and inode of files. When Borg does a new backup and starts processing a file, it first looks whether the file has changed (compared to the values stored in the files cache). If the values are the same, the file is assumed unchanged and thus its contents won't get chunked (again).

Borg can't keep an infinite history of files of course, thus entries in the files cache have a "maximum time to live" which is set via the environment variable BORG_FILES_CACHE_TTL (and defaults to 20). Every time you do a backup (on the same machine, using the same user), the cache entries' ttl values of files that were not "seen" are incremented by 1 and if they reach BORG_FILES_CACHE_TTL, the entry is removed from the cache.

So, for example, if you do daily backups of 26 different data sets A, B, C, ..., Z on one machine (using the default TTL), the files from A will be already forgotten when you repeat the same backups on the next day and it will be slow because it would chunk all the files each time. If you set BORG_FILES_CACHE_TTL to at least 26 (or maybe even a small multiple of that), it would be much faster.

Another possible reason is that files don't always have the same path, for example if you mount a filesystem without stable mount points for each backup or if you are running the backup from a filesystem snapshot whose name is not stable. If the directory where you mount a filesystem is different every time, Borg assume they are different files.

Is there a way to limit bandwidth with Borg?

To limit upload (i.e. *borg create*) bandwidth, use the `--remote-ratelimit` option.

There is no built-in way to limit *download* (i.e. *borg extract*) bandwidth, but limiting download bandwidth can be accomplished with pipeviewer[94]:

Create a wrapper script: /usr/local/bin/pv-wrapper

```
#!/bin/sh
    ## -q, --quiet              do not output any transfer information at all
    ## -L, --rate-limit RATE    limit transfer to RATE bytes per second
RATE=307200
pv -q -L $RATE  | "$@"
```

Add BORG_RSH environment variable to use pipeviewer wrapper script with ssh.

```
export BORG_RSH='/usr/local/bin/pv-wrapper ssh'
```

Now Borg will be bandwidth limited. Nice thing about pv is that you can change rate-limit on the fly:

```
pv -R $(pidof pv) -L 102400
```

I am having troubles with some network/FUSE/special filesystem, why?

Borg is doing nothing special in the filesystem, it only uses very common and compatible operations (even the locking is just "mkdir").

So, if you are encountering issues like slowness, corruption or malfunction when using a specific filesystem, please try if you can reproduce the issues with a local (non-network) and proven filesystem (like ext4 on Linux).

If you can't reproduce the issue then, you maybe have found an issue within the filesystem code you used (not with Borg). For this case, it is recommended that you talk to the developers / support of the network fs and maybe open an issue in their issue tracker. Do not file an issue in the Borg issue tracker.

If you can reproduce the issue with the proven filesystem, please file an issue in the Borg issue tracker about that.

Why does running 'borg check –repair' warn about data loss?

Repair usually works for recovering data in a corrupted archive. However, it's impossible to predict all modes of corruption. In some very rare instances, such as malfunctioning storage hardware, additional repo corruption may occur. If you can't afford to lose the repo, it's strongly recommended that you perform repair on a copy of the repo.

In other words, the warning is there to emphasize that Borg:

- Will perform automated routines that modify your backup repository
- Might not actually fix the problem you are experiencing
- Might, in very rare cases, further corrupt your repository

In the case of malfunctioning hardware, such as a drive or USB hub corrupting data when read or written, it's best to diagnose and fix the cause of the initial corruption before attempting to repair the repo. If the corruption is caused by a one time event such as a power outage, running *borg check –repair* will fix most problems.

---

[94] http://www.ivarch.com/programs/pv.shtml

Why isn't there more progress / ETA information displayed?

Some borg runs take quite a bit, so it would be nice to see a progress display, maybe even including a ETA (expected time of "arrival" [here rather "completion"]).

For some functionality, this can be done: if the total amount of work is more or less known, we can display progress. So check if there is a `--progress` option.

But sometimes, the total amount is unknown (e.g. for `borg create` we just do a single pass over the filesystem, so we do not know the total file count or data volume before reaching the end). Adding another pass just to determine that would take additional time and could be incorrect, if the filesystem is changing.

Even if the fs does not change and we knew count and size of all files, we still could not compute the `borg create` ETA as we do not know the amount of changed chunks, how the bandwidth of source and destination or system performance might fluctuate.

You see, trying to display ETA would be futile. The borg developers prefer to rather not implement progress / ETA display than doing futile attempts.

See also: https://xkcd.com/612/

Miscellaneous

Requirements for the borg single-file binary, esp. (g)libc?

We try to build the binary on old, but still supported systems - to keep the minimum requirement for the (g)libc low. The (g)libc can't be bundled into the binary as it needs to fit your kernel and OS, but Python and all other required libraries will be bundled into the binary.

If your system fulfills the minimum (g)libc requirement (see the README that is released with the binary), there should be no problem. If you are slightly below the required version, maybe just try. Due to the dynamic loading (or not loading) of some shared libraries, it might still work depending on what libraries are actually loaded and used.

In the borg git repository, there is scripts/glibc_check.py that can determine (based on the symbols' versions they want to link to) whether a set of given (Linux) binaries works with a given glibc version.

Why was Borg forked from Attic?

Borg was created in May 2015 in response to the difficulty of getting new code or larger changes incorporated into Attic and establishing a bigger developer community / more open development.

More details can be found in ticket 217[95] that led to the fork.

Borg intends to be:

- simple:
    - as simple as possible, but no simpler
    - do the right thing by default, but offer options
- open:
    - welcome feature requests
    - accept pull requests of good quality and coding style
    - give feedback on PRs that can't be accepted "as is"
    - discuss openly, don't work in the dark
- changing:

---

[95] https://github.com/jborg/attic/issues/217

- Borg is not compatible with Attic

- do not break compatibility accidentally, without a good reason or without warning. allow compatibility breaking for other cases.

- if major version number changes, it may have incompatible changes

Migrating from Attic

What are the differences between Attic and Borg?

Borg is a fork of Attic[96] and maintained by "The Borg collective[97]".

Here's a (incomplete) list of some major changes:

- lots of attic issues fixed (see issue #5[98]), including critical data corruption bugs and security issues.

- more open, faster paced development (see issue #1[99])

- less chunk management overhead (less memory and disk usage for chunks index)

- faster remote cache resync (useful when backing up multiple machines into same repo)

- compression: no, lz4, zlib or lzma compression, adjustable compression levels

- repokey replaces problematic passphrase mode (you can't change the passphrase nor the pbkdf2 iteration count in "passphrase" mode)

- simple sparse file support, great for virtual machine disk files

- can read special files (e.g. block devices) or from stdin, write to stdout

- mkdir-based locking is more compatible than attic's posix locking

- uses fadvise to not spoil / blow up the fs cache

- better error messages / exception handling

- better logging, screen output, progress indication

- tested on misc. Linux systems, 32 and 64bit, FreeBSD, OpenBSD, NetBSD, macOS

Please read the *Changelog* (or `docs/changes.rst` in the source distribution) for more information.

Borg is not compatible with original Attic (but there is a one-way conversion).

How do I migrate from Attic to Borg?

Use *borg upgrade*. This is a one-way process that cannot be reversed.

There are some caveats:

- The upgrade can only be performed on local repositories. It cannot be performed on remote repositories.

- If the repository is in "keyfile" encryption mode, the keyfile must exist locally or it must be manually moved after performing the upgrade:

    1. Locate the repository ID, contained in the `config` file in the repository.

    2. Locate the attic key file at `~/.attic/keys/`. The correct key for the repository starts with the line `ATTIC_KEY <repository id>`.

    3. Copy the attic key file to `~/.config/borg/keys/`

---

[96] https://github.com/jborg/attic
[97] https://borgbackup.readthedocs.org/en/latest/authors.html
[98] https://github.com/borgbackup/borg/issues/5
[99] https://github.com/borgbackup/borg/issues/1

4. Change the first line from `ATTIC_KEY ...` to `BORG_KEY ...`.

5. Verify that the repository is now accessible (e.g. `borg list <repository>`).

- Attic and Borg use different *"chunker params"*. This means that data added by Borg won't deduplicate with the existing data stored by Attic. The effect is lessened if the files cache is used with Borg.

- Repositories in "passphrase" mode *must* be migrated to "repokey" mode using *Upgrading a passphrase encrypted attic repo*. Borg does not support the "passphrase" mode any other way.

Why is my backup bigger than with attic?

Attic was rather unflexible when it comes to compression, it always compressed using zlib level 6 (no way to switch compression off or adjust the level or algorithm).

The default in Borg is lz4, which is fast enough to not use significant CPU time in most cases, but can only achieve modest compression. It still compresses easily compressed data fairly well.

zlib compression with all levels (1-9) as well as LZMA (1-6) are available as well, for cases where they are worth it.

Which choice is the best option depends on a number of factors, like bandwidth to the repository, how well the data compresses, available CPU power and so on.

CHAPTER 7

Internals

The internals chapter describes and analyses most of the inner workings of Borg.

Borg uses a low-level, key-value store, the *Repository*, and implements a more complex data structure on top of it, which is made up of the *manifest*, *archives*, *items* and data *Chunks*.

Each repository can hold multiple *archives*, which represent individual backups that contain a full archive of the files specified when the backup was performed.

Deduplication is performed globally across all data in the repository (multiple backups and even multiple hosts), both on data and file metadata, using *Chunks* created by the chunker using the Buzhash[100] algorithm.

To actually perform the repository-wide deduplication, a hash of each chunk is checked against the *chunks cache*, which is a hash-table of all chunks that already exist.

---

[100] https://en.wikipedia.org/wiki/Buzhash

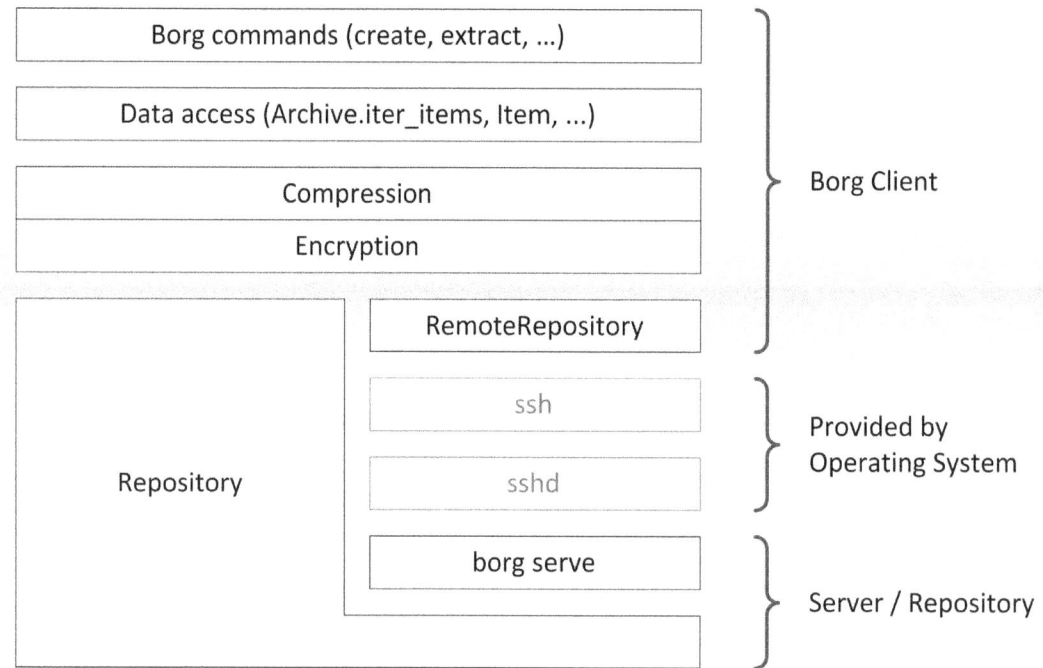

Fig. 7.1: Layers in Borg. On the very top commands are implemented, using a data access layer provided by the Archive and Item classes. The "key" object provides both compression and authenticated encryption used by the data access layer. The "key" object represents the sole trust boundary in Borg. The lowest layer is the repository, either accessed directly (Repository) or remotely (RemoteRepository).

Security

Cryptography in Borg

Attack model

The attack model of Borg is that the environment of the client process (e.g. `borg create`) is trusted and the repository (server) is not. The attacker has any and all access to the repository, including interactive manipulation (man-in-the-middle) for remote repositories.

Furthermore the client environment is assumed to be persistent across attacks (practically this means that the security database cannot be deleted between attacks).

Under these circumstances Borg guarantees that the attacker cannot

1. modify the data of any archive without the client detecting the change

2. rename, remove or add an archive without the client detecting the change

3. recover plain-text data

4. recover definite (heuristics based on access patterns are possible) structural information such as the object graph (which archives refer to what chunks)

The attacker can always impose a denial of service per definition (he could forbid connections to the repository, or delete it entirely).

Structural Authentication

Borg is fundamentally based on an object graph structure (see *Internals*), where the root object is called the manifest.

Borg follows the Horton principle[101], which states that not only the message must be authenticated, but also its meaning (often expressed through context), because every object used is referenced by a parent object through its object ID up to the manifest. The object ID in Borg is a MAC of the object's plaintext, therefore this ensures that an attacker cannot change the context of an object without forging the MAC.

In other words, the object ID itself only authenticates the plaintext of the object and not its context or meaning. The latter is established by a different object referring to an object ID, thereby assigning a particular meaning to an object. For example, an archive item contains a list of object IDs that represent packed file metadata. On their own it's not clear that these objects would represent what they do, but by the archive item referring to them in a particular part of its own data structure assigns this meaning.

This results in a directed acyclic graph of authentication from the manifest to the data chunks of individual files.

Authenticating the manifest

Since the manifest has a fixed ID (000...000) the aforementioned authentication does not apply to it, indeed, cannot apply to it; it is impossible to authenticate the root node of a DAG through its edges, since the root node has no incoming edges.

With the scheme as described so far an attacker could easily replace the manifest, therefore Borg includes a tertiary authentication mechanism (TAM) that is applied to the manifest since version 1.0.9 (see *Pre-1.0.9 manifest spoofing vulnerability (CVE-2016-10099)*).

TAM works by deriving a separate key through HKDF[102] from the other encryption and authentication keys and calculating the HMAC of the metadata to authenticate[104]:

```
# RANDOM(n) returns n random bytes
salt = RANDOM(64)

ikm = id_key || enc_key || enc_hmac_key
# *context* depends on the operation, for manifest authentication it is
# the ASCII string "borg-metadata-authentication-manifest".
tam_key = HKDF-SHA-512(ikm, salt, context)

# *data* is a dict-like structure
data[hmac] = zeroes
packed = pack(data)
data[hmac] = HMAC(tam_key, packed)
packed_authenticated = pack(data)
```

Since an attacker cannot gain access to this key and also cannot make the client authenticate arbitrary data using this mechanism, the attacker is unable to forge the authentication.

This effectively 'anchors' the manifest to the key, which is controlled by the client, thereby anchoring the entire DAG, making it impossible for an attacker to add, remove or modify any part of the DAG without Borg being able to detect the tampering.

Note that when using BORG_PASSPHRASE the attacker cannot swap the *entire* repository against a new repository with e.g. repokey mode and no passphrase, because Borg will abort access when BORG_PASSPRHASE is incorrect.

However, interactively a user might not notice this kind of attack immediately, if she assumes that the reason for the absent passphrase prompt is a set BORG_PASSPHRASE. See issue #2169[103] for details.

---

[101] https://en.wikipedia.org/wiki/Horton_Principle
[102] https://tools.ietf.org/html/rfc5869
[104] The reason why the authentication tag is stored in the packed data itself is that older Borg versions can still read the manifest this way, while a changed layout would have broken compatibility.
[103] https://github.com/borgbackup/borg/issues/2169

Encryption

Encryption is currently based on the Encrypt-then-MAC construction, which is generally seen as the most robust way to create an authenticated encryption scheme from encryption and message authentication primitives.

Every operation (encryption, MAC / authentication, chunk ID derivation) uses independent, random keys generated by os.urandom[105][107].

Borg does not support unauthenticated encryption – only authenticated encryption schemes are supported. No unauthenticated encryption schemes will be added in the future.

Depending on the chosen mode (see *borg init*) different primitives are used:

- The actual encryption is currently always AES-256 in CTR mode. The counter is added in plaintext, since it is needed for decryption, and is also tracked locally on the client to avoid counter reuse.

- The authentication primitive is either HMAC-SHA-256 or BLAKE2b-256 in a keyed mode. HMAC-SHA-256 uses 256 bit keys, while BLAKE2b-256 uses 512 bit keys.

  The latter is secure not only because BLAKE2b itself is not susceptible to length extension[106], but also since it truncates the hash output from 512 bits to 256 bits, which would make the construction safe even if BLAKE2b were broken regarding length extension or similar attacks.

- The primitive used for authentication is always the same primitive that is used for deriving the chunk ID, but they are always used with independent keys.

Encryption:

```
id = AUTHENTICATOR(id_key, data)
compressed = compress(data)

iv = reserve_iv()
encrypted = AES-256-CTR(enc_key, 8-null-bytes || iv, compressed)
authenticated = type-byte || AUTHENTICATOR(enc_hmac_key, encrypted) || iv ||
↪encrypted
```

Decryption:

```
# Given: input *authenticated* data, possibly a *chunk-id* to assert
type-byte, mac, iv, encrypted = SPLIT(authenticated)

ASSERT(type-byte is correct)
ASSERT( CONSTANT-TIME-COMPARISON( mac, AUTHENTICATOR(enc_hmac_key, encrypted) ) )

decrypted = AES-256-CTR(enc_key, 8-null-bytes || iv, encrypted)
decompressed = decompress(decrypted)

ASSERT( CONSTANT-TIME-COMPARISON( chunk-id, AUTHENTICATOR(id_key, decompressed) ) )
```

The client needs to track which counter values have been used, since encrypting a chunk requires a starting counter value and no two chunks may have overlapping counter ranges (otherwise the bitwise XOR of the overlapping plaintexts is revealed).

The client does not directly track the counter value, because it changes often (with each encrypted chunk), instead it commits a "reservation" to the security database and the repository by taking the current counter value and adding 4 GiB / 16 bytes (the block size) to the counter. Thus the client only needs to commit a new reservation every few gigabytes of encrypted data.

This mechanism also avoids reusing counter values in case the client crashes or the connection to the repository is severed, since any reservation would have been committed to both the security database and the repository before

---

[105] https://docs.python.org/3/library/os.html#os.urandom

[107] Using the *borg key migrate-to-repokey* command a user can convert repositories created using Attic in "passphrase" mode to "repokey" mode. In this case the keys were directly derived from the user's passphrase at some point using PBKDF2.

Borg does not support "passphrase" mode otherwise any more.

[106] https://en.wikipedia.org/wiki/Length_extension_attack

any data is encrypted. Borg uses its standard mechanism (SaveFile) to ensure that reservations are durable (on most hardware / storage systems), therefore a crash of the client's host would not impact tracking of reservations.

However, this design is not infallible, and requires synchronization between clients, which is handled through the repository. Therefore in a multiple-client scenario a repository can trick a client into reusing counter values by ignoring counter reservations and replaying the manifest (which will fail if the client has seen a more recent manifest or has a more recent nonce reservation). If the repository is untrusted, but a trusted synchronization channel exists between clients, the security database could be synchronized between them over said trusted channel. This is not part of Borgs functionality.

Offline key security

Borg cannot secure the key material while it is running, because the keys are needed in plain to decrypt/encrypt repository objects.

For offline storage of the encryption keys they are encrypted with a user-chosen passphrase.

A 256 bit key encryption key (KEK) is derived from the passphrase using PBKDF2-HMAC-SHA256 with a random 256 bit salt which is then used to Encrypt-*and*-MAC (unlike the Encrypt-*then*-MAC approach used otherwise) a packed representation of the keys with AES-256-CTR with a constant initialization vector of 0. A HMAC-SHA256 of the plaintext is generated using the same KEK and is stored alongside the ciphertext, which is converted to base64 in its entirety.

This base64 blob (commonly referred to as *keyblob*) is then stored in the key file or in the repository config (keyfile and repokey modes respectively).

This scheme, and specifically the use of a constant IV with the CTR mode, is secure because an identical passphrase will result in a different derived KEK for every key encryption due to the salt.

The use of Encrypt-and-MAC instead of Encrypt-then-MAC is seen as uncritical (but not ideal) here, since it is combined with AES-CTR mode, which is not vulnerable to padding attacks.

See also:

Refer to the *Key files* section for details on the format.

Refer to issue #747[108] for suggested improvements of the encryption scheme and password-based key derivation.

Implementations used

We do not implement cryptographic primitives ourselves, but rely on widely used libraries providing them:

- AES-CTR and HMAC-SHA-256 from OpenSSL 1.0 / 1.1 are used, which is also linked into the static binaries we provide. We think this is not an additional risk, since we don't ever use OpenSSL's networking, TLS or X.509 code, but only their primitives implemented in libcrypto.

- SHA-256 and SHA-512 from Python's hashlib[109] standard library module are used. Borg requires a Python built with OpenSSL support (due to PBKDF2), therefore these functions are delegated to OpenSSL by Python.

- HMAC, PBKDF2 and a constant-time comparison from Python's hmac[110] standard library module is used. While the HMAC implementation is written in Python, the PBKDF2 implementation is provided by OpenSSL. The constant-time comparison (`compare_digest`) is written in C and part of Python.

- BLAKE2b is either provided by the system's libb2, an official implementation, or a bundled copy of the BLAKE2 reference implementation (written in C).

Implemented cryptographic constructions are:

- Encrypt-then-MAC based on AES-256-CTR and either HMAC-SHA-256 or keyed BLAKE2b256 as described above under *Encryption*.

---

[108] https://github.com/borgbackup/borg/issues/747
[109] https://docs.python.org/3/library/hashlib.html
[110] https://docs.python.org/3/library/hmac.html

- Encrypt-and-MAC based on AES-256-CTR and HMAC-SHA-256 as described above under *Offline key security*.

- HKDF[111]-SHA-512

Remote RPC protocol security

Note: This section could be further expanded / detailed.

The RPC protocol is fundamentally based on msgpack'd messages exchanged over an encrypted SSH channel (the system's SSH client is used for this by piping data from/to it).

This means that the authorization and transport security properties are inherited from SSH and the configuration of the SSH client and the SSH server – Borg RPC does not contain *any* networking code. Networking is done by the SSH client running in a separate process, Borg only communicates over the standard pipes (stdout, stderr and stdin) with this process. This also means that Borg doesn't have to directly use a SSH client (or SSH at all). For example, `sudo` or `qrexec` could be used as an intermediary.

By using the system's SSH client and not implementing a (cryptographic) network protocol Borg sidesteps many security issues that would normally impact distributing statically linked / standalone binaries.

The remainder of this section will focus on the security of the RPC protocol within Borg.

The assumed worst-case a server can inflict to a client is a denial of repository service.

The situation were a server can create a general DoS on the client should be avoided, but might be possible by e.g. forcing the client to allocate large amounts of memory to decode large messages (or messages that merely indicate a large amount of data follows). The RPC protocol code uses a limited msgpack Unpacker to prohibit this.

We believe that other kinds of attacks, especially critical vulnerabilities like remote code execution are inhibited by the design of the protocol:

1. The server cannot send requests to the client on its own accord, it only can send responses. This avoids "unexpected inversion of control" issues.

2. msgpack serialization does not allow embedding or referencing code that is automatically executed. Incoming messages are unpacked by the msgpack unpacker into native Python data structures (like tuples and dictionaries), which are then passed to the rest of the program.

   Additional verification of the correct form of the responses could be implemented.

3. Remote errors are presented in two forms:

   (a) A simple plain-text *stderr* channel. A prefix string indicates the kind of message (e.g. WARNING, INFO, ERROR), which is used to suppress it according to the log level selected in the client.

   A server can send arbitrary log messages, which may confuse a user. However, log messages are only processed when server requests are in progress, therefore the server cannot interfere / confuse with security critical dialogue like the password prompt.

   (b) Server-side exceptions passed over the main data channel. These follow the general pattern of server-sent responses and are sent instead of response data for a request.

The msgpack implementation used (msgpack-python) has a good security track record, a large test suite and no issues found by fuzzing. It is based on the msgpack-c implementation, sharing the unpacking engine and some support code. msgpack-c has a good track record as well. Some issues[112] in the past were located in code not included in msgpack-python. Borg does not use msgpack-c.

---

[111] https://tools.ietf.org/html/rfc5869

[112]

- MessagePack fuzzing
- Fixed integer overflow and EXT size problem
- Fixed array and map size overflow

Using OpenSSL

Borg uses the OpenSSL library for most cryptography (see *Implementations used* above). OpenSSL is bundled with static releases, thus the bundled copy is not updated with system updates.

OpenSSL is a large and complex piece of software and has had its share of vulnerabilities, however, it is important to note that Borg links against `libcrypto` **not** `libssl`. libcrypto is the low-level cryptography part of OpenSSL, while libssl implements TLS and related protocols.

The latter is not used by Borg (cf. *Remote RPC protocol security*, Borg itself does not implement any network access) and historically contained most vulnerabilities, especially critical ones. The static binaries released by the project contain neither libssl nor the Python ssl/_ssl modules.

Data structures and file formats

This page documents the internal data structures and storage mechanisms of Borg. It is partly based on mailing list discussion about internals[116] and also on static code analysis.

Repository

Borg stores its data in a *Repository*, which is a file system based transactional key-value store. Thus the repository does not know about the concept of archives or items.

Each repository has the following file structure:

README simple text file telling that this is a Borg repository

config repository configuration

data/ directory where the actual data is stored

hints.%d hints for repository compaction

index.%d repository index

lock.roster and lock.exclusive/* used by the locking system to manage shared and exclusive locks

Transactionality is achieved by using a log (aka journal) to record changes. The log is a series of numbered files called *segments*. Each segment is a series of log entries. The segment number together with the offset of each entry relative to its segment start establishes an ordering of the log entries. This is the "definition" of time for the purposes of the log.

Config file

Each repository has a `config` file which which is a `INI`-style file and looks like this:

```
[repository]
version = 1
segments_per_dir = 1000
max_segment_size = 524288000
id = 57d6c1d52ce76a836b532b0e42e677dec6af9fca3673db511279358828a21ed6
```

This is where the `repository.id` is stored. It is a unique identifier for repositories. It will not change if you move the repository around so you can make a local transfer then decide to move the repository to another (even remote) location at a later time.

---

[116] http://librelist.com/browser/attic/2014/5/6/questions-and-suggestions-about-inner-working-of-attic\T1\textgreater{}

Keys

Repository keys are byte-strings of fixed length (32 bytes), they don't have a particular meaning (except for the *Manifest*).

Normally the keys are computed like this:

```
key = id = id_hash(unencrypted_data)
```

The id_hash function depends on the *encryption mode*.

As the id / key is used for deduplication, id_hash must be a cryptographically strong hash or MAC.

Segments

Objects referenced by a key are stored inline in files (*segments*) of approx. 500 MB size in numbered subdirectories of `repo/data`. The number of segments per directory is controlled by the value of `segments_per_dir`. If you change this value in a non-empty repository, you may also need to relocate the segment files manually.

A segment starts with a magic number (`BORG_SEG` as an eight byte ASCII string), followed by a number of log entries. Each log entry consists of:

- size of the entry
- CRC32 of the entire entry (for a PUT this includes the data)
- entry tag: PUT, DELETE or COMMIT
- PUT and DELETE follow this with the 32 byte key
- PUT follow the key with the data

Those files are strictly append-only and modified only once.

Tag is either `PUT`, `DELETE`, or `COMMIT`.

When an object is written to the repository a `PUT` entry is written to the file containing the object id and data. If an object is deleted a `DELETE` entry is appended with the object id.

A `COMMIT` tag is written when a repository transaction is committed. The segment number of the segment containing a commit is the **transaction ID**.

When a repository is opened any `PUT` or `DELETE` operations not followed by a `COMMIT` tag are discarded since they are part of a partial/uncommitted transaction.

Index, hints and integrity

The **repository index** is stored in `index.<TRANSACTION_ID>` and is used to determine an object's location in the repository. It is a *HashIndex*, a hash table using open addressing. It maps object *keys* to two unsigned 32-bit integers; the first integer gives the segment number, the second indicates the offset of the object's entry within the segment.

The **hints file** is a msgpacked file named `hints.<TRANSACTION_ID>`. It contains:

- version
- list of segments
- compact

The **integrity file** is a msgpacked file named `integrity.<TRANSACTION_ID>`. It contains checksums of the index and hints files and is described in the *Checksumming data structures* section below.

If the index or hints are corrupted, they are re-generated automatically. If they are outdated, segments are replayed from the index state to the currently committed transaction.

Compaction

For a given key only the last entry regarding the key, which is called current (all other entries are called superseded), is relevant: If there is no entry or the last entry is a DELETE then the key does not exist. Otherwise the last PUT defines the value of the key.

By superseding a PUT (with either another PUT or a DELETE) the log entry becomes obsolete. A segment containing such obsolete entries is called sparse, while a segment containing no such entries is called compact.

Since writing a `DELETE` tag does not actually delete any data and thus does not free disk space any log-based data store will need a compaction strategy (somewhat analogous to a garbage collector). Borg uses a simple forward compacting algorithm, which avoids modifying existing segments. Compaction runs when a commit is issued (unless the *Append-only mode* is active). One client transaction can manifest as multiple physical transactions, since compaction is transacted, too, and Borg does not distinguish between the two:

```
Perspective| Time -->
-----------+--------------
Client     | Begin transaction - Modify Data - Commit | <client waits for⌴
↪repository> (done)
Repository | Begin transaction - Modify Data - Commit | Compact segments - Commit ⌴
↪ | (done)
```

The compaction algorithm requires two inputs in addition to the segments themselves:

1. Which segments are sparse, to avoid scanning all segments (impractical). Further, Borg uses a conditional compaction strategy: Only those segments that exceed a threshold sparsity are compacted.

   To implement the threshold condition efficiently, the sparsity has to be stored as well. Therefore, Borg stores a mapping `(segment id,) -> (number of sparse bytes,)`.

   The 1.0.x series used a simpler non-conditional algorithm, which only required the list of sparse segments. Thus, it only stored a list, not the mapping described above.

2. Each segment's reference count, which indicates how many live objects are in a segment. This is not strictly required to perform the algorithm. Rather, it is used to validate that a segment is unused before deleting it. If the algorithm is incorrect, or the reference count was not accounted correctly, then an assertion failure occurs.

These two pieces of information are stored in the hints file (*hints.N*) next to the index (*index.N*).

When loading a hints file, Borg checks the version contained in the file. The 1.0.x series writes version 1 of the format (with the segments list instead of the mapping, mentioned above). Since Borg 1.0.4, version 2 is read as well. The 1.1.x series writes version 2 of the format and reads either version. When reading a version 1 hints file, Borg 1.1.x will read all sparse segments to determine their sparsity.

This process may take some time if a repository is kept in the append-only mode, which causes the number of sparse segments to grow. Repositories not in append-only mode have no sparse segments in 1.0.x, since compaction is unconditional.

Compaction processes sparse segments from oldest to newest; sparse segments which don't contain enough deleted data to justify compaction are skipped. This avoids doing e.g. 500 MB of writing current data to a new segment when only a couple kB were deleted in a segment.

Segments that are compacted are read in entirety. Current entries are written to a new segment, while superseded entries are omitted. After each segment an intermediary commit is written to the new segment. Then, the old segment is deleted (asserting that the reference count diminished to zero), freeing disk space.

A simplified example (excluding conditional compaction and with simpler commit logic) showing the principal operation of compaction:

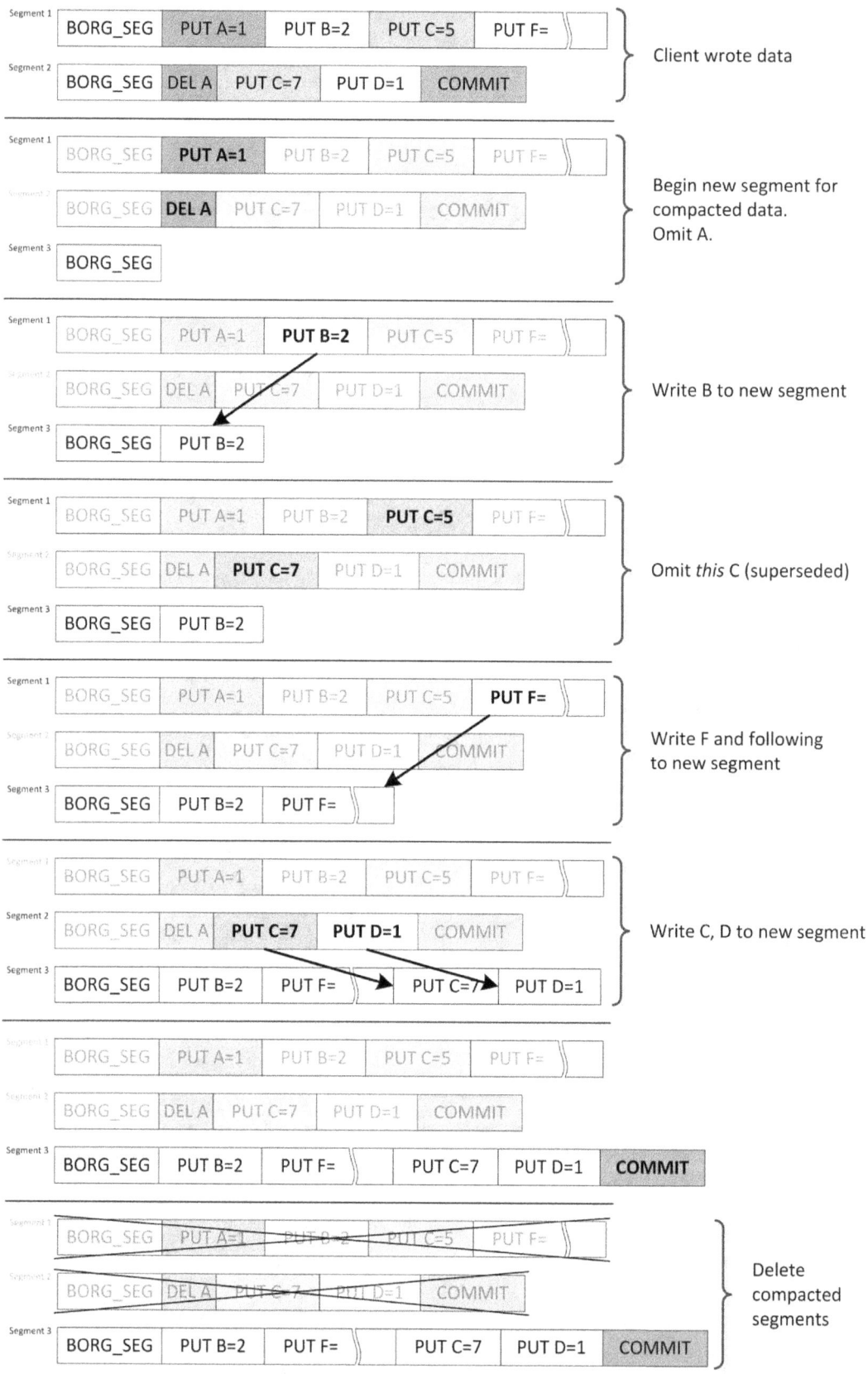

(The actual algorithm is more complex to avoid various consistency issues, refer to the `borg.repository` module for more comments and documentation on these issues.)

Storage quotas

Quotas are implemented at the Repository level. The active quota of a repository is determined by the `storage_quota` *config* entry or a run-time override (via *borg serve*). The currently used quota is stored in the hints file. Operations (PUT and DELETE) during a transaction modify the currently used quota:

- A PUT adds the size of the *log entry* to the quota, i.e. the length of the data plus the 41 byte header.
- A DELETE subtracts the size of the deleted log entry from the quota, which includes the header.

Thus, PUT and DELETE are symmetric and cancel each other out precisely.

The quota does not track on-disk size overheads (due to conditional compaction or append-only mode). In normal operation the inclusion of the log entry headers in the quota act as a faithful proxy for index and hints overheads.

By tracking effective content size, the client can *always* recover from a full quota by deleting archives. This would not be possible if the quota tracked on-disk size, since journaling DELETEs requires extra disk space before space is freed. Tracking effective size on the other hand accounts DELETEs immediately as freeing quota.

Enforcing the quota

The storage quota is meant as a robust mechanism for service providers, therefore *borg serve* has to enforce it without loopholes (e.g. modified clients). The following sections refer to using quotas on remotely accessed repositories. For local access, consider *client* and *serve* the same. Accordingly, quotas cannot be enforced with local access, since the quota can be changed in the repository config.

The quota is enforcible only if *all borg serve* versions accessible to clients support quotas (see next section). Further, quota is per repository. Therefore, ensure clients can only access a defined set of repositories with their quotas set, using `--restrict-to-repository`.

If the client exceeds the storage quota the `StorageQuotaExceeded` exception is raised. Normally a client could ignore such an exception and just send a `commit()` command anyway, circumventing the quota. However, when `StorageQuotaExceeded` is raised, it is stored in the `transaction_doomed` attribute of the repository. If the transaction is doomed, then commit will re-raise this exception, aborting the commit.

The transaction_doomed indicator is reset on a rollback (which erases the quota-exceeding state).

Compatibility with older servers and enabling quota after-the-fact

If no quota data is stored in the hints file, Borg assumes zero quota is used. Thus, if a repository with an enabled quota is written to with an older `borg serve` version that does not understand quotas, then the quota usage will be erased.

The client version is irrelevant to the storage quota and has no part in it. The form of error messages due to exceeding quota varies with client versions.

A similar situation arises when upgrading from a Borg release that did not have quotas. Borg will start tracking quota use from the time of the upgrade, starting at zero.

If the quota shall be enforced accurately in these cases, either

- delete the `index.N` and `hints.N` files, forcing Borg to rebuild both, re-acquiring quota data in the process, or
- edit the msgpacked `hints.N` file (not recommended and thus not documented further).

The object graph

On top of the simple key-value store offered by the *Repository*, Borg builds a much more sophisticated data structure that is essentially a completely encrypted object graph. Objects, such as *archives*, are referenced by their chunk ID, which is cryptographically derived from their contents. More on how this helps security in *Structural Authentication*.

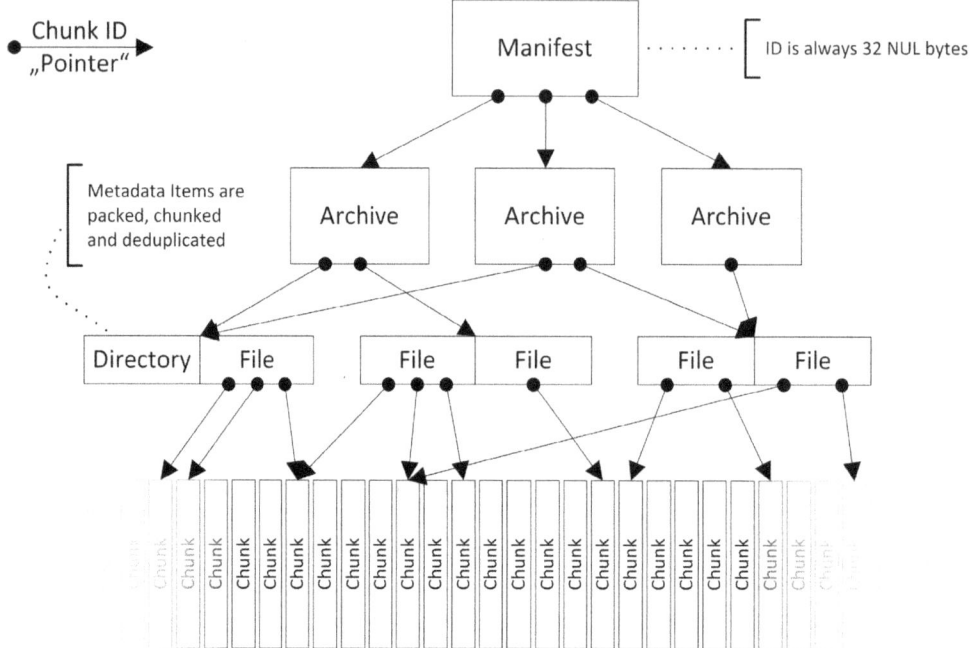

The manifest

The manifest is the root of the object hierarchy. It references all archives in a repository, and thus all data in it. Since no object references it, it cannot be stored under its ID key. Instead, the manifest has a fixed all-zero key.

The manifest is rewritten each time an archive is created, deleted, or modified. It looks like this:

```
{
    b'version': 1,
    b'timestamp': b'2017-05-05T12:42:23.042864',
    b'item_keys': [b'acl_access', b'acl_default', ...],
    b'config': {},
    b'archives': {
        b'2017-05-05-system-backup': {
            b'id': b'<32 byte binary object ID>',
            b'time': b'2017-05-05T12:42:22.942864',
        },
    },
    b'tam': ...,
}
```

The *version* field can be either 1 or 2. The versions differ in the way feature flags are handled, described below.

The *timestamp* field is used to avoid logical replay attacks where the server just resets the repository to a previous state.

item_keys is a list containing all *Item* keys that may be encountered in the repository. It is used by *borg check*, which verifies that all keys in all items are a subset of these keys. Thus, an older version of *borg check* supporting this mechanism can correctly detect keys introduced in later versions.

The *tam* key is part of the *tertiary authentication mechanism* (formerly known as "tertiary authentication for metadata") and authenticates the manifest, since an ID check is not possible.

config is a general-purpose location for additional metadata. All versions of Borg preserve its contents (it may have been a better place for *item_keys*, which is not preserved by unaware Borg versions, releases predating 1.0.4).

Feature flags

Feature flags are used to add features to data structures without causing corruption if older versions are used to access or modify them. The main issues to consider for a feature flag oriented design are flag granularity, flag storage, and *cache* invalidation.

Feature flags are divided in approximately three categories, detailed below. Due to the nature of ID-based dedupli-cation, write (i.e. creating archives) and read access are not symmetric; it is possible to create archives referencing chunks that are not readable with the current feature set. The third category are operations that require accurate reference counts, for example archive deletion and check.

As the manifest is always updated and always read, it is the ideal place to store feature flags, comparable to the super-block of a file system. The only problem is to recover from a lost manifest, i.e. how is it possible to detect which feature flags are enabled, if there is no manifest to tell. This issue is left open at this time, but is not expected to be a major hurdle; it doesn't have to be handled efficiently, it just needs to be handled.

Lastly, *cache* invalidation is handled by noting which feature flags were and which were not understood while manipulating a cache. This allows to detect whether the cache needs to be invalidated, i.e. rebuilt from scratch. See *Cache feature flags* below.

The *config* key stores the feature flags enabled on a repository:

```
config = {
    b'feature_flags': {
        b'read': {
            b'mandatory': [b'some_feature'],
        },
        b'check': {
            b'mandatory': [b'other_feature'],
        }
        b'write': ...,
        b'delete': ...
    },
}
```

The top-level distinction for feature flags is the operation the client intends to perform,

the *read* operation includes extraction and listing of archives,

the *write* operation includes creating new archives,

the *delete* (archives) operation,

the *check* operation requires full understanding of everything in the repository.

These are weakly set-ordered; *check* will include everything required for *delete*, *delete* will likely include *write* and *read*. However, *read* may require more features than *write* (due to ID-based deduplication, *write* does not necessarily require reading/understanding repository contents).

Each operation can contain several sets of feature flags. Only one set, the *mandatory* set is currently defined.

Upon reading the manifest, the Borg client has already determined which operation should be performed. If feature flags are found in the manifest, the set of feature flags supported by the client is compared to the mandatory set

---

found in the manifest. If any unsupported flags are found (i.e. the mandatory set is not a subset of the features supported by the Borg client used), the operation is aborted with a *MandatoryFeatureUnsupported* error:

Unsupported repository feature(s) {'some_feature'}. A newer version of borg is required to access this repository.

Older Borg releases do not have this concept and do not perform feature flags checks. These can be locked out with manifest version 2. Thus, the only difference between manifest versions 1 and 2 is that the latter is only accepted by Borg releases implementing feature flags.

Therefore, as soon as any mandatory feature flag is enabled in a repository, the manifest version must be switched to version 2 in order to lock out all Borg releases unaware of feature flags.

Cache feature flags

The cache does not have its separate set of feature flags. Instead, Borg stores which flags were used to create or modify a cache.

All mandatory manifest features from all operations are gathered in one set. Then, two sets of features are computed;

- those features that are supported by the client and mandated by the manifest are added to the *mandatory_features* set,

- the *ignored_features* set comprised of those features mandated by the manifest, but not supported by the client.

Because the client previously checked compliance with the mandatory set of features required for the particular operation it is executing, the *mandatory_features* set will contain all necessary features required for using the cache safely.

Conversely, the *ignored_features* set contains only those features which were not relevant to operating the cache. Otherwise, the client would not pass the feature set test against the manifest.

When opening a cache and the *mandatory_features* set is not a subset of the features supported by the client, the cache is wiped out and rebuilt, since a client not supporting a mandatory feature that the cache was built with would be unable to update it correctly. The assumption behind this behaviour is that any of the unsupported features could have been reflected in the cache and there is no way for the client to discern whether that is the case. Meanwhile, it may not be practical for every feature to have clients using it track whether the feature had an impact on the cache. Therefore, the cache is wiped.

When opening a cache and the intersection of *ignored_features* and the features supported by the client contains any elements, i.e. the client possesses features that the previous client did not have and those new features are enabled in the repository, the cache is wiped out and rebuilt.

While the former condition likely requires no tweaks, the latter condition is formulated in an especially conservative way to play it safe. It seems likely that specific features might be exempted from the latter condition.

Defined feature flags

Currently no feature flags are defined.

From currently planned features, some examples follow, these may/may not be implemented and purely serve as examples.

- A mandatory *read* feature could be using a different encryption scheme (e.g. session keys). This may not be mandatory for the *write* operation - reading data is not strictly required for creating an archive.

- Any additions to the way chunks are referenced (e.g. to support larger archives) would become a mandatory *delete* and *check* feature; *delete* implies knowing correct reference counts, so all object references need to be understood. *check* must discover the entire object graph as well, otherwise the "orphan chunks check" could delete data still in use.

Archives

Each archive is an object referenced by the manifest. The archive object itself does not store any of the data contained in the archive it describes.

Instead, it contains a list of chunks which form a msgpacked stream of *items*. The archive object itself further contains some metadata:

- *version*
- *name*, which might differ from the name set in the manifest. When *borg check* rebuilds the manifest (e.g. if it was corrupted) and finds more than one archive object with the same name, it adds a counter to the name in the manifest, but leaves the *name* field of the archives as it was.
- *items*, a list of chunk IDs containing item metadata (size: count * ~34B)
- *cmdline*, the command line which was used to create the archive
- *hostname*
- *username*
- *time* and *time_end* are the start and end timestamps, respectively
- *comment*, a user-specified archive comment
- *chunker_params* are the *chunker-params* used for creating the archive. This is used by *borg recreate* to determine whether a given archive needs rechunking.
- Some other pieces of information related to recreate.

Note about archive limitations

The archive is currently stored as a single object in the repository and thus limited in size to MAX_OBJECT_SIZE (20MiB).

As one chunk list entry is ~40B, that means we can reference ~500.000 item metadata stream chunks per archive.

Each item metadata stream chunk is ~128kiB (see hardcoded ITEMS_CHUNKER_PARAMS).

So that means the whole item metadata stream is limited to ~64GiB chunks. If compression is used, the amount of storable metadata is bigger - by the compression factor.

If the medium size of an item entry is 100B (small size file, no ACLs/xattrs), that means a limit of ~640 million files/directories per archive.

If the medium size of an item entry is 2kB (~100MB size files or more ACLs/xattrs), the limit will be ~32 million files/directories per archive.

If one tries to create an archive object bigger than MAX_OBJECT_SIZE, a fatal IntegrityError will be raised.

A workaround is to create multiple archives with less items each, see also #1452[117].

Items

Each item represents a file, directory or other file system item and is stored as a dictionary created by the Item class that contains:

- path
- list of data chunks (size: count * ~40B)
- user
- group

---

[117] https://github.com/borgbackup/borg/issues/1452

- uid

- gid

- mode (item type + permissions)

- source (for symlinks, and for hardlinks within one archive)

- rdev (for device files)

- mtime, atime, ctime in nanoseconds

- xattrs

- acl (various OS-dependent fields)

- bsdflags

All items are serialized using msgpack and the resulting byte stream is fed into the same chunker algorithm as used for regular file data and turned into deduplicated chunks. The reference to these chunks is then added to the archive metadata. To achieve a finer granularity on this metadata stream, we use different chunker params for this chunker, which result in smaller chunks.

A chunk is stored as an object as well, of course.

Chunks

The Borg chunker uses a rolling hash computed by the Buzhash[118] algorithm. It triggers (chunks) when the last HASH_MASK_BITS bits of the hash are zero, producing chunks of 2^HASH_MASK_BITS Bytes on average.

Buzhash is **only** used for cutting the chunks at places defined by the content, the buzhash value is **not** used as the deduplication criteria (we use a cryptographically strong hash/MAC over the chunk contents for this, the id_hash).

`borg create --chunker-params CHUNK_MIN_EXP,CHUNK_MAX_EXP,HASH_MASK_BITS,` `HASH_WINDOW_SIZE` can be used to tune the chunker parameters, the default is:

- CHUNK_MIN_EXP = 19 (minimum chunk size = 2^19 B = 512 kiB)

- CHUNK_MAX_EXP = 23 (maximum chunk size = 2^23 B = 8 MiB)

- HASH_MASK_BITS = 21 (statistical medium chunk size ~= 2^21 B = 2 MiB)

- HASH_WINDOW_SIZE = 4095 [B] (*0xFFF*)

The buzhash table is altered by XORing it with a seed randomly generated once for the archive, and stored encrypted in the keyfile. This is to prevent chunk size based fingerprinting attacks on your encrypted repo contents (to guess what files you have based on a specific set of chunk sizes).

For some more general usage hints see also `--chunker-params`.

The cache

The **files cache** is stored in `cache/files` and is used at backup time to quickly determine whether a given file is unchanged and we have all its chunks.

In memory, the files cache is a key -> value mapping (a Python *dict*) and contains:

- key: id_hash of the encoded, absolute file path

- value:

    - file inode number

    - file size

    - file mtime_ns

---

[118] https://en.wikipedia.org/wiki/Buzhash

- age (0 [newest], 1, 2, 3, ..., BORG_FILES_CACHE_TTL - 1)

- list of chunk ids representing the file's contents

To determine whether a file has not changed, cached values are looked up via the key in the mapping and compared to the current file attribute values.

If the file's size, mtime_ns and inode number is still the same, it is considered to not have changed. In that case, we check that all file content chunks are (still) present in the repository (we check that via the chunks cache).

If everything is matching and all chunks are present, the file is not read / chunked / hashed again (but still a file metadata item is written to the archive, made from fresh file metadata read from the filesystem). This is what makes borg so fast when processing unchanged files.

If there is a mismatch or a chunk is missing, the file is read / chunked / hashed. Chunks already present in repo won't be transferred to repo again.

The inode number is stored and compared to make sure we distinguish between different files, as a single path may not be unique across different archives in different setups.

Not all filesystems have stable inode numbers. If that is the case, borg can be told to ignore the inode number in the check via –ignore-inode.

The age value is used for cache management. If a file is "seen" in a backup run, its age is reset to 0, otherwise its age is incremented by one. If a file was not seen in BORG_FILES_CACHE_TTL backups, its cache entry is removed. See also: *It always chunks all my files, even unchanged ones!* and *I am seeing 'A' (added) status for an unchanged file!?*

The files cache is a python dictionary, storing python objects, which generates a lot of overhead.

Borg can also work without using the files cache (saves memory if you have a lot of files or not much RAM free), then all files are assumed to have changed. This is usually much slower than with files cache.

The on-disk format of the files cache is a stream of msgpacked tuples (key, value). Loading the files cache involves reading the file, one msgpack object at a time, unpacking it, and msgpacking the value (in an effort to save memory).

The **chunks cache** is stored in `cache/chunks` and is used to determine whether we already have a specific chunk, to count references to it and also for statistics.

The chunks cache is a key -> value mapping and contains:

- key:

    - chunk id_hash

- value:

    - reference count

    - size

    - encrypted/compressed size

The chunks cache is a *HashIndex*. Due to some restrictions of HashIndex, the reference count of each given chunk is limited to a constant, MAX_VALUE (introduced below in *HashIndex*), approximately 2**32. If a reference count hits MAX_VALUE, decrementing it yields MAX_VALUE again, i.e. the reference count is pinned to MAX_VALUE.

Indexes / Caches memory usage

Here is the estimated memory usage of Borg - it's complicated:

```
chunk_count ~= total_file_size / 2 ^ HASH_MASK_BITS

repo_index_usage = chunk_count * 40

chunks_cache_usage = chunk_count * 44
```

```
files_cache_usage = total_file_count * 240 + chunk_count * 80

mem_usage ~= repo_index_usage + chunks_cache_usage + files_cache_usage
           = chunk_count * 164 + total_file_count * 240
```

Due to the hashtables, the best/usual/worst cases for memory allocation can be estimated like that:

```
mem_allocation = mem_usage / load_factor  # l_f = 0.25 .. 0.75

mem_allocation_peak = mem_allocation * (1 + growth_factor)  # g_f = 1.1 .. 2
```

All units are Bytes.

It is assuming every chunk is referenced exactly once (if you have a lot of duplicate chunks, you will have less chunks than estimated above).

It is also assuming that typical chunk size is 2^HASH_MASK_BITS (if you have a lot of files smaller than this statistical medium chunk size, you will have more chunks than estimated above, because 1 file is at least 1 chunk).

If a remote repository is used the repo index will be allocated on the remote side.

The chunks cache, files cache and the repo index are all implemented as hash tables. A hash table must have a significant amount of unused entries to be fast - the so-called load factor gives the used/unused elements ratio.

When a hash table gets full (load factor getting too high), it needs to be grown (allocate new, bigger hash table, copy all elements over to it, free old hash table) - this will lead to short-time peaks in memory usage each time this happens. Usually does not happen for all hashtables at the same time, though. For small hash tables, we start with a growth factor of 2, which comes down to ~1.1x for big hash tables.

E.g. backing up a total count of 1 Mi (IEC binary prefix i.e. 2^20) files with a total size of 1TiB.

1. with `create --chunker-params 10,23,16,4095` (custom, like borg < 1.0 or attic):

   mem_usage = 2.8GiB

2. with `create --chunker-params 19,23,21,4095` (default):

   mem_usage = 0.31GiB

Note: There is also the `--files-cache=disabled` option to disable the files cache. You'll save some memory, but it will need to read / chunk all the files as it can not skip unmodified files then.

HashIndex

The chunks cache and the repository index are stored as hash tables, with only one slot per bucket, spreading hash collisions to the following buckets. As a consequence the hash is just a start position for a linear search. If a key is looked up that is not in the table, then the hash table is searched from the start position (the hash) until the first empty bucket is reached.

This particular mode of operation is open addressing with linear probing.

When the hash table is filled to 75%, its size is grown. When it's emptied to 25%, its size is shrinked. Operations on it have a variable complexity between constant and linear with low factor, and memory overhead varies between 33% and 300%.

If an element is deleted, and the slot behind the deleted element is not empty, then the element will leave a tombstone, a bucket marked as deleted. Tombstones are only removed by insertions using the tombstone's bucket, or by resizing the table. They present the same load to the hash table as a real entry, but do not count towards the regular load factor.

Thus, if the number of empty slots becomes too low (recall that linear probing for an element not in the index stops at the first empty slot), the hash table is rebuilt. The maximum *effective* load factor, i.e. including tombstones, is 93%.

Data in a HashIndex is always stored in little-endian format, which increases efficiency for almost everyone, since basically no one uses big-endian processors any more.

HashIndex does not use a hashing function, because all keys (save manifest) are outputs of a cryptographic hash or MAC and thus already have excellent distribution. Thus, HashIndex simply uses the first 32 bits of the key as its "hash".

The format is easy to read and write, because the buckets array has the same layout in memory and on disk. Only the header formats differ. The on-disk header is `struct HashHeader`:

- First, the HashIndex magic, the eight byte ASCII string "BORG_IDX".

- Second, the signed 32-bit number of entries (i.e. buckets which are not deleted and not empty).

- Third, the signed 32-bit number of buckets, i.e. the length of the buckets array contained in the file, and the modulus for index calculation.

- Fourth, the signed 8-bit length of keys.

- Fifth, the signed 8-bit length of values. This has to be at least four bytes.

All fields are packed.

The HashIndex is *not* a general purpose data structure. The value size must be at least 4 bytes, and these first bytes are used for in-band signalling in the data structure itself.

The constant MAX_VALUE (defined as 2**32-1025 = 4294966271) defines the valid range for these 4 bytes when interpreted as an uint32_t from 0 to MAX_VALUE (inclusive). The following reserved values beyond MAX_VALUE are currently in use (byte order is LE):

- 0xffffffff marks empty buckets in the hash table

- 0xfffffffe marks deleted buckets in the hash table

HashIndex is implemented in C and wrapped with Cython in a class-based interface. The Cython wrapper checks every passed value against these reserved values and raises an AssertionError if they are used.

Encryption

See also:

The *Cryptography in Borg* section for an in-depth review.

AES[119]-256 is used in CTR mode (so no need for padding). A 64 bit initialization vector is used, a MAC is computed on the encrypted chunk and both are stored in the chunk. Encryption and MAC use two different keys. Each chunk consists of `TYPE(1) + MAC(32) + NONCE(8) + CIPHERTEXT`:

---

[119] https://en.wikipedia.org/wiki/Advanced_Encryption_Standard

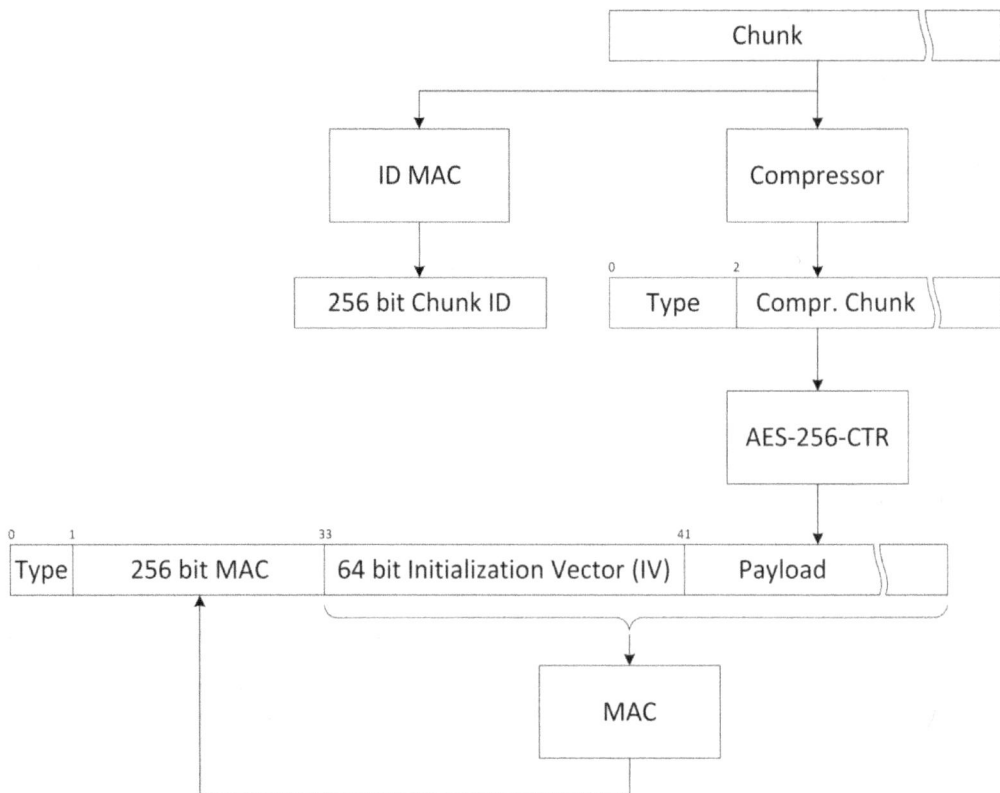

In AES-CTR mode you can think of the IV as the start value for the counter. The counter itself is incremented by one after each 16 byte block. The IV/counter is not required to be random but it must NEVER be reused. So to accomplish this Borg initializes the encryption counter to be higher than any previously used counter value before encrypting new data.

To reduce payload size, only 8 bytes of the 16 bytes nonce is saved in the payload, the first 8 bytes are always zeros. This does not affect security but limits the maximum repository capacity to only 295 exabytes (2**64 * 16 bytes).

Encryption keys (and other secrets) are kept either in a key file on the client ('keyfile' mode) or in the repository config on the server ('repokey' mode). In both cases, the secrets are generated from random and then encrypted by a key derived from your passphrase (this happens on the client before the key is stored into the keyfile or as repokey).

The passphrase is passed through the `BORG_PASSPHRASE` environment variable or prompted for interactive usage.

Key files

See also:

The *Offline key security* section for an in-depth review of the key encryption.

When initialized with the `init -e keyfile` command, Borg needs an associated file in `$HOME/.config/borg/keys` to read and write the repository. The format is based on msgpack[120], base64 encoding and PBKDF2[121] SHA256 hashing, which is then encoded again in a msgpack[122].

---

[120] https://msgpack.org/
[121] https://en.wikipedia.org/wiki/PBKDF2
[122] https://msgpack.org/

The same data structure is also used in the "repokey" modes, which store it in the repository in the configuration file.

The internal data structure is as follows:

version currently always an integer, 1

repository_id the `id` field in the `config` INI file of the repository.

enc_key the key used to encrypt data with AES (256 bits)

enc_hmac_key the key used to HMAC the encrypted data (256 bits)

id_key the key used to HMAC the plaintext chunk data to compute the chunk's id

chunk_seed the seed for the buzhash chunking table (signed 32 bit integer)

These fields are packed using msgpack[123]. The utf-8 encoded passphrase is processed with PBKDF2[124] (SHA256[125], 100000 iterations, random 256 bit salt) to derive a 256 bit key encryption key (KEK).

A HMAC-SHA256[126] checksum of the packed fields is generated with the KEK, then the KEK is also used to encrypt the same packed fields using AES-CTR.

The result is stored in a another msgpack[127] formatted as follows:

version currently always an integer, 1

salt random 256 bits salt used to process the passphrase

iterations number of iterations used to process the passphrase (currently 100000)

algorithm the hashing algorithm used to process the passphrase and do the HMAC checksum (currently the string `sha256`)

hash HMAC-SHA256 of the *plaintext* of the packed fields.

data The encrypted, packed fields.

The resulting msgpack[128] is then encoded using base64 and written to the key file, wrapped using the standard `textwrap` module with a header. The header is a single line with a MAGIC string, a space and a hexadecimal representation of the repository id.

Compression

Borg supports the following compression methods:

- none (no compression, pass through data 1:1)

- lz4 (low compression, but super fast)

- zlib (level 0-9, level 0 is no compression [but still adding zlib overhead], level 1 is low, level 9 is high compression)

- lzma (level 0-9, level 0 is low, level 9 is high compression).

Speed: none > lz4 > zlib > lzma Compression: lzma > zlib > lz4 > none

Be careful, higher zlib and especially lzma compression levels might take a lot of resources (CPU and memory).

The overall speed of course also depends on the speed of your target storage. If that is slow, using a higher compression level might yield better overall performance. You need to experiment a bit. Maybe just watch your CPU load, if that is relatively low, increase compression until 1 core is 70-100% loaded.

---

[123] https://msgpack.org/
[124] https://en.wikipedia.org/wiki/PBKDF2
[125] https://en.wikipedia.org/wiki/SHA-256
[126] https://en.wikipedia.org/wiki/HMAC
[127] https://msgpack.org/
[128] https://msgpack.org/

Even if your target storage is rather fast, you might see interesting effects: while doing no compression at all (none) is a operation that takes no time, it likely will need to store more data to the storage compared to using lz4. The time needed to transfer and store the additional data might be much more than if you had used lz4 (which is super fast, but still might compress your data about 2:1). This is assuming your data is compressible (if you backup already compressed data, trying to compress them at backup time is usually pointless).

Compression is applied after deduplication, thus using different compression methods in one repo does not influence deduplication.

See `borg create --help` about how to specify the compression level and its default.

Lock files

Borg uses locks to get (exclusive or shared) access to the cache and the repository.

The locking system is based on creating a directory *lock.exclusive* (for exclusive locks). Inside the lock directory, there is a file indicating hostname, process id and thread id of the lock holder.

There is also a json file *lock.roster* that keeps a directory of all shared and exclusive lockers.

If the process can create the *lock.exclusive* directory for a resource, it has the lock for it. If creation fails (because the directory has already been created by some other process), lock acquisition fails.

The cache lock is usually in *~/.cache/borg/REPOID/lock.**. The repository lock is in *repository/lock.**.

In case you run into troubles with the locks, you can use the `borg break-lock` command after you first have made sure that no Borg process is running on any machine that accesses this resource. Be very careful, the cache or repository might get damaged if multiple processes use it at the same time.

Checksumming data structures

As detailed in the previous sections, Borg generates and stores various files containing important meta data, such as the repository index, repository hints, chunks caches and files cache.

Data corruption in these files can damage the archive data in a repository, e.g. due to wrong reference counts in the chunks cache. Only some parts of Borg were designed to handle corrupted data structures, so a corrupted files cache may cause crashes or write incorrect archives.

Therefore, Borg calculates checksums when writing these files and tests checksums when reading them. Checksums are generally 64-bit XXH64 hashes. The canonical xxHash representation is used, i.e. big-endian. Checksums are stored as hexadecimal ASCII strings.

For compatibility, checksums are not required and absent checksums do not trigger errors. The mechanisms have been designed to avoid false-positives when various Borg versions are used alternately on the same repositories.

Checksums are a data safety mechanism. They are not a security mechanism.

Choice of algorithm

XXH64 has been chosen for its high speed on all platforms, which avoids performance degradation in CPU-limited parts (e.g. cache synchronization). Unlike CRC32, it neither requires hardware support (crc32c or CLMUL) nor vectorized code nor large, cache-unfriendly lookup tables to achieve good performance. This simplifies deployment of it considerably (cf. src/borg/algorithms/crc32...).

Further, XXH64 is a non-linear hash function and thus has a "more or less" good chance to detect larger burst errors, unlike linear CRCs where the probability of detection decreases with error size.

The 64-bit checksum length is considered sufficient for the file sizes typically checksummed (individual files up to a few GB, usually less). xxHash was expressly designed for data blocks of these sizes.

Lower layer — file_integrity

To accommodate the different transaction models used for the cache and repository, there is a lower layer (borg.crypto.file_integrity.IntegrityCheckedFile) wrapping a file-like object, performing streaming calculation and comparison of checksums. Checksum errors are signalled by raising an exception (borg.crypto.file_integrity.FileIntegrityError) at the earliest possible moment.

Calculating checksums

Before feeding the checksum algorithm any data, the file name (i.e. without any path) is mixed into the checksum, since the name encodes the context of the data for Borg.

The various indices used by Borg have separate header and main data parts. IntegrityCheckedFile allows to checksum them independently, which avoids even reading the data when the header is corrupted. When a part is signalled, the length of the part name is mixed into the checksum state first (encoded as an ASCII string via *%10d* printf format), then the name of the part is mixed in as an UTF-8 string. Lastly, the current position (length) in the file is mixed in as well.

The checksum state is not reset at part boundaries.

A final checksum is always calculated in the same way as the parts described above, after seeking to the end of the file. The final checksum cannot prevent code from processing corrupted data during reading, however, it prevents use of the corrupted data.

Serializing checksums

All checksums are compiled into a simple JSON structure called *integrity data*:

```
{
    "algorithm": "XXH64",
    "digests": {
        "HashHeader": "eab6802590ba39e3",
        "final": "e2a7f132fc2e8b24"
    }
}
```

The *algorithm* key notes the used algorithm. When reading, integrity data containing an unknown algorithm is not inspected further.

The *digests* key contains a mapping of part names to their digests.

Integrity data is generally stored by the upper layers, introduced below. An exception is the DetachedIntegrityCheckedFile, which automatically writes and reads it from a ".integrity" file next to the data file. It is used for archive chunks indexes in chunks.archive.d.

Upper layer

Storage of integrity data depends on the component using it, since they have different transaction mechanisms, and integrity data needs to be transacted with the data it is supposed to protect.

Main cache files: chunks and files cache

The integrity data of the `chunks` and `files` caches is stored in the cache `config`, since all three are transacted together.

The `[integrity]` section is used:

```
[cache]
version = 1
repository = 3c4...e59
manifest = 10e...21c
timestamp = 2017-06-01T21:31:39.699514
key_type = 2
previous_location = /path/to/repo

[integrity]
manifest = 10e...21c
chunks = {"algorithm": "XXH64", "digests": {"HashHeader": "eab...39e3", "final":
↪"e2a...b24"}}
```

The manifest ID is duplicated in the integrity section due to the way all Borg versions handle the config file. Instead of creating a "new" config file from an internal representation containing only the data understood by Borg, the config file is read in entirety (using the Python ConfigParser) and modified. This preserves all sections and values not understood by the Borg version modifying it.

Thus, if an older versions uses a cache with integrity data, it would preserve the integrity section and its contents. If a integrity-aware Borg version would read this cache, it would incorrectly report checksum errors, since the older version did not update the checksums.

However, by duplicating the manifest ID in the integrity section, it is easy to tell whether the checksums concern the current state of the cache.

Integrity errors are fatal in these files, terminating the program, and are not automatically corrected at this time.

chunks.archive.d

Indices in chunks.archive.d are not transacted and use DetachedIntegrityCheckedFile, which writes the integrity data to a separate ".integrity" file.

Integrity errors result in deleting the affected index and rebuilding it. This logs a warning and increases the exit code to WARNING (1).

Repository index and hints

The repository associates index and hints files with a transaction by including the transaction ID in the file names. Integrity data is stored in a third file ("integrity.<TRANSACTION_ID>"). Like the hints file, it is msgpacked:

```
{
    b'version': 2,
    b'hints': b'{"algorithm": "XXH64", "digests": {"final": "411208db2aa13f1a"}}',
    b'index': b'{"algorithm": "XXH64", "digests": {"HashHeader": "846b7315f91b8e48
↪", "final": "cb3e26cadc173e40"}}'
}
```

The *version* key started at 2, the same version used for the hints. Since Borg has many versioned file formats, this keeps the number of different versions in use a bit lower.

The other keys map an auxiliary file, like *index* or *hints* to their integrity data. Note that the JSON is stored as-is, and not as part of the msgpack structure.

Integrity errors result in deleting the affected file(s) (index/hints) and rebuilding the index, which is the same action taken when corruption is noticed in other ways (e.g. HashIndex can detect most corrupted headers, but not data corruption). A warning is logged as well. The exit code is not influenced, since remote repositories cannot perform that action. Raising the exit code would be possible for local repositories, but is not implemented.

Unlike the cache design this mechanism can have false positives whenever an older version *rewrites* the auxiliary files for a transaction created by a newer version, since that might result in a different index (due to hash-table resizing) or hints file (hash ordering, or the older version 1 format), while not invalidating the integrity file.

For example, using 1.1 on a repository, noticing corruption or similar issues and then running `borg-1.0 check --repair`, which rewrites the index and hints, results in this situation. Borg 1.1 would erroneously report checksum errors in the hints and/or index files and trigger an automatic rebuild of these files.

All about JSON: How to develop frontends

Borg does not have a public API on the Python level. That does not keep you from writing `import borg`, but does mean that there are no release-to-release guarantees on what you might find in that package, not even for point releases (1.1.x), and there is no documentation beyond the code and the internals documents.

Borg does on the other hand provide an API on a command-line level. In other words, a frontend should to (for example) create a backup archive just invoke *borg create*, give commandline parameters/options as needed and parse JSON output from borg.

Important: JSON output is expected to be UTF-8, but currently borg depends on the locale being configured for that (must be a UTF-8 locale and *not* "C" or "ascii"), so that Python will choose to encode to UTF-8. The same applies to any inputs read by borg, they are expected to be UTF-8 encoded also.

We consider this a bug (see #2273[129]) and might fix it later, so borg will use UTF-8 independent of the locale.

On POSIX systems, you can usually set environment vars to choose a UTF-8 locale:

```
export LANG=en_US.UTF-8
export LC_CTYPE=en_US.UTF-8
```

Logging

Especially for graphical frontends it is important to be able to convey and reformat progress information in meaningful ways. The `--log-json` option turns the stderr stream of Borg into a stream of JSON lines, where each line is a JSON object. The *type* key of the object determines its other contents.

Since JSON can only encode text, any string representing a file system path may miss non-text parts.

The following types are in use. Progress information is governed by the usual rules for progress information, it is not produced unless `--progress` is specified.

archive_progress Output during operations creating archives (*borg create* and *borg recreate*). The following keys exist, each represents the current progress.

> **original_size** Original size of data processed so far (before compression and deduplication)
>
> **compressed_size** Compressed size
>
> **deduplicated_size** Deduplicated size
>
> **nfiles** Number of (regular) files processed so far
>
> **path** Current path
>
> **time** Unix timestamp (float)

progress_message A message-based progress information with no concrete progress information, just a message saying what is currently being worked on.

> **operation** unique, opaque integer ID of the operation
>
> *msgid* Message ID of the operation (may be *null*)
>
> **finished** boolean indicating whether the operation has finished, only the last object for an *operation* can have this property set to *true*.
>
> **message** current progress message (may be empty/absent)

---

[129] https://github.com/borgbackup/borg/issues/2273

time Unix timestamp (float)

progress_percent Absolute progress information with defined end/total and current value.

> **operation** unique, opaque integer ID of the operation
>
> *msgid* Message ID of the operation (may be *null*)
>
> **finished** boolean indicating whether the operation has finished, only the last object for an *operation* can have this property set to *true*.
>
> **message** A formatted progress message, this will include the percentage and perhaps other information
>
> **current** Current value (always less-or-equal to *total*)
>
> **info** Array that describes the current item, may be *null*, contents depend on *msgid*
>
> **total** Total value
>
> **time** Unix timestamp (float)

file_status This is only output by *borg create* and *borg recreate* if `--list` is specified. The usual rules for the file listing applies, including the `--filter` option.

> **status** Single-character status as for regular list output
>
> **path** Path of the file system object

log_message Any regular log output invokes this type. Regular log options and filtering applies to these as well.

> **time** Unix timestamp (float)
>
> **levelname** Upper-case log level name (also called severity). Defined levels are: DEBUG, INFO, WARN-ING, ERROR, CRITICAL
>
> **name** Name of the emitting entity
>
> **message** Formatted log message
>
> *msgid* Message ID, may be *null* or absent

See *Prompts* for the types used by prompts.

Examples (reformatted, each object would be on exactly one line)

borg extract progress:

```
{"message": "100.0% Extracting: src/borgbackup.egg-info/entry_points.txt",
 "current": 13000228, "total": 13004993, "info": ["src/borgbackup.egg-info/entry_
↪points.txt"],
 "operation": 1, "msgid": "extract", "type": "progress_percent", "finished": false}
{"message": "100.0% Extracting: src/borgbackup.egg-info/SOURCES.txt",
 "current": 13004993, "total": 13004993, "info": ["src/borgbackup.egg-info/SOURCES.
↪txt"],
 "operation": 1, "msgid": "extract", "type": "progress_percent", "finished": false}
{"operation": 1, "msgid": "extract", "type": "progress_percent", "finished": true}
```

borg create file listing with progress:

```
{"original_size": 0, "compressed_size": 0, "deduplicated_size": 0, "nfiles": 0,
↪"type": "archive_progress", "path": "src"}
{"type": "file_status", "status": "U", "path": "src/borgbackup.egg-info/entry_
↪points.txt"}
{"type": "file_status", "status": "U", "path": "src/borgbackup.egg-info/SOURCES.txt
↪"}
{"type": "file_status", "status": "d", "path": "src/borgbackup.egg-info"}
{"type": "file_status", "status": "d", "path": "src"}
{"original_size": 13176040, "compressed_size": 11386863, "deduplicated_size": 503,
↪"nfiles": 277, "type": "archive_progress", "path": ""}
```

Internal transaction progress:

```
{"message": "Saving files cache", "operation": 2, "msgid": "cache.commit", "type":
↪"progress_message", "finished": false}
{"message": "Saving cache config", "operation": 2, "msgid": "cache.commit", "type
↪": "progress_message", "finished": false}
{"message": "Saving chunks cache", "operation": 2, "msgid": "cache.commit", "type
↪": "progress_message", "finished": false}
{"operation": 2, "msgid": "cache.commit", "type": "progress_message", "finished":
↪true}
```

A debug log message:

```
{"message": "35 self tests completed in 0.08 seconds",
 "type": "log_message", "created": 1488278449.5575905, "levelname": "DEBUG", "name
↪": "borg.archiver"}
```

Prompts

Prompts assume a JSON form as well when the `--log-json` option is specified. Responses are still read verbatim from *stdin*, while prompts are JSON messages printed to *stderr*, just like log messages.

Prompts use the *question_prompt* and *question_prompt_retry* types for the prompt itself, and *question_invalid_answer*, *question_accepted_default*, *question_accepted_true*, *question_accepted_false* and *question_env_answer* types for information about prompt processing.

The *message* property contains the same string displayed regularly in the same situation, while the *msgid* property may contain a *msgid*, typically the name of the environment variable that can be used to override the prompt. It is the same for all JSON messages pertaining to the same prompt.

Examples (reformatted, each object would be on exactly one line)

Providing an invalid answer:

```
{"type": "question_prompt", "msgid": "BORG_CHECK_I_KNOW_WHAT_I_AM_DOING",
 "message": "... Type 'YES' if you understand this and want to continue: "}
incorrect answer  # input on stdin
{"type": "question_invalid_answer", "msgid": "BORG_CHECK_I_KNOW_WHAT_I_AM_DOING",
↪"is_prompt": false,
 "message": "Invalid answer, aborting."}
```

Providing a false (negative) answer:

```
{"type": "question_prompt", "msgid": "BORG_CHECK_I_KNOW_WHAT_I_AM_DOING",
 "message": "... Type 'YES' if you understand this and want to continue: "}
NO  # input on stdin
{"type": "question_accepted_false", "msgid": "BORG_CHECK_I_KNOW_WHAT_I_AM_DOING",
 "message": "Aborting.", "is_prompt": false}
```

Providing a true (affirmative) answer:

```
{"type": "question_prompt", "msgid": "BORG_CHECK_I_KNOW_WHAT_I_AM_DOING",
 "message": "... Type 'YES' if you understand this and want to continue: "}
YES # input on stdin
# no further output, just like the prompt without --log-json
```

Passphrase prompts

Passphrase prompts should be handled differently. Use the environment variables *BORG_PASSPHRASE* and *BORG_NEW_PASSPHRASE* (see *Environment Variables* for reference) to pass passphrases to Borg, don't use the interactive passphrase prompts.

When setting a new passphrase (*borg init*, *borg key change-passphrase*) normally Borg prompts whether it should display the passphrase. This can be suppressed by setting the environment variable *BORG_DISPLAY_PASSPHRASE* to *no*.

When "confronted" with an unknown repository, where the application does not know whether the repository is encrypted, the following algorithm can be followed to detect encryption:

1. Set *BORG_PASSPHRASE* to gibberish (for example a freshly generated UUID4, which cannot possibly be the passphrase)

2. Invoke `borg list repository ...`

3. If this fails, due the repository being encrypted and the passphrase obviously being wrong, you'll get an error with the *PassphraseWrong* msgid.

   The repository is encrypted, for further access the application will need the passphrase.

4. If this does not fail, then the repository is not encrypted.

Standard output

stdout is different and more command-dependent than logging. Commands like *borg info*, *borg create* and *borg list* implement a `--json` option which turns their regular output into a single JSON object.

Dates are formatted according to ISO 8601 in local time. No explicit time zone is specified *at this time* (subject to change). The equivalent strftime format string is '%Y-%m-%dT%H:%M:%S.%f', e.g. `2017-08-07T12:27:20.123456`.

The root object at least contains a *repository* key with an object containing:

id The ID of the repository, normally 64 hex characters

location Canonicalized repository path, thus this may be different from what is specified on the command line

last_modified Date when the repository was last modified by the Borg client

The *encryption* key, if present, contains:

mode Textual encryption mode name (same as *borg init* `--encryption` names)

keyfile Path to the local key file used for access. Depending on *mode* this key may be absent.

The *cache* key, if present, contains:

path Path to the local repository cache

stats Object containing cache stats:

> **total_chunks** Number of chunks
>
> **total_unique_chunks** Number of unique chunks
>
> **total_size** Total uncompressed size of all chunks multiplied with their reference counts
>
> **total_csize** Total compressed and encrypted size of all chunks multiplied with their reference counts
>
> **unique_size** Uncompressed size of all chunks
>
> **unique_csize** Compressed and encrypted size of all chunks

Example *borg info* output:

```
{
    "cache": {
        "path": "/home/user/.cache/borg/
↪0cbe6166b46627fd26b97f8831e2ca97584280a46714ef84d2b668daf8271a23",
        "stats": {
            "total_chunks": 511533,
            "total_csize": 17948017540,
            "total_size": 22635749792,
            "total_unique_chunks": 54892,
            "unique_csize": 1920405405,
            "unique_size": 2449675468
        }
    },
    "encryption": {
        "mode": "repokey"
    },
    "repository": {
        "id": "0cbe6166b46627fd26b97f8831e2ca97584280a46714ef84d2b668daf8271a23",
        "last_modified": "2017-08-07T12:27:20.789123",
        "location": "/home/user/testrepo"
    },
    "security_dir": "/home/user/.config/borg/security/
↪0cbe6166b46627fd26b97f8831e2ca97584280a46714ef84d2b668daf8271a23",
    "archives": []
}
```

Archive formats

borg info uses an extended format for archives, which is more expensive to retrieve, while *borg list* uses a simpler format that is faster to retrieve. Either return archives in an array under the *archives* key, while *borg create* returns a single archive object under the *archive* key.

Both formats contain a *name* key with the archive name, the *id* key with the hexadecimal archive ID, and the *start* key with the start timestamp.

borg info and *borg create* further have:

end End timestamp

duration Duration in seconds between start and end in seconds (float)

stats Archive statistics (freshly calculated, this is what makes "info" more expensive)

> **original_size** Size of files and metadata before compression
>
> **compressed_size** Size after compression
>
> **deduplicated_size** Deduplicated size (against the current repository, not when the archive was created)
>
> **nfiles** Number of regular files in the archive

limits Object describing the utilization of Borg limits

> **max_archive_size** Float between 0 and 1 describing how large this archive is relative to the maximum size allowed by Borg

command_line Array of strings of the command line that created the archive

> The note about paths from above applies here as well.

borg info further has:

hostname Hostname of the creating host

username Name of the creating user

comment Archive comment, if any

Example of a simple archive listing (`borg list --last 1 --json`):

```
{
    "archives": [
        {
            "id": "80cd07219ad725b3c5f665c1dcf119435c4dee1647a560ecac30f8d40221a46a
↪",
            "name": "host-system-backup-2017-02-27",
            "start": "2017-08-07T12:27:20.789123"
        }
    ],
    "encryption": {
        "mode": "repokey"
    },
    "repository": {
        "id": "0cbe6166b46627fd26b97f8831e2ca97584280a46714ef84d2b668daf8271a23",
        "last_modified": "2017-08-07T12:27:20.789123",
        "location": "/home/user/repository"
    }
}
```

The same archive with more information (`borg info --last 1 --json`):

```
{
    "archives": [
        {
            "command_line": [
                "/home/user/.local/bin/borg",
                "create",
                "/home/user/repository",
                "..."
            ],
            "comment": "",
            "duration": 5.641542,
            "end": "2017-02-27T12:27:20.789123",
            "hostname": "host",
            "id": "80cd07219ad725b3c5f665c1dcf119435c4dee1647a560ecac30f8d40221a46a
↪",
            "limits": {
                "max_archive_size": 0.0001330855110409714
            },
            "name": "host-system-backup-2017-02-27",
            "start": "2017-02-27T12:27:20.789123",
            "stats": {
                "compressed_size": 1880961894,
                "deduplicated_size": 2791,
                "nfiles": 53669,
                "original_size": 2400471280
            },
            "username": "user"
        }
    ],
    "cache": {
        "path": "/home/user/.cache/borg/
↪0cbe6166b46627fd26b97f8831e2ca97584280a46714ef84d2b668daf8271a23",
        "stats": {
            "total_chunks": 511533,
            "total_csize": 17948017540,
            "total_size": 22635749792,
            "total_unique_chunks": 54892,
            "unique_csize": 1920405405,
            "unique_size": 2449675468
        }
    }
}
```

```
    },
    "encryption": {
        "mode": "repokey"
    },
    "repository": {
        "id": "0cbe6166b46627fd26b97f8831e2ca97584280a46714ef84d2b668daf8271a23",
        "last_modified": "2017-08-07T12:27:20.789123",
        "location": "/home/user/repository"
    }
}
```

File listings

Listing the contents of an archive can produce *a lot* of JSON. Since many JSON implementations don't support a streaming mode of operation, which is pretty much required to deal with this amount of JSON, output is generated in the JSON lines[130] format, which is simply a number of JSON objects separated by new lines.

Each item (file, directory, ...) is described by one object in the *borg list* output. Refer to the *borg list* documentation for the available keys and their meaning.

Example (excerpt) of `borg list --json-lines`:

```
{"type": "d", "mode": "drwxr-xr-x", "user": "user", "group": "user", "uid": 1000,
 "gid": 1000, "path": "linux", "healthy": true, "source": "", "linktarget": "",
 "flags": null, "mtime": "2017-02-27T12:27:20.023407", "size": 0}
{"type": "d", "mode": "drwxr-xr-x", "user": "user", "group": "user", "uid": 1000,
 "gid": 1000, "path": "linux/baz", "healthy": true, "source": "", "linktarget": "
", "flags": null, "mtime": "2017-02-27T12:27:20.585407", "size": 0}
```

Message IDs

Message IDs are strings that essentially give a log message or operation a name, without actually using the full text, since texts change more frequently. Message IDs are unambiguous and reduce the need to parse log messages.

Assigned message IDs are:

Errors

> **Archive.AlreadyExists** Archive {} already exists
>
> **Archive.DoesNotExist** Archive {} does not exist
>
> **Archive.IncompatibleFilesystemEncodingError** Failed to encode filename "{}" into file system encoding "{}". Consider configuring the LANG environment variable.
>
> **Cache.CacheInitAbortedError** Cache initialization aborted
>
> **Cache.EncryptionMethodMismatch** Repository encryption method changed since last access, refusing to continue
>
> **Cache.RepositoryAccessAborted** Repository access aborted
>
> **Cache.RepositoryIDNotUnique** Cache is newer than repository - do you have multiple, independently updated repos with same ID?
>
> **Cache.RepositoryReplay** Cache is newer than repository - this is either an attack or unsafe (multiple repos with same ID)
>
> **Buffer.MemoryLimitExceeded** Requested buffer size {} is above the limit of {}.
>
> **ExtensionModuleError** The Borg binary extension modules do not seem to be properly installed

---

[130] http://jsonlines.org/

IntegrityError Data integrity error: {}

NoManifestError Repository has no manifest.

PlaceholderError Formatting Error: "{}".format({}): {}({})

KeyfileInvalidError Invalid key file for repository {} found in {}.

KeyfileMismatchError Mismatch between repository {} and key file {}.

KeyfileNotFoundError No key file for repository {} found in {}.

PassphraseWrong passphrase supplied in BORG_PASSPHRASE is incorrect

PasswordRetriesExceeded exceeded the maximum password retries

RepoKeyNotFoundError No key entry found in the config of repository {}.

UnsupportedManifestError Unsupported manifest envelope. A newer version is required to access this repository.

UnsupportedPayloadError Unsupported payload type {}. A newer version is required to access this repository.

NotABorgKeyFile This file is not a borg key backup, aborting.

RepoIdMismatch This key backup seems to be for a different backup repository, aborting.

UnencryptedRepo Keymanagement not available for unencrypted repositories.

UnknownKeyType Keytype {0} is unknown.

LockError Failed to acquire the lock {}.

LockErrorT Failed to acquire the lock {}.

ConnectionClosed Connection closed by remote host

InvalidRPCMethod RPC method {} is not valid

PathNotAllowed Repository path not allowed

RemoteRepository.RPCServerOutdated Borg server is too old for {}. Required version {}

UnexpectedRPCDataFormatFromClient Borg {}: Got unexpected RPC data format from client.

UnexpectedRPCDataFormatFromServer Got unexpected RPC data format from server: {}

Repository.AlreadyExists Repository {} already exists.

Repository.CheckNeeded Inconsistency detected. Please run "borg check {}".

Repository.DoesNotExist Repository {} does not exist.

Repository.InsufficientFreeSpaceError Insufficient free space to complete transaction (required: {}, available: {}).

Repository.InvalidRepository {} is not a valid repository. Check repo config.

Repository.AtticRepository Attic repository detected. Please run "borg upgrade {}".

Repository.ObjectNotFound Object with key {} not found in repository {}.

Operations

- cache.begin_transaction
- cache.download_chunks, appears with `borg create --no-cache-sync`
- cache.commit
- cache.sync

  info is one string element, the name of the archive currently synced.

- repository.compact_segments

- repository.replay_segments

- repository.check_segments

- check.verify_data

- extract

  info is one string element, the name of the path currently extracted.

- extract.permissions

- archive.delete

Prompts

BORG_UNKNOWN_UNENCRYPTED_REPO_ACCESS_IS_OK For "Warning: Attempting to access a previously unknown unencrypted repository"

BORG_RELOCATED_REPO_ACCESS_IS_OK For "Warning: The repository at location ... was previously located at ..."

BORG_CHECK_I_KNOW_WHAT_I_AM_DOING For "Warning: 'check –repair' is an experimental feature that might result in data loss."

BORG_DELETE_I_KNOW_WHAT_I_AM_DOING For "You requested to completely DELETE the repository *including* all archives it contains:"

BORG_RECREATE_I_KNOW_WHAT_I_AM_DOING For "recreate is an experimental feature."

CHAPTER 8

Development

This chapter will get you started with Borg development.

Borg is written in Python (with a little bit of Cython and C for the performance critical parts).

Contributions

... are welcome!

Some guidance for contributors:

- discuss about changes on github issue tracker, IRC or mailing list

- make your PRs on the `master` branch (see *Branching Model* for details)

- do clean changesets:

  - focus on some topic, resist changing anything else.

  - do not do style changes mixed with functional changes.

  - try to avoid refactorings mixed with functional changes.

  - if you need to fix something after commit/push:

    * if there are ongoing reviews: do a fixup commit you can merge into the bad commit later.

    * if there are no ongoing reviews or you did not push the bad commit yet: edit the commit to include your fix or merge the fixup commit before pushing.

  - have a nice, clear, typo-free commit comment

  - if you fixed an issue, refer to it in your commit comment

  - follow the style guide (see below)

- if you write new code, please add tests and docs for it

- run the tests, fix anything that comes up

- make a pull request on github

- wait for review by other developers

Branching model

Borg development happens on the `master` branch and uses GitHub pull requests (if you don't have GitHub or don't want to use it you can send smaller patches via the borgbackup *Mailing list* to the maintainers).

Stable releases are maintained on maintenance branches named x.y-maint, eg. the maintenance branch of the 1.0.x series is 1.0-maint.

Most PRs should be made against the `master` branch. Only if an issue affects **only** a particular maintenance branch a PR should be made against it directly.

While discussing / reviewing a PR it will be decided whether the change should be applied to maintenance branch(es). Each maintenance branch has a corresponding *backport/x.y-maint* label, which will then be applied.

Changes that are typically considered for backporting:

- Data loss, corruption and inaccessibility fixes

- Security fixes

- Forward-compatibility improvements

- Documentation corrections

Maintainer part

From time to time a maintainer will backport the changes for a maintenance branch, typically before a release or if enough changes were collected:

1. Notify others that you're doing this to avoid duplicate work.

2. Branch a backporting branch off the maintenance branch.

3. Cherry pick and backport the changes from each labelled PR, remove the label for each PR you've backported.

   To preserve authorship metadata, do not follow the `git cherry-pick` instructions to use `git commit` after resolving conflicts. Instead, stage conflict resolutions and run `git cherry-pick --continue`, much like using `git rebase`.

   To avoid merge issues (a cherry pick is a form of merge), use these options (similar to the `git merge` options used previously, the `-x` option adds a reference to the original commit):

   ```
   git cherry-pick --strategy recursive -X rename-threshold=5% -x
   ```

4. Make a PR of the backporting branch against the maintenance branch for backport review. Mention the backported PRs in this PR, e.g.:

   Includes changes from #2055 #2057 #2381

   This way GitHub will automatically show in these PRs where they were backported.

Historic model

Previously (until release 1.0.10) Borg used a "merge upwards"[131] model where most minor changes and fixes where committed to a maintenance branch (eg. 1.0-maint), and the maintenance branch(es) were regularly merged back into the main development branch. This became more and more troublesome due to merges growing more conflict-heavy and error-prone.

---

[131] https://git-scm.com/docs/gitworkflows#_merging_upwards

Code and issues

Code is stored on Github, in the Borgbackup organization[132]. Issues[133] and pull requests[134] should be sent there as well. See also the *Support* section for more details.

Style guide

We generally follow pep8[135], with 120 columns instead of 79. We do *not* use form-feed (^L) characters to separate sections either. Compliance is tested automatically when you run the tests.

Continuous Integration

All pull requests go through Travis-CI[136], which runs the tests on Linux and Mac OS X as well as the flake8 style checker. Windows builds run on AppVeyor[137], while additional Unix-like platforms are tested on Golem[138].

Output and Logging

When writing logger calls, always use correct log level (debug only for debugging, info for informative messages, warning for warnings, error for errors, critical for critical errors/states).

When directly talking to the user (e.g. Y/N questions), do not use logging, but directly output to stderr (not: stdout, it could be connected to a pipe).

To control the amount and kinds of messages output emitted at info level, use flags like `--stats` or `--list`, then create a topic logger for messages controlled by that flag. See `_setup_implied_logging()` in `borg/archiver.py` for the entry point to topic logging.

Building a development environment

First, just install borg into a virtual env as described before.

To install some additional packages needed for running the tests, activate your virtual env and run:

```
pip install -r requirements.d/development.txt
```

Running the tests

The tests are in the borg/testsuite package.

To run all the tests, you need to have fakeroot installed. If you do not have fakeroot, you still will be able to run most tests, just leave away the *fakeroot -u* from the given command lines.

To run the test suite use the following command:

---

[132] https://github.com/borgbackup/borg/
[133] https://github.com/borgbackup/borg/issues
[134] https://github.com/borgbackup/borg/pulls
[135] https://www.python.org/dev/peps/pep-0008/
[136] https://travis-ci.org/borgbackup/borg
[137] https://ci.appveyor.com/project/borgbackup/borg/
[138] https://golem.enkore.de/view/Borg/

```
fakeroot -u tox    # run all tests
```

Some more advanced examples:

```
# verify a changed tox.ini (run this after any change to tox.ini):
fakeroot -u tox --recreate

fakeroot -u tox -e py34   # run all tests, but only on python 3.4

fakeroot -u tox borg.testsuite.locking   # only run 1 test module

fakeroot -u tox borg.testsuite.locking -- -k '"not Timer"'   # exclude some tests

fakeroot -u tox borg.testsuite -- -v   # verbose py.test
```

Important notes:

- When using `--` to give options to py.test, you MUST also give `borg.testsuite[.module]`.

Running more checks using coala

First install coala and some checkers ("bears"):

    pip install -r requirements.d/coala.txt

You can now run coala from the toplevel directory; it will read its settings from `.coafile` there:

    coala

Some bears have additional requirements and they usually tell you about them in case they are missing.

Documentation

Generated files

Usage documentation (found in `docs/usage/`) and man pages (`docs/man/`) are generated automatically from the command line parsers declared in the program and their documentation, which is embedded in the program (see archiver.py). These are committed to git for easier use by packagers downstream.

When a command is added, a commandline flag changed, added or removed, the usage docs need to be rebuilt as well:

```
python setup.py build_usage
python setup.py build_man
```

However, we prefer to do this as part of our *Creating a new release* preparations, so it is generally not necessary to update these when submitting patches that change something about the command line.

Building the docs with Sphinx

The documentation (in reStructuredText format, .rst) is in docs/.

To build the html version of it, you need to have Sphinx installed (in your Borg virtualenv with Python 3):

```
pip install -r requirements.d/docs.txt
```

Now run:

```
cd docs/
make html
```

Then point a web browser at docs/_build/html/index.html.

The website is updated automatically by ReadTheDocs through GitHub web hooks on the main repository.

Using Vagrant

We use Vagrant for the automated creation of testing environments and borgbackup standalone binaries for various platforms.

For better security, there is no automatic sync in the VM to host direction. The plugin *vagrant-scp* is useful to copy stuff from the VMs to the host.

The "windows10" box requires the *reload* plugin (`vagrant plugin install vagrant-reload`).

Usage:

```
# To create and provision the VM:
vagrant up OS
# same, but use 6 VM cpus and 12 workers for pytest:
VMCPUS=6 XDISTN=12 vagrant up OS
# To create an ssh session to the VM:
vagrant ssh OS
# To execute a command via ssh in the VM:
vagrant ssh OS -c "command args"
# To shut down the VM:
vagrant halt OS
# To shut down and destroy the VM:
vagrant destroy OS
# To copy files from the VM (in this case, the generated binary):
vagrant scp OS:/vagrant/borg/borg.exe .
```

Creating standalone binaries

Make sure you have everything built and installed (including llfuse and fuse). When using the Vagrant VMs, pyinstaller will already be installed.

With virtual env activated:

```
pip install pyinstaller  # or git checkout master
pyinstaller -F -n borg-PLATFORM borg/__main__.py
for file in dist/borg-*; do gpg --armor --detach-sign $file; done
```

If you encounter issues, see also our *Vagrantfile* for details.

Note: Standalone binaries built with pyinstaller are supposed to work on same OS, same architecture (x86 32bit, amd64 64bit) without external dependencies.

Creating a new release

Checklist:

- make sure all issues for this milestone are closed or moved to the next milestone

---

- find and fix any low hanging fruit left on the issue tracker
- check that Travis CI is happy
- update `CHANGES.rst`, based on `git log $PREVIOUS_RELEASE..`
- check version number of upcoming release in `CHANGES.rst`
- verify that `MANIFEST.in` and `setup.py` are complete
- `python setup.py build_usage ; python setup.py build_man` and commit (be sure to build with Python 3.4 or 3.5 as Python 3.6 added more guaranteed hashing algorithms[139])
- tag the release:

```
git tag -s -m "tagged/signed release X.Y.Z" X.Y.Z
```

- create a clean repo and use it for the following steps:

```
git clone borg borg-clean
```

This makes sure no uncommitted files get into the release archive. It also will find if you forgot to commit something that is needed. It also makes sure the vagrant machines only get committed files and do a fresh start based on that.

- run tox and/or binary builds on all supported platforms via vagrant, check for test failures
- create a release on PyPi:

```
python setup.py register sdist upload --identity="Thomas Waldmann" --sign
```

- close release milestone on Github
- announce on:
- Mailing list
- Twitter
- IRC channel (change `/topic`)
- create a Github release, include:
  - standalone binaries (see above for how to create them)
    * for OS X, document the OS X Fuse version in the README of the binaries. OS X FUSE uses a kernel extension that needs to be compatible with the code contained in the binary.
  - a link to `CHANGES.rst`

---

[139] https://github.com/borgbackup/borg/issues/2123

Support

Please first read the docs, the existing issue tracker issues and mailing list posts – a lot of stuff is already documented / explained / discussed / filed there.

Issue Tracker

If you've found a bug or have a concrete feature request, please create a new ticket on the project's issue tracker[140].

For more general questions or discussions, IRC or mailing list are preferred.

Chat (IRC)

Join us on channel #borgbackup on chat.freenode.net.

As usual on IRC, just ask or tell directly and then patiently wait for replies. Stay connected.

You could use the following link (after connecting, you can change the random nickname you get by typing "/nick mydesirednickname"):

http://webchat.freenode.net/?randomnick=1&channels=%23borgbackup&uio=MTY9dHJ1ZSY5PXRydWUa8

Mailing list

To find out about the mailing list, its topic, how to subscribe, how to unsubscribe and where you can find the archives of the list, see the mailing list homepage[141].

Twitter

Follow @borgbackup for announcements. You can also add @borgbackup if you would like to get retweeted for a borg related tweet.

---

[140] https://github.com/borgbackup/borg/issues
[141] https://mail.python.org/mailman/listinfo/borgbackup

Please understand that Twitter is not suitable for longer / more complex discussions - use one of the other channels for that.

Bounties and Fundraisers

We use BountySource[142] to allow monetary contributions to the project and the developers, who push it forward.

There, you can give general funds to the borgbackup members (the developers will then spend the funds as they deem fit). If you do not have some specific bounty (see below), you can use this as a general way to say "Thank You!" and support the software / project you like.

If you want to encourage developers to fix some specific issue or implement some specific feature suggestion, you can post a new bounty or back an existing one (they always refer to an issue in our issue tracker[143]).

As a developer, you can become a Bounty Hunter and win bounties (earn money) by contributing to Borg, a free and open source software project.

We might also use BountySource to fund raise for some bigger goals.

Security

In case you discover a security issue, please use this contact for reporting it privately and please, if possible, use encrypted E-Mail:

Thomas Waldmann <tw@waldmann-edv.de>

GPG Key Fingerprint: 6D5B EF9A DD20 7580 5747 B70F 9F88 FB52 FAF7 B393

The public key can be fetched from any GPG keyserver, but be careful: you must use the **full fingerprint** to check that you got the correct key.

Releases[144] are signed with this GPG key, please use GPG to verify their authenticity.

---

[142] https://www.bountysource.com/teams/borgbackup
[143] https://github.com/borgbackup/borg/issues
[144] https://github.com/borgbackup/borg/releases

Resources

This is a collection of additional resources that are somehow related to borgbackup.

Videos, Talks, Presentations

Some of them refer to attic, but you can do the same stuff (and more) with borgbackup.

- BorgBackup Installation and Basic Usage[145] (english screencast)
- TW's slides for borgbackup talks / lightning talks[146] (just grab the latest ones)
- Attic / Borg Backup talk from GPN 2015 (media.ccc.de)[147]
- Attic / Borg Backup talk from GPN 2015 (youtube)[148]
- Attic talk from Easterhegg 2015 (media.ccc.de)[149]
- Attic talk from Easterhegg 2015 (youtube)[150]
- Attic Backup: Mount your encrypted backups over ssh (youtube)[151]
- Evolution of Borg (youtube)[152]

Software

- BorgWeb - a very simple web UI for BorgBackup[153]
- some other stuff found at the BorgBackup Github organisation[154]

---

[145] https://asciinema.org/a/28691?autoplay=1&speed=2
[146] https://slides.com/thomaswaldmann
[147] https://media.ccc.de/browse/conferences/gpn/gpn15/gpn15-6942-attic_borg_backup.html#video
[148] https://www.youtube.com/watch?v=Nb5nXEKSN-k
[149] https://media.ccc.de/v/eh15_-_49_-__-_saal_-_201504042130_-_attic_-_the_holy_grail_of_backups_-_thomas#video
[150] https://www.youtube.com/watch?v=96VEAAFDtJw
[151] https://www.youtube.com/watch?v=BVXDFv9YMp8
[152] https://www.youtube.com/watch?v=K4k_4wDkG6Q
[153] https://borgweb.readthedocs.io/
[154] https://github.com/borgbackup/

- borgmatic[155] - simple wrapper script for BorgBackup that creates and prunes backups

---

[155] https://torsion.org/borgmatic/

Appendix B. Resources

Important notes

This section provides information about security and corruption issues.

Pre-1.0.9 manifest spoofing vulnerability (CVE-2016-10099)

A flaw in the cryptographic authentication scheme in Borg allowed an attacker to spoof the manifest. The attack requires an attacker to be able to

1. insert files (with no additional headers) into backups

2. gain write access to the repository

This vulnerability does not disclose plaintext to the attacker, nor does it affect the authenticity of existing archives.

The vulnerability allows an attacker to create a spoofed manifest (the list of archives). Creating plausible fake archives may be feasible for small archives, but is unlikely for large archives.

The fix adds a separate authentication tag to the manifest. For compatibility with prior versions this authentication tag is *not* required by default for existing repositories. Repositories created with 1.0.9 and later require it.

Steps you should take:

1. Upgrade all clients to 1.0.9 or later.

2. Run `borg upgrade --tam <repository>` *on every client* for *each* repository.

3. This will list all archives, including archive IDs, for easy comparison with your logs.

4. Done.

Prior versions can access and modify repositories with this measure enabled, however, to 1.0.9 or later their modifications are indiscernible from an attack and will raise an error until the below procedure is followed. We are aware that this can be be annoying in some circumstances, but don't see a way to fix the vulnerability otherwise.

In case a version prior to 1.0.9 is used to modify a repository where above procedure was completed, and now you get an error message from other clients:

1. `borg upgrade --tam --force <repository>` once with *any* client suffices.

This attack is mitigated by:

- Noting/logging `borg list`, `borg info`, or `borg create --stats`, which contain the archive IDs.

We are not aware of others having discovered, disclosed or exploited this vulnerability.

Vulnerability time line:

- 2016-11-14: Vulnerability and fix discovered during review of cryptography by Marian Beermann (@enkore)
- 2016-11-20: First patch
- 2016-12-20: Released fixed version 1.0.9
- 2017-01-02: CVE was assigned
- 2017-01-15: Released fixed version 1.1.0b3 (fix was previously only available from source)

Pre-1.0.9 potential data loss

If you have archives in your repository that were made with attic <= 0.13 (and later migrated to borg), running borg check would report errors in these archives. See issue #1837.

The reason for this is a invalid (and useless) metadata key that was always added due to a bug in these old attic versions.

If you run borg check –repair, things escalate quickly: all archive items with invalid metadata will be killed. Due to that attic bug, that means all items in all archives made with these old attic versions.

Pre-1.0.4 potential repo corruption

Some external errors (like network or disk I/O errors) could lead to corruption of the backup repository due to issue #1138.

A sign that this happened is if "E" status was reported for a file that can not be explained by problems with the source file. If you still have logs from "borg create -v –list", you can check for "E" status.

Here is what could cause corruption and what you can do now:

1. I/O errors (e.g. repo disk errors) while writing data to repo.

This could lead to corrupted segment files.

Fix:

```
# check for corrupt chunks / segments:
borg check -v --repository-only REPO

# repair the repo:
borg check -v --repository-only --repair REPO

# make sure everything is fixed:
borg check -v --repository-only REPO
```

2. Unreliable network / unreliable connection to the repo.

This could lead to archive metadata corruption.

Fix:

```
# check for corrupt archives:
borg check -v --archives-only REPO

# delete the corrupt archives:
borg delete --force REPO::CORRUPT_ARCHIVE
```

```
# make sure everything is fixed:
borg check -v --archives-only REPO
```

3. In case you want to do more intensive checking.

The best check that everything is ok is to run a dry-run extraction:

```
borg extract -v --dry-run REPO::ARCHIVE
```

Changelog

Version 1.1.0 (2017-10-07)

Fixes:

- fix LD_LIBRARY_PATH restoration for subprocesses, #3077
- "auto" compression: make sure expensive compression is actually better, otherwise store lz4 compressed data we already computed.

Other changes:

- docs:
    - FAQ: we do not implement futile attempts of ETA / progress displays
    - manpage: fix typos, update homepage
    - implement simple "issue" role for manpage generation, #3075

Version 1.1.0rc4 (2017-10-01)

Compatibility notes:

- A borg server >= 1.1.0rc4 does not support borg clients 1.1.0b3-b5. #3033
- The files cache is now controlled differently and has a new default mode:
    - the files cache now uses ctime by default for improved file change detection safety. You can still use mtime for more speed and less safety.
    - –ignore-inode is deprecated (use –files-cache=... without "inode")
    - –no-files-cache is deprecated (use –files-cache=disabled)

New features:

- –files-cache - implement files cache mode control, #911 You can now control the files cache mode using this option: –files-cache={ctime,mtime,size,inode,rechunk,disabled} (only some combinations are supported). See the docs for details.

Fixes:

- remote progress/logging: deal with partial lines, #2637

- remote progress: flush json mode output

- fix subprocess environments, #3050 (and more)

Other changes:

- remove client_supports_log_v3 flag, #3033

- exclude broken Cython 0.27(.0) in requirements, #3066

- vagrant:

    - upgrade to FUSE for macOS 3.7.1

    - use Python 3.5.4 to build the binaries

- docs:

    - security: change-passphrase only changes the passphrase, #2990

    - fixed/improved borg create –compression examples, #3034

    - add note about metadata dedup and –no[ac]time, #2518

    - twitter account @borgbackup now, better visible, #2948

    - simplified rate limiting wrapper in FAQ

Version 1.1.0rc3 (2017-09-10)

New features:

- delete: support naming multiple archives, #2958

Fixes:

- repo cleanup/write: invalidate cached FDs, #2982

- fix datetime.isoformat() microseconds issues, #2994

- recover_segment: use mmap(), lower memory needs, #2987

Other changes:

- with-lock: close segment file before invoking subprocess

- keymanager: don't depend on optional readline module, #2976

- docs:

    - fix macOS keychain integration command

    - show/link new screencasts in README, #2936

    - document utf-8 locale requirement for json mode, #2273

- vagrant: clean up shell profile init, user name, #2977

- test_detect_attic_repo: don't test mount, #2975

- add debug logging for repository cleanup

Version 1.1.0rc2 (2017-08-28)

Compatibility notes:

- list: corrected mix-up of "isomtime" and "mtime" formats. Previously, "isomtime" was the default but produced a verbose human format, while "mtime" produced a ISO-8601-like format. The behaviours have been swapped (so "mtime" is human, "isomtime" is ISO-like), and the default is now "mtime". "isomtime" is now a real ISO-8601 format ("T" between date and time, not a space).

New features:

- None.

Fixes:

- list: fix weird mixup of mtime/isomtime
- create –timestamp: set start time, #2957
- ignore corrupt files cache, #2939
- migrate locks to child PID when daemonize is used
- fix exitcode of borg serve, #2910
- only compare contents when chunker params match, #2899
- umount: try fusermount, then try umount, #2863

Other changes:

- JSON: use a more standard ISO 8601 datetime format, #2376
- cache: write_archive_index: truncate_and_unlink on error, #2628
- detect non-upgraded Attic repositories, #1933
- delete various nogil and threading related lines
- coala / pylint related improvements
- docs:
  - renew asciinema/screencasts, #669
  - create: document exclusion through nodump, #2949
  - minor formatting fixes
  - tar: tarpipe example
  - improve "with-lock" and "info" docs, #2869
  - detail how to use macOS/GNOME/KDE keyrings for repo passwords, #392
- travis: only short-circuit docs-only changes for pull requests
- vagrant:
  - netbsd: bash is already installed
  - fix netbsd version in PKG_PATH
  - add exe location to PATH when we build an exe

Version 1.1.0rc1 (2017-07-24)

Compatibility notes:

- delete: removed short option for –cache-only

New features:

- support borg list repo –format {comment} {bcomment} {end}, #2081
- key import: allow reading from stdin, #2760

Fixes:

- with-lock: avoid creating segment files that might be overwritten later, #1867

- prune: fix checkpoints processing with –glob-archives

- FUSE: versions view: keep original file extension at end, #2769

- fix –last, –first: do not accept values <= 0, fix reversed archive ordering with –last

- include testsuite data (attic.tar.gz) when installing the package

- use limited unpacker for outer key, for manifest (both security precautions), #2174 #2175

- fix bashism in shell scripts, #2820, #2816

- cleanup endianness detection, create _endian.h, fixes build on alpine linux, #2809

- fix crash with –no-cache-sync (give known chunk size to chunk_incref), #2853

Other changes:

- FUSE: versions view: linear numbering by archive time

- split up interval parsing from filtering for –keep-within, #2610

- add a basic .editorconfig, #2734

- use archive creation time as mtime for FUSE mount, #2834

- upgrade FUSE for macOS (osxfuse) from 3.5.8 to 3.6.3, #2706

- hashindex: speed up by replacing modulo with "if" to check for wraparound

- coala checker / pylint: fixed requirements and .coafile, more ignores

- borg upgrade: name backup directories as 'before-upgrade', #2811

- add .mailmap

- some minor changes suggested by lgtm.com

- docs:

    - better explanation of the –ignore-inode option relevance, #2800

    - fix openSUSE command and add openSUSE section

    - simplify ssh authorized_keys file using "restrict", add legacy note, #2121

    - mount: show usage of archive filters

    - mount: add repository example, #2462

    - info: update and add examples, #2765

    - prune: include example

    - improved style / formatting

    - improved/fixed segments_per_dir docs

    - recreate: fix wrong "remove unwanted files" example

    - reference list of status chars in borg recreate –filter description

    - update source-install docs about doc build dependencies, #2795

    - cleanup installation docs

    - file system requirements, update segs per dir

    - fix checkpoints/parts reference in FAQ, #2859

- code:

    - hashindex: don't pass side effect into macro

- crypto low_level: don't mutate local bytes()

- use dash_open function to open file or "-" for stdin/stdout

- archiver: argparse cleanup / refactoring

- shellpattern: add match_end arg

- tests: added some additional unit tests, some fixes, #2700 #2710

- vagrant: fix setup of cygwin, add Debian 9 "stretch"

- travis: don't perform full travis build on docs-only changes, #2531

Version 1.1.0b6 (2017-06-18)

Compatibility notes:

- Running "borg init" via a "borg serve –append-only" server will *not* create an append-only repository anymore. Use "borg init –append-only" to initialize an append-only repository.

- Repositories in the "repokey" and "repokey-blake2" modes with an empty passphrase are now treated as unencrypted repositories for security checks (e.g. BORG_UNKNOWN_UNENCRYPTED_REPO_ACCESS_IS_OK).

  Previously there would be no prompts nor messages if an unknown repository in one of these modes with an empty passphrase was encountered. This would allow an attacker to swap a repository, if one assumed that the lack of password prompts was due to a set BORG_PASSPHRASE.

  Since the "trick" does not work if BORG_PASSPHRASE is set, this does generally not affect scripts.

- Repositories in the "authenticated" mode are now treated as the unencrypted repositories they are.

- The client-side temporary repository cache now holds unencrypted data for better speed.

- borg init: removed the short form of –append-only (-a).

- borg upgrade: removed the short form of –inplace (-i).

New features:

- reimplemented the RepositoryCache, size-limited caching of decrypted repo contents, integrity checked via xxh64. #2515

- reduced space usage of chunks.archive.d. Existing caches are migrated during a cache sync. #235 #2638

- integrity checking using xxh64 for important files used by borg, #1101:

  - repository: index and hints files

  - cache: chunks and files caches, chunks.archive.d

- improve cache sync speed, #1729

- create: new –no-cache-sync option

- add repository mandatory feature flags infrastructure, #1806

- Verify most operations against SecurityManager. Location, manifest timestamp and key types are now checked for almost all non-debug commands. #2487

- implement storage quotas, #2517

- serve: add –restrict-to-repository, #2589

- BORG_PASSCOMMAND: use external tool providing the key passphrase, #2573

- borg export-tar, #2519

- list: –json-lines instead of –json for archive contents, #2439

- add –debug-profile option (and also "borg debug convert-profile"), #2473
- implement –glob-archives/-a, #2448
- normalize authenticated key modes for better naming consistency:
    - rename "authenticated" to "authenticated-blake2" (uses blake2b)
    - implement "authenticated" mode (uses hmac-sha256)

Fixes:

- hashindex: read/write indices >2 GiB on 32bit systems, better error reporting, #2496
- repository URLs: implement IPv6 address support and also more informative error message when parsing fails.
- mount: check whether llfuse is installed before asking for passphrase, #2540
- mount: do pre-mount checks before opening repository, #2541
- FUSE:
    - fix crash if empty (None) xattr is read, #2534
    - fix read(2) caching data in metadata cache
    - fix negative uid/gid crash (fix crash when mounting archives of external drives made on cygwin), #2674
    - redo ItemCache, on top of object cache
    - use decrypted cache
    - remove unnecessary normpaths
- serve: ignore –append-only when initializing a repository (borg init), #2501
- serve: fix incorrect type of exception_short for Errors, #2513
- fix –exclude and –exclude-from recursing into directories, #2469
- init: don't allow creating nested repositories, #2563
- –json: fix encryption[mode] not being the cmdline name
- remote: propagate Error.traceback correctly
- fix remote logging and progress, #2241
    - implement –debug-topic for remote servers
    - remote: restore "Remote:" prefix (as used in 1.0.x)
    - rpc negotiate: enable v3 log protocol only for supported clients
    - fix –progress and logging in general for remote
- fix parse_version, add tests, #2556
- repository: truncate segments (and also some other files) before unlinking, #2557
- recreate: keep timestamps as in original archive, #2384
- recreate: if single archive is not processed, exit 2
- patterns: don't recurse with ! / –exclude for pf:, #2509
- cache sync: fix n^2 behaviour in lookup_name
- extract: don't write to disk with –stdout (affected non-regular-file items), #2645
- hashindex: implement KeyError, more tests

Other changes:

- remote: show path in PathNotAllowed

- consider repokey w/o passphrase == unencrypted, #2169

- consider authenticated mode == unencrypted, #2503

- restrict key file names, #2560

- document follow_symlinks requirements, check libc, use stat and chown with follow_symlinks=False, #2507

- support common options on the main command, #2508

- support common options on mid-level commands (e.g. borg *key* export)

- make –progress a common option

- increase DEFAULT_SEGMENTS_PER_DIR to 1000

- chunker: fix invalid use of types (function only used by tests)

- chunker: don't do uint32_t >> 32

- FUSE:

    - add instrumentation (–debug and SIGUSR1/SIGINFO)

    - reduced memory usage for repository mounts by lazily instantiating archives

    - improved archive load times

- info: use CacheSynchronizer & HashIndex.stats_against (better performance)

- docs:

    - init: document –encryption as required

    - security: OpenSSL usage

    - security: used implementations; note python libraries

    - security: security track record of OpenSSL and msgpack

    - patterns: document denial of service (regex, wildcards)

    - init: note possible denial of service with "none" mode

    - init: document SHA extension is supported in OpenSSL and thus SHA is faster on AMD Ryzen than blake2b.

    - book: use A4 format, new builder option format.

    - book: create appendices

    - data structures: explain repository compaction

    - data structures: add chunk layout diagram

    - data structures: integrity checking

    - data structures: demingle cache and repo index

    - Attic FAQ: separate section for attic stuff

    - FAQ: I get an IntegrityError or similar - what now?

    - FAQ: Can I use Borg on SMR hard drives?, #2252

    - FAQ: specify "using inline shell scripts"

    - add systemd warning regarding placeholders, #2543

    - xattr: document API

    - add docs/misc/borg-data-flow data flow chart

    - debugging facilities

    - README: how to help the project, #2550

- README: add bountysource badge, #2558

- fresh new theme + tweaking

- logo: vectorized (PDF and SVG) versions

- frontends: use headlines - you can link to them

- mark –pattern, –patterns-from as experimental

- highlight experimental features in online docs

- remove regex based pattern examples, #2458

- nanorst for "borg help TOPIC" and –help

- split deployment

- deployment: hosting repositories

- deployment: automated backups to a local hard drive

- development: vagrant, windows10 requirements

- development: update docs remarks

- split usage docs, #2627

- usage: avoid bash highlight, [options] instead of <options>

- usage: add benchmark page

- helpers: truncate_and_unlink doc

- don't suggest to leak BORG_PASSPHRASE

- internals: columnize rather long ToC [webkit fixup] internals: manifest & feature flags

- internals: more HashIndex details

- internals: fix ASCII art equations

- internals: edited obj graph related sections a bit

- internals: layers image + description

- fix way too small figures in pdf

- index: disable syntax highlight (bash)

- improve options formatting, fix accidental block quotes

- testing / checking:

  - add support for using coala, #1366

  - testsuite: add ArchiverCorruptionTestCase

  - do not test logger name, #2504

  - call setup_logging after destroying logging config

  - testsuite.archiver: normalise pytest.raises vs. assert_raises

  - add test for preserved intermediate folder permissions, #2477

  - key: add round-trip test

  - remove attic dependency of the tests, #2505

  - enable remote tests on cygwin

  - tests: suppress tar's future timestamp warning

  - cache sync: add more refcount tests

  - repository: add tests, including corruption tests

- vagrant:
    - control VM cpus and pytest workers via env vars VMCPUS and XDISTN
    - update cleaning workdir
    - fix openbsd shell
    - add OpenIndiana

- packaging:
    - binaries: don't bundle libssl
    - setup.py clean to remove compiled files
    - fail in borg package if version metadata is very broken (setuptools_scm)

- repo / code structure:
    - create borg.algorithms and borg.crypto packages
    - algorithms: rename crc32 to checksums
    - move patterns to module, #2469
    - gitignore: complete paths for src/ excludes
    - cache: extract CacheConfig class
    - implement IntegrityCheckedFile + Detached variant, #2502 #1688
    - introduce popen_with_error_handling to handle common user errors

Version 1.1.0b5 (2017-04-30)

Compatibility notes:

- BORG_HOSTNAME_IS_UNIQUE is now on by default.
- removed –compression-from feature
- recreate: add –recompress flag, unify –always-recompress and –recompress

Fixes:

- catch exception for os.link when hardlinks are not supported, #2405
- borg rename / recreate: expand placeholders, #2386
- generic support for hardlinks (files, devices, FIFOs), #2324
- extract: also create parent dir for device files, if needed, #2358
- extract: if a hardlink master is not in the to-be-extracted subset, the "x" status was not displayed for it, #2351
- embrace y2038 issue to support 32bit platforms: clamp timestamps to int32, #2347
- verify_data: fix IntegrityError handling for defect chunks, #2442
- allow excluding parent and including child, #2314

Other changes:

- refactor compression decision stuff
- change global compression default to lz4 as well, to be consistent with –compression defaults.
- placeholders: deny access to internals and other unspecified stuff
- clearer error message for unrecognized placeholder

- more clear exception if borg check does not help, #2427

- vagrant: upgrade FUSE for macOS to 3.5.8, #2346

- linux binary builds: get rid of glibc 2.13 dependency, #2430

- docs:

    - placeholders: document escaping

    - serve: env vars in original commands are ignored

    - tell what kind of hardlinks we support

    - more docs about compression

    - LICENSE: use canonical formulation ("copyright holders and contributors" instead of "author")

    - document borg init behaviour via append-only borg serve, #2440

    - be clear about what buzhash is used for, #2390

    - add hint about chunker params, #2421

    - clarify borg upgrade docs, #2436

    - FAQ to explain warning when running borg check –repair, #2341

    - repository file system requirements, #2080

    - pre-install considerations

    - misc. formatting / crossref fixes

- tests:

    - enhance travis setuptools_scm situation

    - add extra test for the hashindex

    - fix invalid param issue in benchmarks

These belong to 1.1.0b4 release, but did not make it into changelog by then:

- vagrant: increase memory for parallel testing

- lz4 compress: lower max. buffer size, exception handling

- add docstring to do_benchmark_crud

- patterns help: mention path full-match in intro

Version 1.1.0b4 (2017-03-27)

Compatibility notes:

- init: the –encryption argument is mandatory now (there are several choices)

- moved "borg migrate-to-repokey" to "borg key migrate-to-repokey".

- "borg change-passphrase" is deprecated, use "borg key change-passphrase" instead.

- the –exclude-if-present option now supports tagging a folder with any filesystem object type (file, folder, etc), instead of expecting only files as tags, #1999

- the –keep-tag-files option has been deprecated in favor of the new –keep-exclude-tags, to account for the change mentioned above.

- use lz4 compression by default, #2179

New features:

- JSON API to make developing frontends and automation easier (see *All about JSON: How to develop frontends*)

    - add JSON output to commands: *borg create/list/info –json ....*

    - add –log-json option for structured logging output.

    - add JSON progress information, JSON support for confirmations (yes()).

- add two new options –pattern and –patterns-from as discussed in #1406

- new path full match pattern style (pf:) for very fast matching, #2334

- add 'debug dump-manifest' and 'debug dump-archive' commands

- add 'borg benchmark crud' command, #1788

- new 'borg delete –force –force' to delete severely corrupted archives, #1975

- info: show utilization of maximum archive size, #1452

- list: add dsize and dcsize keys, #2164

- paperkey.html: Add interactive html template for printing key backups.

- key export: add qr html export mode

- securely erase config file (which might have old encryption key), #2257

- archived file items: add size to metadata, 'borg extract' and 'borg check' do check the file size for consistency, FUSE uses precomputed size from Item.

Fixes:

- fix remote speed regression introduced in 1.1.0b3, #2185

- fix regression handling timestamps beyond 2262 (revert bigint removal), introduced in 1.1.0b3, #2321

- clamp (nano)second values to unproblematic range, #2304

- hashindex: rebuild hashtable if we have too little empty buckets (performance fix), #2246

- Location regex: fix bad parsing of wrong syntax

- ignore posix_fadvise errors in repository.py, #2095

- borg rpc: use limited msgpack.Unpacker (security precaution), #2139

- Manifest: Make sure manifest timestamp is strictly monotonically increasing.

- create: handle BackupOSError on a per-path level in one spot

- create: clarify -x option / meaning of "same filesystem"

- create: don't create hard link refs to failed files

- archive check: detect and fix missing all-zero replacement chunks, #2180

- files cache: update inode number when –ignore-inode is used, #2226

- fix decompression exceptions crashing `check --verify-data` and others instead of reporting integrity error, #2224 #2221

- extract: warning for unextracted big extended attributes, #2258, #2161

- mount: umount on SIGINT/^C when in foreground

- mount: handle invalid hard link refs

- mount: fix huge RAM consumption when mounting a repository (saves number of archives * 8 MiB), #2308

- hashindex: detect mingw byte order #2073

- hashindex: fix wrong skip_hint on hashindex_set when encountering tombstones, the regression was introduced in #1748

- fix ChunkIndex.__contains__ assertion for big-endian archs

- fix borg key/debug/benchmark crashing without subcommand, #2240

- Location: accept //servername/share/path

- correct/refactor calculation of unique/non-unique chunks

- extract: fix missing call to ProgressIndicator.finish

- prune: fix error msg, it is –keep-within, not –within

- fix "auto" compression mode bug (not compressing), #2331

- fix symlink item fs size computation, #2344

Other changes:

- remote repository: improved async exception processing, #2255 #2225

- with –compression auto,C, only use C if lz4 achieves at least 3% compression

- PatternMatcher: only normalize path once, #2338

- hashindex: separate endian-dependent defs from endian detection

- migrate-to-repokey: ask using canonical_path() as we do everywhere else.

- SyncFile: fix use of fd object after close

- make LoggedIO.close_segment reentrant

- creating a new segment: use "xb" mode, #2099

- redo key_creator, key_factory, centralise key knowledge, #2272

- add return code functions, #2199

- list: only load cache if needed

- list: files->items, clarifications

- list: add "name" key for consistency with info cmd

- ArchiveFormatter: add "start" key for compatibility with "info"

- RemoteRepository: account rx/tx bytes

- setup.py build_usage/build_man/build_api fixes

- Manifest.in: simplify, exclude .so, .dll and .orig, #2066

- FUSE: get rid of chunk accounting, st_blocks = ceil(size / blocksize).

- tests:

  - help python development by testing 3.6-dev

  - test for borg delete –force

- vagrant:

  - freebsd: some fixes, #2067

  - darwin64: use osxfuse 3.5.4 for tests / to build binaries

  - darwin64: improve VM settings

  - use python 3.5.3 to build binaries, #2078

  - upgrade pyinstaller from 3.1.1+ to 3.2.1

  - pyinstaller: use fixed AND freshly compiled bootloader, #2002

  - pyinstaller: automatically builds bootloader if missing

- docs:

- create really nice man pages

- faq: mention –remote-ratelimit in bandwidth limit question

- fix caskroom link, #2299

- docs/security: reiterate that RPC in Borg does no networking

- docs/security: counter tracking, #2266

- docs/development: update merge remarks

- address SSH batch mode in docs, #2202 #2270

- add warning about running build_usage on Python >3.4, #2123

- one link per distro in the installation page

- improve –exclude-if-present and –keep-exclude-tags, #2268

- improve automated backup script in doc, #2214

- improve remote-path description

- update docs for create -C default change (lz4)

- document relative path usage, #1868

- document snapshot usage, #2178

- corrected some stuff in internals+security

- internals: move toctree to after the introduction text

- clarify metadata kind, manifest ops

- key enc: correct / clarify some stuff, link to internals/security

- datas: enc: 1.1.x mas different MACs

- datas: enc: correct factual error – no nonce involved there.

- make internals.rst an index page and edit it a bit

- add "Cryptography in Borg" and "Remote RPC protocol security" sections

- document BORG_HOSTNAME_IS_UNIQUE, #2087

- FAQ by categories as proposed by @anarcat in #1802

- FAQ: update Which file types, attributes, etc. are *not* preserved?

- development: new branching model for git repository

- development: define "ours" merge strategy for auto-generated files

- create: move –exclude note to main doc

- create: move item flags to main doc

- fix examples using borg init without -e/–encryption

- list: don't print key listings in fat (html + man)

- remove Python API docs (were very incomplete, build problems on RTFD)

- added FAQ section about backing up root partition

Version 1.0.10 (2017-02-13)

Bug fixes:

- Manifest timestamps are now monotonically increasing, this fixes issues when the system clock jumps backwards or is set inconsistently across computers accessing the same repository, #2115

- Fixed testing regression in 1.0.10rc1 that lead to a hard dependency on py.test >= 3.0, #2112

New features:

- "key export" can now generate a printable HTML page with both a QR code and a human-readable "paperkey" representation (and custom text) through the `--qr-html` option.

  The same functionality is also available through paperkey.html, which is the same HTML page generated by `--qr-html`. It works with existing "key export" files and key files.

Other changes:

- docs:

  - language clarification - "borg create –one-file-system" option does not respect mount points, but considers different file systems instead, #2141

- setup.py: build_api: sort file list for determinism

Version 1.1.0b3 (2017-01-15)

Compatibility notes:

- borg init: removed the default of "–encryption/-e", #1979 This was done so users do a informed decision about -e mode.

Bug fixes:

- borg recreate: don't rechunkify unless explicitly told so

- borg info: fixed bug when called without arguments, #1914

- borg init: fix free space check crashing if disk is full, #1821

- borg debug delete/get obj: fix wrong reference to exception

- fix processing of remote ~/ and ~user/ paths (regressed since 1.1.0b1), #1759

- posix platform module: only build / import on non-win32 platforms, #2041

New features:

- new CRC32 implementations that are much faster than the zlib one used previously, #1970

- add blake2b key modes (use blake2b as MAC). This links against system libb2, if possible, otherwise uses bundled code

- automatically remove stale locks - set BORG_HOSTNAME_IS_UNIQUE env var to enable stale lock killing. If set, stale locks in both cache and repository are deleted. #562 #1253

- borg info <repo>: print general repo information, #1680

- borg check –first / –last / –sort / –prefix, #1663

- borg mount –first / –last / –sort / –prefix, #1542

- implement "health" item formatter key, #1749

- BORG_SECURITY_DIR to remember security related infos outside the cache. Key type, location and manifest timestamp checks now survive cache deletion. This also means that you can now delete your cache and avoid previous warnings, since Borg can still tell it's safe.

- implement BORG_NEW_PASSPHRASE, #1768

Other changes:

- borg recreate:

- – remove special-cased –dry-run

- – update –help

- – remove bloat: interruption blah, autocommit blah, resuming blah

- – re-use existing checkpoint functionality

- – archiver tests: add check_cache tool - lints refcounts

- fixed cache sync performance regression from 1.1.0b1 onwards, #1940

- syncing the cache without chunks.archive.d (see *The borg cache eats way too much disk space, what can I do?*) now avoids any merges and is thus faster, #1940

- borg check –verify-data: faster due to linear on-disk-order scan

- borg debug-xxx commands removed, we use "debug xxx" subcommands now, #1627

- improve metadata handling speed

- shortcut hashindex_set by having hashindex_lookup hint about address

- improve / add progress displays, #1721

- check for index vs. segment files object count mismatch

- make RPC protocol more extensible: use named parameters.

- RemoteRepository: misc. code cleanups / refactors

- clarify cache/repository README file

- docs:

  - – quickstart: add a comment about other (remote) filesystems

  - – quickstart: only give one possible ssh url syntax, all others are documented in usage chapter.

  - – mention file://

  - – document repo URLs / archive location

  - – clarify borg diff help, #980

  - – deployment: synthesize alternative –restrict-to-path example

  - – improve cache / index docs, esp. files cache docs, #1825

  - – document using "git merge 1.0-maint -s recursive -X rename-threshold=20%" for avoiding troubles when merging the 1.0-maint branch into master.

- tests:

  - – FUSE tests: catch ENOTSUP on freebsd

  - – FUSE tests: test troublesome xattrs last

  - – fix byte range error in test, #1740

  - – use monkeypatch to set env vars, but only on pytest based tests.

  - – point XDG_*_HOME to temp dirs for tests, #1714

  - – remove all BORG_* env vars from the outer environment

Version 1.0.10rc1 (2017-01-29)

Bug fixes:

- borg serve: fix transmission data loss of pipe writes, #1268 This affects only the cygwin platform (not Linux, BSD, OS X).

- Avoid triggering an ObjectiveFS bug in xattr retrieval, #1992

- When running out of buffer memory when reading xattrs, only skip the current file, #1993

- Fixed "borg upgrade –tam" crashing with unencrypted repositories. Since *the issue* is not relevant for unencrypted repositories, it now does nothing and prints an error, #1981.

- Fixed change-passphrase crashing with unencrypted repositories, #1978

- Fixed "borg check repo::archive" indicating success if "archive" does not exist, #1997

- borg check: print non-exit-code warning if –last or –prefix aren't fulfilled

- fix bad parsing of wrong repo location syntax

- create: don't create hard link refs to failed files, mount: handle invalid hard link refs, #2092

- detect mingw byte order, #2073

- creating a new segment: use "xb" mode, #2099

- mount: umount on SIGINT/^C when in foreground, #2082

Other changes:

- binary: use fixed AND freshly compiled pyinstaller bootloader, #2002

- xattr: ignore empty names returned by llistxattr(2) et al

- Enable the fault handler: install handlers for the SIGSEGV, SIGFPE, SIGABRT, SIGBUS and SIGILL signals to dump the Python traceback.

- Also print a traceback on SIGUSR2.

- borg change-passphrase: print key location (simplify making a backup of it)

- officially support Python 3.6 (setup.py: add Python 3.6 qualifier)

- tests:

  - vagrant / travis / tox: add Python 3.6 based testing

  - vagrant: fix openbsd repo, #2042

  - vagrant: fix the freebsd64 machine, #2037 #2067

  - vagrant: use python 3.5.3 to build binaries, #2078

  - vagrant: use osxfuse 3.5.4 for tests / to build binaries vagrant: improve darwin64 VM settings

  - travis: fix osxfuse install (fixes OS X testing on Travis CI)

  - travis: require succeeding OS X tests, #2028

  - travis: use latest pythons for OS X based testing

  - use pytest-xdist to parallelize testing

  - fix xattr test race condition, #2047

  - setup.cfg: fix pytest deprecation warning, #2050

- docs:

  - language clarification - VM backup FAQ

  - borg create: document how to backup stdin, #2013

  - borg upgrade: fix incorrect title levels

  - add CVE numbers for issues fixed in 1.0.9, #2106

- fix typos (taken from Debian package patch)

- remote: include data hexdump in "unexpected RPC data" error message

- remote: log SSH command line at debug level

- API_VERSION: use numberspaces, #2023

- remove .github from pypi package, #2051

- add pip and setuptools to requirements file, #2030

- SyncFile: fix use of fd object after close (cosmetic)

- Manifest.in: simplify, exclude *.{so,dll,orig}, #2066

- ignore posix_fadvise errors in repository.py, #2095 (works around issues with docker on ARM)

- make LoggedIO.close_segment reentrant, avoid reentrance

Version 1.0.9 (2016-12-20)

Security fixes:

- A flaw in the cryptographic authentication scheme in Borg allowed an attacker to spoof the manifest. See *Pre-1.0.9 manifest spoofing vulnerability (CVE-2016-10099)* above for the steps you should take.

  CVE-2016-10099 was assigned to this vulnerability.

- borg check: When rebuilding the manifest (which should only be needed very rarely) duplicate archive names would be handled on a "first come first serve" basis, allowing an attacker to apparently replace archives.

  CVE-2016-10100 was assigned to this vulnerability.

Bug fixes:

- borg check:

  - rebuild manifest if it's corrupted

  - skip corrupted chunks during manifest rebuild

- fix TypeError in integrity error handler, #1903, #1894

- fix location parser for archives with @ char (regression introduced in 1.0.8), #1930

- fix wrong duration/timestamps if system clock jumped during a create

- fix progress display not updating if system clock jumps backwards

- fix checkpoint interval being incorrect if system clock jumps

Other changes:

- docs:

  - add python3-devel as a dependency for cygwin-based installation

  - clarify extract is relative to current directory

  - FAQ: fix link to changelog

  - markup fixes

- tests:

  - test_get_(cache|keys)_dir: clean env state, #1897

  - get back pytest's pretty assertion failures, #1938

- setup.py build_usage:

  - fixed build_usage not processing all commands

  - fixed build_usage not generating includes for debug commands

Version 1.0.9rc1 (2016-11-27)

Bug fixes:

- files cache: fix determination of newest mtime in backup set (which is used in cache cleanup and led to wrong "A" [added] status for unchanged files in next backup), #1860.
- borg check:
  - fix incorrectly reporting attic 0.13 and earlier archives as corrupt
  - handle repo w/o objects gracefully and also bail out early if repo is *completely* empty, #1815.
- fix tox/pybuild in 1.0-maint
- at xattr module import time, loggers are not initialized yet

New features:

- borg umount <mountpoint> exposed already existing umount code via the CLI api, so users can use it, which is more consistent than using borg to mount and fusermount -u (or umount) to un-mount, #1855.
- implement borg create –noatime –noctime, fixes #1853

Other changes:

- docs:
  - display README correctly on PyPI
  - improve cache / index docs, esp. files cache docs, fixes #1825
  - different pattern matching for –exclude, #1779
  - datetime formatting examples for {now} placeholder, #1822
  - clarify passphrase mode attic repo upgrade, #1854
  - clarify –umask usage, #1859
  - clarify how to choose PR target branch
  - clarify prune behavior for different archive contents, #1824
  - fix PDF issues, add logo, fix authors, headings, TOC
  - move security verification to support section
  - fix links in standalone README (:ref: tags)
  - add link to security contact in README
  - add FAQ about security
  - move fork differences to FAQ
  - add more details about resource usage
- tests: skip remote tests on cygwin, #1268
- travis:
  - allow OS X failures until the brew cask osxfuse issue is fixed
  - caskroom osxfuse-beta gone, it's osxfuse now (3.5.3)
- vagrant:
  - upgrade OSXfuse / FUSE for macOS to 3.5.3
  - remove llfuse from tox.ini at a central place
  - do not try to install llfuse on centos6
  - fix FUSE test for darwin, #1546

– add windows virtual machine with cygwin

– Vagrantfile cleanup / code deduplication

Version 1.1.0b2 (2016-10-01)

Bug fixes:

- fix incorrect preservation of delete tags, leading to "object count mismatch" on borg check, #1598. This only occurred with 1.1.0b1 (not with 1.0.x) and is normally fixed by running another borg create/delete/prune.

- fix broken –progress for double-cell paths (e.g. CJK), #1624

- borg recreate: also catch SIGHUP

- FUSE:

  – fix hardlinks in versions view, #1599

  – add parameter check to ItemCache.get to make potential failures more clear

New features:

- Archiver, RemoteRepository: add –remote-ratelimit (send data)

- borg help compression, #1582

- borg check: delete chunks with integrity errors, #1575, so they can be "repaired" immediately and maybe healed later.

- archives filters concept (refactoring/unifying older code)

  – covers –first/–last/–prefix/–sort-by options

  – currently used for borg list/info/delete

Other changes:

- borg check –verify-data slightly tuned (use get_many())

- change {utcnow} and {now} to ISO-8601 format ("T" date/time separator)

- repo check: log transaction IDs, improve object count mismatch diagnostic

- Vagrantfile: use TW's fresh-bootloader pyinstaller branch

- fix module names in api.rst

- hashindex: bump api_version

Version 1.1.0b1 (2016-08-28)

New features:

- new commands:

  – borg recreate: re-create existing archives, #787 #686 #630 #70, also see #757, #770.

    * selectively remove files/dirs from old archives

    * re-compress data

    * re-chunkify data, e.g. to have upgraded Attic / Borg 0.xx archives deduplicate with Borg 1.x archives or to experiment with chunker-params.

  – borg diff: show differences between archives

  – borg with-lock: execute a command with the repository locked, #990

- borg create:

  - Flexible compression with pattern matching on path/filename, and LZ4 heuristic for deciding compressibility, #810, #1007

  - visit files in inode order (better speed, esp. for large directories and rotating disks)

  - in-file checkpoints, #1217

  - increased default checkpoint interval to 30 minutes (was 5 minutes), #896

  - added uuid archive format tag, #1151

  - save mountpoint directories with –one-file-system, makes system restore easier, #1033

  - Linux: added support for some BSD flags, #1050

  - add 'x' status for excluded paths, #814

    * also means files excluded via UF_NODUMP, #1080

- borg check:

  - will not produce the "Checking segments" output unless new –progress option is passed, #824.

  - –verify-data to verify data cryptographically on the client, #975

- borg list, #751, #1179

  - removed {formatkeys}, see "borg list –help"

  - –list-format is deprecated, use –format instead

  - –format now also applies to listing archives, not only archive contents, #1179

  - now supports the usual [PATH [PATHS. . .]] syntax and excludes

  - new keys: csize, num_chunks, unique_chunks, NUL

  - supports guaranteed_available hashlib hashes (to avoid varying functionality depending on environment), which includes the SHA1 and SHA2 family as well as MD5

- borg prune:

  - to better visualize the "thinning out", we now list all archives in reverse time order. rephrase and reorder help text.

  - implement –keep-last N via –keep-secondly N, also –keep-minutely. assuming that there is not more than 1 backup archive made in 1s, –keep-last N and –keep-secondly N are equivalent, #537

  - cleanup checkpoints except the latest, #1008

- borg extract:

  - added –progress, #1449

  - Linux: limited support for BSD flags, #1050

- borg info:

  - output is now more similar to borg create –stats, #977

- borg mount:

  - provide "borgfs" wrapper for borg mount, enables usage via fstab, #743

  - "versions" mount option - when used with a repository mount, this gives a merged, versioned view of the files in all archives, #729

- repository:

  - added progress information to commit/compaction phase (often takes some time when deleting/pruning), #1519

  - automatic recovery for some forms of repository inconsistency, #858

- check free space before going forward with a commit, #1336

- improved write performance (esp. for rotating media), #985

  * new IO code for Linux

  * raised default segment size to approx 512 MiB

- improved compaction performance, #1041

- reduced client CPU load and improved performance for remote repositories, #940

- options that imply output (–show-rc, –show-version, –list, –stats, –progress) don't need -v/–info to have that output displayed, #865

- add archive comments (via borg (re)create –comment), #842

- borg list/prune/delete: also output archive id, #731

- –show-version: shows/logs the borg version, #725

- added –debug-topic for granular debug logging, #1447

- use atomic file writing/updating for configuration and key files, #1377

- BORG_KEY_FILE environment variable, #1001

- self-testing module, #970

Bug fixes:

- list: fixed default output being produced if –format is given with empty parameter, #1489

- create: fixed overflowing progress line with CJK and similar characters, #1051

- prune: fixed crash if –prefix resulted in no matches, #1029

- init: clean up partial repo if passphrase input is aborted, #850

- info: quote cmdline arguments that have spaces in them

- fix hardlinks failing in some cases for extracting subtrees, #761

Other changes:

- replace stdlib hmac with OpenSSL, zero-copy decrypt (10-15% increase in performance of hash-lists and extract).

- improved chunker performance, #1021

- open repository segment files in exclusive mode (fail-safe), #1134

- improved error logging, #1440

- Source:

  - pass meta-data around, #765

  - move some constants to new constants module

  - better readability and less errors with namedtuples, #823

  - moved source tree into src/ subdirectory, #1016

  - made borg.platform a package, #1113

  - removed dead crypto code, #1032

  - improved and ported parts of the test suite to py.test, #912

  - created data classes instead of passing dictionaries around, #981, #1158, #1161

  - cleaned up imports, #1112

- Docs:

  - better help texts and sphinx reproduction of usage help:

* Group options

* Nicer list of options in Sphinx

* Deduplicate 'Common options' (including –help)

- chunker: added some insights by "Voltara", #903

- clarify what "deduplicated size" means

- fix / update / add package list entries

- added a SaltStack usage example, #956

- expanded FAQ

- new contributors in AUTHORS!

• Tests:

- vagrant: add ubuntu/xenial 64bit - this box has still some issues

- ChunkBuffer: add test for leaving partial chunk in buffer, fixes #945

Version 1.0.8 (2016-10-29)

Bug fixes:

• RemoteRepository: Fix busy wait in call_many, #940

New features:

• implement borgmajor/borgminor/borgpatch placeholders, #1694 {borgversion} was already there (full version string). With the new placeholders you can now also get e.g. 1 or 1.0 or 1.0.8.

Other changes:

• avoid previous_location mismatch, #1741

due to the changed canonicalization for relative paths in PR #1711 / #1655 (implement ./ relpath hack), there would be a changed repo location warning and the user would be asked if this is ok. this would break automation and require manual intervention, which is unwanted.

thus, we automatically fix the previous_location config entry, if it only changed in the expected way, but still means the same location.

• docs:

- deployment.rst: do not use bare variables in ansible snippet

- add clarification about append-only mode, #1689

- setup.py: add comment about requiring llfuse, #1726

- update usage.rst / api.rst

- repo url / archive location docs + typo fix

- quickstart: add a comment about other (remote) filesystems

• vagrant / tests:

- no chown when rsyncing (fixes boxes w/o vagrant group)

- fix FUSE permission issues on linux/freebsd, #1544

- skip FUSE test for borg binary + fakeroot

- ignore security.selinux xattrs, fixes tests on centos, #1735

Version 1.0.8rc1 (2016-10-17)

Bug fixes:

- fix signal handling (SIGINT, SIGTERM, SIGHUP), #1620 #1593 Fixes e.g. leftover lock files for quickly repeated signals (e.g. Ctrl-C Ctrl-C) or lost connections or systemd sending SIGHUP.

- progress display: adapt formatting to narrow screens, do not crash, #1628

- borg create –read-special - fix crash on broken symlink, #1584. also correctly processes broken symlinks. before this regressed to a crash (5b45385) a broken symlink would've been skipped.

- process_symlink: fix missing backup_io() Fixes a chmod/chown/chgrp/unlink/rename/... crash race between getting dirents and dispatching to process_symlink.

- yes(): abort on wrong answers, saying so, #1622

- fixed exception borg serve raised when connection was closed before reposiory was openend. add an error message for this.

- fix read-from-closed-FD issue, #1551 (this seems not to get triggered in 1.0.x, but was discovered in master)

- hashindex: fix iterators (always raise StopIteration when exhausted) (this seems not to get triggered in 1.0.x, but was discovered in master)

- enable relative paths in ssh:// repo URLs, via /./relpath hack, #1655

- allow repo paths with colons, #1705

- update changed repo location immediately after acceptance, #1524

- fix debug get-obj / delete-obj crash if object not found and remote repo, #1684

- pyinstaller: use a spec file to build borg.exe binary, exclude osxfuse dylib on Mac OS X (avoids mismatch lib <-> driver), #1619

New features:

- add "borg key export" / "borg key import" commands, #1555, so users are able to backup / restore their encryption keys more easily.

  Supported formats are the keyfile format used by borg internally and a special "paper" format with by line checksums for printed backups. For the paper format, the import is an interactive process which checks each line as soon as it is input.

- add "borg debug-refcount-obj" to determine a repo objects' referrer counts, #1352

Other changes:

- add "borg debug ..." subcommands (borg debug-* still works, but will be removed in borg 1.1)

- setup.py: Add subcommand support to build_usage.

- remote: change exception message for unexpected RPC data format to indicate dataflow direction.

- improved messages / error reporting:

  - IntegrityError: add placeholder for message, so that the message we give appears not only in the traceback, but also in the (short) error message, #1572

  - borg.key: include chunk id in exception msgs, #1571

  - better messages for cache newer than repo, #1700

- vagrant (testing/build VMs):

  - upgrade OSXfuse / FUSE for macOS to 3.5.2

  - update Debian Wheezy boxes, #1686

  - openbsd / netbsd: use own boxes, fixes misc rsync installation and FUSE/llfuse related testing issues, #1695 #1696 #1670 #1671 #1728

- docs:

  - add docs for "key export" and "key import" commands, #1641

  - fix inconsistency in FAQ (pv-wrapper).

  - fix second block in "Easy to use" section not showing on GitHub, #1576

  - add bestpractices badge

  - link reference docs and faq about BORG_FILES_CACHE_TTL, #1561

  - improve borg info –help, explain size infos, #1532

  - add release signing key / security contact to README, #1560

  - add contribution guidelines for developers

  - development.rst: add sphinx_rtd_theme to the sphinx install command

  - adjust border color in borg.css

  - add debug-info usage help file

  - internals.rst: fix typos

  - setup.py: fix build_usage to always process all commands

  - added docs explaining multiple –restrict-to-path flags, #1602

  - add more specific warning about write-access debug commands, #1587

  - clarify FAQ regarding backup of virtual machines, #1672

- tests:

  - work around FUSE xattr test issue with recent fakeroot

  - simplify repo/hashindex tests

  - travis: test FUSE-enabled borg, use trusty to have a recent FUSE

  - re-enable FUSE tests for RemoteArchiver (no deadlocks any more)

  - clean env for pytest based tests, #1714

  - fuse_mount contextmanager: accept any options

Version 1.0.7 (2016-08-19)

Security fixes:

- borg serve: fix security issue with remote repository access, #1428 If you used e.g. –restrict-to-path
  /path/client1/ (with or without trailing slash does not make a difference), it acted like a path prefix match using /path/client1 (note the missing trailing slash) - the code then also allowed working in e.g. /path/client13
  or /path/client1000.

  As this could accidentally lead to major security/privacy issues depending on the paths you use, the behaviour was changed to be a strict directory match. That means –restrict-to-path /path/client1 (with or
  without trailing slash does not make a difference) now uses /path/client1/ internally (note the trailing slash
  here!) for matching and allows precisely that path AND any path below it. So, /path/client1 is allowed,
  /path/client1/repo1 is allowed, but not /path/client13 or /path/client1000.

  If you willingly used the undocumented (dangerous) previous behaviour, you may need to rearrange your
  –restrict-to-path paths now. We are sorry if that causes work for you, but we did not want a potentially
  dangerous behaviour in the software (not even using a for-backwards-compat option).

Bug fixes:

- fixed repeated LockTimeout exceptions when borg serve tried to write into a already write-locked repo (e.g. by a borg mount), #502 part b) This was solved by the fix for #1220 in 1.0.7rc1 already.

- fix cosmetics + file leftover for "not a valid borg repository", #1490

- Cache: release lock if cache is invalid, #1501

- borg extract –strip-components: fix leak of preloaded chunk contents

- Repository, when a InvalidRepository exception happens:

    - fix spurious, empty lock.roster

    - fix repo not closed cleanly

New features:

- implement borg debug-info, fixes #1122 (just calls already existing code via cli, same output as below tracebacks)

Other changes:

- skip the O_NOATIME test on GNU Hurd, fixes #1315 (this is a very minor issue and the GNU Hurd project knows the bug)

- document using a clean repo to test / build the release

Version 1.0.7rc2 (2016-08-13)

Bug fixes:

- do not write objects to repository that are bigger than the allowed size, borg will reject reading them, #1451.

    Important: if you created archives with many millions of files or directories, please verify if you can open them successfully, e.g. try a "borg list REPO::ARCHIVE".

- lz4 compression: dynamically enlarge the (de)compression buffer, the static buffer was not big enough for archives with extremely many items, #1453

- larger item metadata stream chunks, raise archive item limit by 8x, #1452

- fix untracked segments made by moved DELETEs, #1442

    Impact: Previously (metadata) segments could become untracked when deleting data, these would never be cleaned up.

- extended attributes (xattrs) related fixes:

    - fixed a race condition in xattrs querying that led to the entire file not being backed up (while logging the error, exit code = 1), #1469

    - fixed a race condition in xattrs querying that led to a crash, #1462

    - raise OSError including the error message derived from errno, deal with path being a integer FD

Other changes:

- print active env var override by default, #1467

- xattr module: refactor code, deduplicate, clean up

- repository: split object size check into too small and too big

- add a transaction_id assertion, so borg init on a broken (inconsistent) filesystem does not look like a coding error in borg, but points to the real problem.

- explain confusing TypeError caused by compat support for old servers, #1456

- add forgotten usage help file from build_usage

- refactor/unify buffer code into helpers.Buffer class, add tests

- docs:

    - document archive limitation, #1452

    - improve prune examples

Version 1.0.7rc1 (2016-08-05)

Bug fixes:

- fix repo lock deadlocks (related to lock upgrade), #1220

- catch unpacker exceptions, resync, #1351

- fix borg break-lock ignoring BORG_REPO env var, #1324

- files cache performance fixes (fixes unnecessary re-reading/chunking/ hashing of unmodified files for some use cases):

    - fix unintended file cache eviction, #1430

    - implement BORG_FILES_CACHE_TTL, update FAQ, raise default TTL from 10 to 20, #1338

- FUSE:

    - cache partially read data chunks (performance), #965, #966

    - always create a root dir, #1125

- use an OrderedDict for helptext, making the build reproducible, #1346

- RemoteRepository init: always call close on exceptions, #1370 (cosmetic)

- ignore stdout/stderr broken pipe errors (cosmetic), #1116

New features:

- better borg versions management support (useful esp. for borg servers wanting to offer multiple borg versions and for clients wanting to choose a specific server borg version), #1392:

    - add BORG_VERSION environment variable before executing "borg serve" via ssh

    - add new placeholder {borgversion}

    - substitute placeholders in –remote-path

- borg init –append-only option (makes using the more secure append-only mode more convenient. when used remotely, this requires 1.0.7+ also on the borg server), #1291.

Other changes:

- Vagrantfile:

    - darwin64: upgrade to FUSE for macOS 3.4.1 (aka osxfuse), #1378

    - xenial64: use user "ubuntu", not "vagrant" (as usual), #1331

- tests:

    - fix FUSE tests on OS X, #1433

- docs:

    - FAQ: add backup using stable filesystem names recommendation

    - FAQ about glibc compatibility added, #491, glibc-check improved

    - FAQ: 'A' unchanged file; remove ambiguous entry age sentence.

    - OS X: install pkg-config to build with FUSE support, fixes #1400

    - add notes about shell/sudo pitfalls with env. vars, #1380

– added platform feature matrix

- implement borg debug-dump-repo-objs

Version 1.0.6 (2016-07-12)

Bug fixes:

- Linux: handle multiple LD_PRELOAD entries correctly, #1314, #1111
- Fix crash with unclear message if the libc is not found, #1314, #1111

Other changes:

- tests:
    - Fixed O_NOATIME tests for Solaris and GNU Hurd, #1315
    - Fixed sparse file tests for (file) systems not supporting it, #1310
- docs:
    - Fixed syntax highlighting, #1313
    - misc docs: added data processing overview picture

Version 1.0.6rc1 (2016-07-10)

New features:

- borg check –repair: heal damaged files if missing chunks re-appear (e.g. if the previously missing chunk was added again in a later backup archive), #148. (*) Also improved logging.

Bug fixes:

- sync_dir: silence fsync() failing with EINVAL, #1287 Some network filesystems (like smbfs) don't support this and we use this in repository code.
- borg mount (FUSE):
    - fix directories being shadowed when contained paths were also specified, #1295
    - raise I/O Error (EIO) on damaged files (unless -o allow_damaged_files is used), #1302. (*)
- borg extract: warn if a damaged file is extracted, #1299. (*)
- Added some missing return code checks (ChunkIndex._add, hashindex resize).
- borg check: fix/optimize initial hash table size, avoids resize of the table.

Other changes:

- tests:
    - add more FUSE tests, #1284
    - deduplicate FUSE (u)mount code
    - fix borg binary test issues, #862
- docs:
    - changelog: added release dates to older borg releases
    - fix some sphinx (docs generator) warnings, #881

Notes:

(*) Some features depend on information (chunks_healthy list) added to item metadata when a file with missing chunks was "repaired" using all-zero replacement chunks. The chunks_healthy list is generated since borg 1.0.4, thus borg can't recognize such "repaired" (but content-damaged) files if the repair was done with an older borg version.

Version 1.0.5 (2016-07-07)

Bug fixes:

- borg mount: fix FUSE crash in xattr code on Linux introduced in 1.0.4, #1282

Other changes:

- backport some FAQ entries from master branch
- add release helper scripts
- Vagrantfile:
    - centos6: no FUSE, don't build binary
    - add xz for redhat-like dists

Version 1.0.4 (2016-07-07)

New features:

- borg serve –append-only, #1168 This was included because it was a simple change (append-only functionality was already present via repository config file) and makes better security now practically usable.
- BORG_REMOTE_PATH environment variable, #1258 This was included because it was a simple change (–remote-path cli option was already present) and makes borg much easier to use if you need it.
- Repository: cleanup incomplete transaction on "no space left" condition. In many cases, this can avoid a 100% full repo filesystem (which is very problematic as borg always needs free space - even to delete archives).

Bug fixes:

- Fix wrong handling and reporting of OSErrors in borg create, #1138. This was a serious issue: in the context of "borg create", errors like repository I/O errors (e.g. disk I/O errors, ssh repo connection errors) were handled badly and did not lead to a crash (which would be good for this case, because the repo transaction would be incomplete and trigger a transaction rollback to clean up). Now, error handling for source files is cleanly separated from every other error handling, so only problematic input files are logged and skipped.
- Implement fail-safe error handling for borg extract. Note that this isn't nearly as critical as the borg create error handling bug, since nothing is written to the repo. So this was "merely" misleading error reporting.
- Add missing error handler in directory attr restore loop.
- repo: make sure write data hits disk before the commit tag (#1236) and also sync the containing directory.
- FUSE: getxattr fail must use errno.ENOATTR, #1126 (fixes Mac OS X Finder malfunction: "zero bytes" file length, access denied)
- borg check –repair: do not lose information about the good/original chunks. If we do not lose the original chunk IDs list when "repairing" a file (replacing missing chunks with all-zero chunks), we have a chance to "heal" the file back into its original state later, in case the chunks re-appear (e.g. in a fresh backup). Healing is not implemented yet, see #148.
- fixes for –read-special mode:
    - ignore known files cache, #1241

- fake regular file mode, #1214

- improve symlinks handling, #1215

- remove passphrase from subprocess environment, #1105

- Ignore empty index file (will trigger index rebuild), #1195

- add missing placeholder support for –prefix, #1027

- improve exception handling for placeholder replacement

- catch and format exceptions in arg parsing

- helpers: fix "undefined name 'e'" in exception handler

- better error handling for missing repo manifest, #1043

- borg delete:

  - make it possible to delete a repo without manifest

  - borg delete –forced allows to delete corrupted archives, #1139

- borg check:

  - make borg check work for empty repo

  - fix resync and msgpacked item qualifier, #1135

  - rebuild_manifest: fix crash if 'name' or 'time' key were missing.

  - better validation of item metadata dicts, #1130

  - better validation of archive metadata dicts

- close the repo on exit - even if rollback did not work, #1197. This is rather cosmetic, it avoids repo closing in the destructor.

- tests:

  - fix sparse file test, #1170

  - flake8: ignore new F405, #1185

  - catch "invalid argument" on cygwin, #257

  - fix sparseness assertion in test prep, #1264

Other changes:

- make borg build/work on OpenSSL 1.0 and 1.1, #1187

- docs / help:

  - fix / clarify prune help, #1143

  - fix "patterns" help formatting

  - add missing docs / help about placeholders

  - resources: rename atticmatic to borgmatic

  - document sshd settings, #545

  - more details about checkpoints, add split trick, #1171

  - support docs: add freenode web chat link, #1175

  - add prune visualization / example, #723

  - add note that Fnmatch is default, #1247

  - make clear that lzma levels > 6 are a waste of cpu cycles

  - add a "do not edit" note to auto-generated files, #1250

- update cygwin installation docs
- repository interoperability with borg master (1.1dev) branch:
  - borg check: read item metadata keys from manifest, #1147
  - read v2 hints files, #1235
  - fix hints file "unknown version" error handling bug
- tests: add tests for format_line
- llfuse: update version requirement for freebsd
- Vagrantfile:
  - use openbsd 5.9, #716
  - do not install llfuse on netbsd (broken)
  - update OSXfuse to version 3.3.3
  - use Python 3.5.2 to build the binaries
- glibc compatibility checker: scripts/glibc_check.py
- add .eggs to .gitignore

Version 1.0.3 (2016-05-20)

Bug fixes:

- prune: avoid that checkpoints are kept and completed archives are deleted in a prune run), #997
- prune: fix commandline argument validation - some valid command lines were considered invalid (annoying, but harmless), #942
- fix capabilities extraction on Linux (set xattrs last, after chown()), #1069
- repository: fix commit tags being seen in data
- when probing key files, do binary reads. avoids crash when non-borg binary files are located in borg's key files directory.
- handle SIGTERM and make a clean exit - avoids orphan lock files.
- repository cache: don't cache large objects (avoid using lots of temp. disk space), #1063

Other changes:

- Vagrantfile: OS X: update osxfuse / install lzma package, #933
- setup.py: add check for platform_darwin.c
- setup.py: on freebsd, use a llfuse release that builds ok
- docs / help:
  - update readthedocs URLs, #991
  - add missing docs for "borg break-lock", #992
  - borg create help: add some words to about the archive name
  - borg create help: document format tags, #894

Version 1.0.2 (2016-04-16)

Bug fixes:

- fix malfunction and potential corruption on (nowadays rather rare) big-endian architectures or bi-endian archs in (rare) BE mode. #886, #889

  cache resync / index merge was malfunctioning due to this, potentially leading to data loss. borg info had cosmetic issues (displayed wrong values).

  note: all (widespread) little-endian archs (like x86/x64) or bi-endian archs in (widespread) LE mode (like ARMEL, MIPSEL, ...) were NOT affected.

- add overflow and range checks for 1st (special) uint32 of the hashindex values, switch from int32 to uint32.

- fix so that refcount will never overflow, but just stick to max. value after a overflow would have occurred.

- borg delete: fix –cache-only for broken caches, #874

  Makes –cache-only idempotent: it won't fail if the cache is already deleted.

- fixed borg create –one-file-system erroneously traversing into other filesystems (if starting fs device number was 0), #873

- workround a bug in Linux fadvise FADV_DONTNEED, #907

Other changes:

- better test coverage for hashindex, incl. overflow testing, checking correct computations so endianness issues would be discovered.

- reproducible doc for ProgressIndicator*, make the build reproducible.

- use latest llfuse for vagrant machines

- docs:

  - use /path/to/repo in examples, fixes #901

  - fix confusing usage of "repo" as archive name (use "arch")

Version 1.0.1 (2016-04-08)

New features:

Usually there are no new features in a bugfix release, but these were added due to their high impact on security/safety/speed or because they are fixes also:

- append-only mode for repositories, #809, #36 (see docs)

- borg create: add –ignore-inode option to make borg detect unmodified files even if your filesystem does not have stable inode numbers (like sshfs and possibly CIFS).

- add options –warning, –error, –critical for missing log levels, #826. it's not recommended to suppress warnings or errors, but the user may decide this on his own. note: –warning is not given to borg serve so a <= 1.0.0 borg will still work as server (it is not needed as it is the default). do not use –error or –critical when using a <= 1.0.0 borg server.

Bug fixes:

- fix silently skipping EIO, #748

- add context manager for Repository (avoid orphan repository locks), #285

- do not sleep for >60s while waiting for lock, #773

- unpack file stats before passing to FUSE

- fix build on illumos

- don't try to backup doors or event ports (Solaris and derivates)
- remove useless/misleading libc version display, #738
- test suite: reset exit code of persistent archiver, #844
- RemoteRepository: clean up pipe if remote open() fails
- Remote: don't print tracebacks for Error exceptions handled downstream, #792
- if BORG_PASSPHRASE is present but wrong, don't prompt for password, but fail instead, #791
- ArchiveChecker: move "orphaned objects check skipped" to INFO log level, #826
- fix capitalization, add ellipses, change log level to debug for 2 messages, #798

Other changes:

- update llfuse requirement, llfuse 1.0 works
- update OS / dist packages on build machines, #717
- prefer showing –info over -v in usage help, #859
- docs:
    - fix cygwin requirements (gcc-g++)
    - document how to debug / file filesystem issues, #664
    - fix reproducible build of api docs
    - RTD theme: CSS !important overwrite, #727
    - Document logo font. Recreate logo png. Remove GIMP logo file.

Version 1.0.0 (2016-03-05)

The major release number change (0.x -> 1.x) indicates bigger incompatible changes, please read the compatibility notes, adapt / test your scripts and check your backup logs.

Compatibility notes:

- drop support for python 3.2 and 3.3, require 3.4 or 3.5, #221 #65 #490 note: we provide binaries that include python 3.5.1 and everything else needed. they are an option in case you are stuck with < 3.4 otherwise.
- change encryption to be on by default (using "repokey" mode)
- moved keyfile keys from ~/.borg/keys to ~/.config/borg/keys, you can either move them manually or run "borg upgrade <REPO>"
- remove support for –encryption=passphrase, use borg migrate-to-repokey to switch to repokey mode, #97
- remove deprecated –compression <number>, use –compression zlib,<number> instead in case of 0, you could also use –compression none
- remove deprecated –hourly/daily/weekly/monthly/yearly use –keep-hourly/daily/weekly/monthly/yearly instead
- remove deprecated –do-not-cross-mountpoints, use –one-file-system instead
- disambiguate -p option, #563:
    - -p now is same as –progress
    - -P now is same as –prefix
- remove deprecated "borg verify", use "borg extract –dry-run" instead

- cleanup environment variable semantics, #355 the environment variables used to be "yes sayers" when set, this was conceptually generalized to "automatic answerers" and they just give their value as answer (as if you typed in that value when being asked). See the "usage" / "Environment Variables" section of the docs for details.

- change the builtin default for –chunker-params, create 2MiB chunks, #343 –chunker-params new default: 19,23,21,4095 - old default: 10,23,16,4095

  one of the biggest issues with borg < 1.0 (and also attic) was that it had a default target chunk size of 64kiB, thus it created a lot of chunks and thus also a huge chunk management overhead (high RAM and disk usage).

  please note that the new default won't change the chunks that you already have in your repository. the new big chunks do not deduplicate with the old small chunks, so expect your repo to grow at least by the size of every changed file and in the worst case (e.g. if your files cache was lost / is not used) by the size of every file (minus any compression you might use).

  in case you want to immediately see a much lower resource usage (RAM / disk) for chunks management, it might be better to start with a new repo than continuing in the existing repo (with an existing repo, you'ld have to wait until all archives with small chunks got pruned to see a lower resource usage).

  if you used the old –chunker-params default value (or if you did not use –chunker-params option at all) and you'ld like to continue using small chunks (and you accept the huge resource usage that comes with that), just explicitly use borg create –chunker-params=10,23,16,4095.

- archive timestamps: the 'time' timestamp now refers to archive creation start time (was: end time), the new 'time_end' timestamp refers to archive creation end time. This might affect prune if your backups take rather long. if you give a timestamp via cli this is stored into 'time', therefore it now needs to mean archive creation start time.

New features:

- implement password roundtrip, #695

Bug fixes:

- remote end does not need cache nor keys directories, do not create them, #701
- added retry counter for passwords, #703

Other changes:

- fix compiler warnings, #697
- docs:
    - update README.rst to new changelog location in docs/changes.rst
    - add Teemu to AUTHORS
    - changes.rst: fix old chunker params, #698
    - FAQ: how to limit bandwidth

Version 1.0.0rc2 (2016-02-28)

New features:

- format options for location: user, pid, fqdn, hostname, now, utcnow, user
- borg list –list-format
- borg prune -v –list enables the keep/prune list output, #658

Bug fixes:

- fix _open_rb noatime handling, #657
- add a simple archivename validator, #680

- borg create –stats: show timestamps in localtime, use same labels/formatting as borg info, #651

- llfuse compatibility fixes (now compatible with: 0.40, 0.41, 0.42)

Other changes:

- it is now possible to use "pip install borgbackup[fuse]" to automatically install the llfuse dependency using the correct version requirement for it. you still need to care about having installed the FUSE / build related OS package first, though, so that building llfuse can succeed.

- Vagrant: drop Ubuntu Precise (12.04) - does not have Python >= 3.4

- Vagrant: use pyinstaller v3.1.1 to build binaries

- docs:

  - borg upgrade: add to docs that only LOCAL repos are supported

  - borg upgrade also handles borg 0.xx -> 1.0

  - use pip extras or requirements file to install llfuse

  - fix order in release process

  - updated usage docs and other minor / cosmetic fixes

  - verified borg examples in docs, #644

  - freebsd dependency installation and FUSE configuration, #649

  - add example how to restore a raw device, #671

  - add a hint about the dev headers needed when installing from source

  - add examples for delete (and handle delete after list, before prune), #656

  - update example for borg create -v –stats (use iso datetime format), #663

  - added example to BORG_RSH docs

  - "connection closed by remote": add FAQ entry and point to issue #636

Version 1.0.0rc1 (2016-02-07)

New features:

- borg migrate-to-repokey ("passphrase" -> "repokey" encryption key mode)

- implement –short for borg list REPO, #611

- implement –list for borg extract (consistency with borg create)

- borg serve: overwrite client's –restrict-to-path with ssh forced command's option value (but keep everything else from the client commandline), #544

- use $XDG_CONFIG_HOME/keys for keyfile keys (~/.config/borg/keys), #515

- "borg upgrade" moves the keyfile keys to the new location

- display both archive creation start and end time in "borg info", #627

Bug fixes:

- normalize trailing slashes for the repository path, #606

- Cache: fix exception handling in __init__, release lock, #610

Other changes:

- suppress unneeded exception context (PEP 409), simpler tracebacks

Appendix D. Changelog

- removed special code needed to deal with imperfections / incompatibilities / missing stuff in py 3.2/3.3, simplify code that can be done simpler in 3.4

- removed some version requirements that were kept on old versions because newer did not support py 3.2 any more

- use some py 3.4+ stdlib code instead of own/openssl/pypi code:

  - use os.urandom instead of own cython openssl RAND_bytes wrapper, #493

  - use hashlib.pbkdf2_hmac from py stdlib instead of own openssl wrapper

  - use hmac.compare_digest instead of == operator (constant time comparison)

  - use stat.filemode instead of homegrown code

  - use "mock" library from stdlib, #145

  - remove borg.support (with non-broken argparse copy), it is ok in 3.4+, #358

- Vagrant: copy CHANGES.rst as symlink, #592

- cosmetic code cleanups, add flake8 to tox/travis, #4

- docs / help:

  - make "borg -h" output prettier, #591

  - slightly rephrase prune help

  - add missing example for –list option of borg create

  - quote exclude line that includes an asterisk to prevent shell expansion

  - fix dead link to license

  - delete Ubuntu Vivid, it is not supported anymore (EOL)

  - OS X binary does not work for older OS X releases, #629

  - borg serve's special support for forced/original ssh commands, #544

  - misc. updates and fixes

Version 0.30.0 (2016-01-23)

Compatibility notes:

- you may need to use -v (or –info) more often to actually see output emitted at INFO log level (because it is suppressed at the default WARNING log level). See the "general" section in the usage docs.

- for borg create, you need –list (additionally to -v) to see the long file list (was needed so you can have e.g. –stats alone without the long list)

- see below about BORG_DELETE_I_KNOW_WHAT_I_AM_DOING (was: BORG_CHECK_I_KNOW_WHAT_I_AM_DOING)

Bug fixes:

- fix crash when using borg create –dry-run –keep-tag-files, #570

- make sure teardown with cleanup happens for Cache and RepositoryCache, avoiding leftover locks and TEMP dir contents, #285 (partially), #548

- fix locking KeyError, partial fix for #502

- log stats consistently, #526

- add abbreviated weekday to timestamp format, fixes #496

- strip whitespace when loading exclusions from file

- unset LD_LIBRARY_PATH before invoking ssh, fixes strange OpenSSL library version warning when using the borg binary, #514

- add some error handling/fallback for C library loading, #494

- added BORG_DELETE_I_KNOW_WHAT_I_AM_DOING for check in "borg delete", #503

- remove unused "repair" rpc method name

New features:

- borg create: implement exclusions using regular expression patterns.

- borg create: implement inclusions using patterns.

- borg extract: support patterns, #361

- support different styles for patterns:

  - fnmatch (*fm:* prefix, default when omitted), like borg <= 0.29.

  - shell (*sh:* prefix) with * not matching directory separators and **/ matching 0..n directories

  - path prefix (*pp:* prefix, for unifying borg create pp1 pp2 into the patterns system), semantics like in borg <= 0.29

  - regular expression (*re:*), new!

- –progress option for borg upgrade (#291) and borg delete <archive>

- update progress indication more often (e.g. for borg create within big files or for borg check repo), #500

- finer chunker granularity for items metadata stream, #547, #487

- borg create –list now used (additionally to -v) to enable the verbose file list output

- display borg version below tracebacks, #532

Other changes:

- hashtable size (and thus: RAM and disk consumption) follows a growth policy: grows fast while small, grows slower when getting bigger, #527

- Vagrantfile: use pyinstaller 3.1 to build binaries, freebsd sqlite3 fix, fixes #569

- no separate binaries for centos6 any more because the generic linux binaries also work on centos6 (or in general: on systems with a slightly older glibc than debian7

- dev environment: require virtualenv<14.0 so we get a py32 compatible pip

- docs:

  - add space-saving chunks.archive.d trick to FAQ

  - important: clarify -v and log levels in usage -> general, please read!

  - sphinx configuration: create a simple man page from usage docs

  - add a repo server setup example

  - disable unneeded SSH features in authorized_keys examples for security.

  - borg prune only knows "–keep-within" and not "–within"

  - add gource video to resources docs, #507

  - add netbsd install instructions

  - authors: make it more clear what refers to borg and what to attic

  - document standalone binary requirements, #499

  - rephrase the mailing list section

  - development docs: run build_api and build_usage before tagging release

– internals docs: hash table max. load factor is 0.75 now

– markup, typo, grammar, phrasing, clarifications and other fixes.

– add gcc gcc-c++ to redhat/fedora/corora install docs, fixes #583

Version 0.29.0 (2015-12-13)

Compatibility notes:

• when upgrading to 0.29.0 you need to upgrade client as well as server installations due to the locking and commandline interface changes otherwise you'll get an error msg about a RPC protocol mismatch or a wrong commandline option. if you run a server that needs to support both old and new clients, it is suggested that you have a "borg-0.28.2" and a "borg-0.29.0" command. clients then can choose via e.g. "borg –remote-path=borg-0.29.0 ...".

• the default waiting time for a lock changed from infinity to 1 second for a better interactive user experience. if the repo you want to access is currently locked, borg will now terminate after 1s with an error message. if you have scripts that shall wait for the lock for a longer time, use –lock-wait N (with N being the maximum wait time in seconds).

Bug fixes:

• hash table tuning (better chosen hashtable load factor 0.75 and prime initial size of 1031 gave ~1000x speedup in some scenarios)

• avoid creation of an orphan lock for one case, #285

• –keep-tag-files: fix file mode and multiple tag files in one directory, #432

• fixes for "borg upgrade" (attic repo converter), #466

• remove –progress isatty magic (and also –no-progress option) again, #476

• borg init: display proper repo URL

• fix format of umask in help pages, #463

New features:

• implement –lock-wait, support timeout for UpgradableLock, #210

• implement borg break-lock command, #157

• include system info below traceback, #324

• sane remote logging, remote stderr, #461:

– remote log output: intercept it and log it via local logging system, with "Remote: " prefixed to message. log remote tracebacks.

– remote stderr: output it to local stderr with "Remote: " prefixed.

• add –debug and –info (same as –verbose) to set the log level of the builtin logging configuration (which otherwise defaults to warning), #426 note: there are few messages emitted at DEBUG level currently.

• optionally configure logging via env var BORG_LOGGING_CONF

• add –filter option for status characters: e.g. to show only the added or modified files (and also errors), use "borg create -v –filter=AME ...".

• more progress indicators, #394

• use ISO-8601 date and time format, #375

• "borg check –prefix" to restrict archive checking to that name prefix, #206

Other changes:

• hashindex_add C implementation (speed up cache re-sync for new archives)

- increase FUSE read_size to 1024 (speed up metadata operations)

- check/delete/prune –save-space: free unused segments quickly, #239

- increase rpc protocol version to 2 (see also Compatibility notes), #458

- silence borg by default (via default log level WARNING)

- get rid of C compiler warnings, #391

- upgrade OS X FUSE to 3.0.9 on the OS X binary build system

- use python 3.5.1 to build binaries

- docs:

  - new mailing list borgbackup@python.org, #468

  - readthedocs: color and logo improvements

  - load coverage icons over SSL (avoids mixed content)

  - more precise binary installation steps

  - update release procedure docs about OS X FUSE

  - FAQ entry about unexpected 'A' status for unchanged file(s), #403

  - add docs about 'E' file status

  - add "borg upgrade" docs, #464

  - add developer docs about output and logging

  - clarify encryption, add note about client-side encryption

  - add resources section, with videos, talks, presentations, #149

  - Borg moved to Arch Linux [community]

  - fix wrong installation instructions for archlinux

Version 0.28.2 (2015-11-15)

New features:

- borg create –exclude-if-present TAGFILE - exclude directories that have the given file from the backup. You can additionally give –keep-tag-files to preserve just the directory roots and the tag-files (but not backup other directory contents), #395, attic #128, attic #142

Other changes:

- do not create docs sources at build time (just have them in the repo), completely remove have_cython() hack, do not use the "mock" library at build time, #384

- avoid hidden import, make it easier for PyInstaller, easier fix for #218

- docs:

  - add description of item flags / status output, fixes #402

  - explain how to regenerate usage and API files (build_api or build_usage) and when to commit usage files directly into git, #384

  - minor install docs improvements

Version 0.28.1 (2015-11-08)

Bug fixes:

- do not try to build api / usage docs for production install, fixes unexpected "mock" build dependency, #384

Other changes:

- avoid using msgpack.packb at import time
- fix formatting issue in changes.rst
- fix build on readthedocs

Version 0.28.0 (2015-11-08)

Compatibility notes:

- changed return codes (exit codes), see docs. in short: old: 0 = ok, 1 = error. now: 0 = ok, 1 = warning, 2 = error

New features:

- refactor return codes (exit codes), fixes #61
- add –show-rc option enable "terminating with X status, rc N" output, fixes 58, #351
- borg create backups atime and ctime additionally to mtime, fixes #317 - extract: support atime additionally to mtime - FUSE: support ctime and atime additionally to mtime
- support borg –version
- emit a warning if we have a slow msgpack installed
- borg list –prefix=thishostname- REPO, fixes #205
- Debug commands (do not use except if you know what you do: debug-get-obj, debug-put-obj, debug-delete-obj, debug-dump-archive-items.

Bug fixes:

- setup.py: fix bug related to BORG_LZ4_PREFIX processing
- fix "check" for repos that have incomplete chunks, fixes #364
- borg mount: fix unlocking of repository at umount time, fixes #331
- fix reading files without touching their atime, #334
- non-ascii ACL fixes for Linux, FreeBSD and OS X, #277
- fix acl_use_local_uid_gid() and add a test for it, attic #359
- borg upgrade: do not upgrade repositories in place by default, #299
- fix cascading failure with the index conversion code, #269
- borg check: implement 'cmdline' archive metadata value decoding, #311
- fix RobustUnpacker, it missed some metadata keys (new atime and ctime keys were missing, but also bsd-flags). add check for unknown metadata keys.
- create from stdin: also save atime, ctime (cosmetic)
- use default_notty=False for confirmations, fixes #345
- vagrant: fix msgpack installation on centos, fixes #342
- deal with unicode errors for symlinks in same way as for regular files and have a helpful warning message about how to fix wrong locale setup, fixes #382

- add ACL keys the RobustUnpacker must know about

Other changes:

- improve file size displays, more flexible size formatters

- explicitly commit to the units standard, #289

- archiver: add E status (means that an error occurred when processing this (single) item

- do binary releases via "github releases", closes #214

- create: use -x and –one-file-system (was: –do-not-cross-mountpoints), #296

- a lot of changes related to using "logging" module and screen output, #233

- show progress display if on a tty, output more progress information, #303

- factor out status output so it is consistent, fix surrogates removal, maybe fixes #309

- move away from RawConfigParser to ConfigParser

- archive checker: better error logging, give chunk_id and sequence numbers (can be used together with borg debug-dump-archive-items).

- do not mention the deprecated passphrase mode

- emit a deprecation warning for –compression N (giving a just a number)

- misc .coverragerc fixes (and coverage measurement improvements), fixes #319

- refactor confirmation code, reduce code duplication, add tests

- prettier error messages, fixes #307, #57

- tests:

    - add a test to find disk-full issues, #327

    - travis: also run tests on Python 3.5

    - travis: use tox -r so it rebuilds the tox environments

    - test the generated pyinstaller-based binary by archiver unit tests, #215

    - vagrant: tests: announce whether fakeroot is used or not

    - vagrant: add vagrant user to fuse group for debianoid systems also

    - vagrant: llfuse install on darwin needs pkgconfig installed

    - vagrant: use pyinstaller from develop branch, fixes #336

    - benchmarks: test create, extract, list, delete, info, check, help, fixes #146

    - benchmarks: test with both the binary and the python code

    - archiver tests: test with both the binary and the python code, fixes #215

    - make basic test more robust

- docs:

    - moved docs to borgbackup.readthedocs.org, #155

    - a lot of fixes and improvements, use mobile-friendly RTD standard theme

    - use zlib,6 compression in some examples, fixes #275

    - add missing rename usage to docs, closes #279

    - include the help offered by borg help <topic> in the usage docs, fixes #293

    - include a list of major changes compared to attic into README, fixes #224

    - add OS X install instructions, #197

- more details about the release process, #260

- fix linux glibc requirement (binaries built on debian7 now)

- build: move usage and API generation to setup.py

- update docs about return codes, #61

- remove api docs (too much breakage on rtd)

- borgbackup install + basics presentation (asciinema)

- describe the current style guide in documentation

- add section about debug commands

- warn about not running out of space

- add example for rename

- improve chunker params docs, fixes #362

- minor development docs update

Version 0.27.0 (2015-10-07)

New features:

- "borg upgrade" command - attic -> borg one time converter / migration, #21

- temporary hack to avoid using lots of disk space for chunks.archive.d, #235: To use it: rm -rf chunks.archive.d ; touch chunks.archive.d

- respect XDG_CACHE_HOME, attic #181

- add support for arbitrary SSH commands, attic #99

- borg delete –cache-only REPO (only delete cache, not REPO), attic #123

Bug fixes:

- use Debian 7 (wheezy) to build pyinstaller borgbackup binaries, fixes slow down observed when running the Centos6-built binary on Ubuntu, #222

- do not crash on empty lock.roster, fixes #232

- fix multiple issues with the cache config version check, #234

- fix segment entry header size check, attic #352 plus other error handling improvements / code deduplication there.

- always give segment and offset in repo IntegrityErrors

Other changes:

- stop producing binary wheels, remove docs about it, #147

- docs: - add warning about prune - generate usage include files only as needed - development docs: add Vagrant section - update / improve / reformat FAQ - hint to single-file pyinstaller binaries from README

Version 0.26.1 (2015-09-28)

This is a minor update, just docs and new pyinstaller binaries.

- docs update about python and binary requirements

- better docs for –read-special, fix #220

- re-built the binaries, fix #218 and #213 (glibc version issue)

- update web site about single-file pyinstaller binaries

Note: if you did a python-based installation, there is no need to upgrade.

Version 0.26.0 (2015-09-19)

New features:

- Faster cache sync (do all in one pass, remove tar/compression stuff), #163
- BORG_REPO env var to specify the default repo, #168
- read special files as if they were regular files, #79
- implement borg create –dry-run, attic issue #267
- Normalize paths before pattern matching on OS X, #143
- support OpenBSD and NetBSD (except xattrs/ACLs)
- support / run tests on Python 3.5

Bug fixes:

- borg mount repo: use absolute path, attic #200, attic #137
- chunker: use off_t to get 64bit on 32bit platform, #178
- initialize chunker fd to -1, so it's not equal to STDIN_FILENO (0)
- fix reaction to "no" answer at delete repo prompt, #182
- setup.py: detect lz4.h header file location
- to support python < 3.2.4, add less buggy argparse lib from 3.2.6 (#194)
- fix for obtaining `char *` from temporary Python value (old code causes a compile error on Mint 17.2)
- llfuse 0.41 install troubles on some platforms, require < 0.41 (UnicodeDecodeError exception due to non-ascii llfuse setup.py)
- cython code: add some int types to get rid of unspecific python add / subtract operations (avoid `undefined symbol FPE_...` error on some platforms)
- fix verbose mode display of stdin backup
- extract: warn if a include pattern never matched, fixes #209, implement counters for Include/ExcludePatterns
- archive names with slashes are invalid, attic issue #180
- chunker: add a check whether the POSIX_FADV_DONTNEED constant is defined - fixes building on OpenBSD.

Other changes:

- detect inconsistency / corruption / hash collision, #170
- replace versioneer with setuptools_scm, #106
- docs:
    - pkg-config is needed for llfuse installation
    - be more clear about pruning, attic issue #132
- unit tests:
    - xattr: ignore security.selinux attribute showing up
    - ext3 seems to need a bit more space for a sparse file

  – do not test lzma level 9 compression (avoid MemoryError)

  – work around strange mtime granularity issue on netbsd, fixes #204

  – ignore st_rdev if file is not a block/char device, fixes #203

  – stay away from the setgid and sticky mode bits

- use Vagrant to do easy cross-platform testing (#196), currently:

  – Debian 7 "wheezy" 32bit, Debian 8 "jessie" 64bit

  – Ubuntu 12.04 32bit, Ubuntu 14.04 64bit

  – Centos 7 64bit

  – FreeBSD 10.2 64bit

  – OpenBSD 5.7 64bit

  – NetBSD 6.1.5 64bit

  – Darwin (OS X Yosemite)

Version 0.25.0 (2015-08-29)

Compatibility notes:

- lz4 compression library (liblz4) is a new requirement (#156)

- the new compression code is very compatible: as long as you stay with zlib compression, older borg releases will still be able to read data from a repo/archive made with the new code (note: this is not the case for the default "none" compression, use "zlib,0" if you want a "no compression" mode that can be read by older borg). Also the new code is able to read repos and archives made with older borg versions (for all zlib levels 0..9).

Deprecations:

- –compression N (with N being a number, as in 0.24) is deprecated. We keep the –compression 0..9 for now to not break scripts, but it is deprecated and will be removed later, so better fix your scripts now: –compression 0 (as in 0.24) is the same as –compression zlib,0 (now). BUT: if you do not want compression, you rather want –compression none (which is the default). –compression 1 (in 0.24) is the same as –compression zlib,1 (now) –compression 9 (in 0.24) is the same as –compression zlib,9 (now)

New features:

- create –compression none (default, means: do not compress, just pass through data "as is". this is more efficient than zlib level 0 as used in borg 0.24)

- create –compression lz4 (super-fast, but not very high compression)

- create –compression zlib,N (slower, higher compression, default for N is 6)

- create –compression lzma,N (slowest, highest compression, default N is 6)

- honor the nodump flag (UF_NODUMP) and do not backup such items

- list –short just outputs a simple list of the files/directories in an archive

Bug fixes:

- fixed –chunker-params parameter order confusion / malfunction, fixes #154

- close fds of segments we delete (during compaction)

- close files which fell out the lrucache

- fadvise DONTNEED now is only called for the byte range actually read, not for the whole file, fixes #158.

- fix issue with negative "all archives" size, fixes #165

- restore_xattrs: ignore if setxattr fails with EACCES, fixes #162

Other changes:

- remove fakeroot requirement for tests, tests run faster without fakeroot (test setup does not fail any more without fakeroot, so you can run with or without fakeroot), fixes #151 and #91.

- more tests for archiver

- recover_segment(): don't assume we have an fd for segment

- lrucache refactoring / cleanup, add dispose function, py.test tests

- generalize hashindex code for any key length (less hardcoding)

- lock roster: catch file not found in remove() method and ignore it

- travis CI: use requirements file

- improved docs:

    - replace hack for llfuse with proper solution (install libfuse-dev)

    - update docs about compression

    - update development docs about fakeroot

    - internals: add some words about lock files / locking system

    - support: mention BountySource and for what it can be used

    - theme: use a lighter green

    - add pypi, wheel, dist package based install docs

    - split install docs into system-specific preparations and generic instructions

Version 0.24.0 (2015-08-09)

Incompatible changes (compared to 0.23):

- borg now always issues –umask NNN option when invoking another borg via ssh on the repository server. By that, it's making sure it uses the same umask for remote repos as for local ones. Because of this, you must upgrade both server and client(s) to 0.24.

- the default umask is 077 now (if you do not specify via –umask) which might be a different one as you used previously. The default umask avoids that you accidentally give access permissions for group and/or others to files created by borg (e.g. the repository).

Deprecations:

- "–encryption passphrase" mode is deprecated, see #85 and #97. See the new "–encryption repokey" mode for a replacement.

New features:

- borg create –chunker-params ... to configure the chunker, fixes #16 (attic #302, attic #300, and somehow also #41). This can be used to reduce memory usage caused by chunk management overhead, so borg does not create a huge chunks index/repo index and eats all your RAM if you back up lots of data in huge files (like VM disk images). See docs/misc/create_chunker-params.txt for more information.

- borg info now reports chunk counts in the chunk index.

- borg create –compression 0..9 to select zlib compression level, fixes #66 (attic #295).

- borg init –encryption repokey (to store the encryption key into the repo), fixes #85

- improve at-end error logging, always log exceptions and set exit_code=1

- LoggedIO: better error checks / exceptions / exception handling

- implement –remote-path to allow non-default-path borg locations, #125
- implement –umask M and use 077 as default umask for better security, #117
- borg check: give a named single archive to it, fixes #139
- cache sync: show progress indication
- cache sync: reimplement the chunk index merging in C

Bug fixes:

- fix segfault that happened for unreadable files (chunker: n needs to be a signed size_t), #116
- fix the repair mode, #144
- repo delete: add destroy to allowed rpc methods, fixes issue #114
- more compatible repository locking code (based on mkdir), maybe fixes #92 (attic #317, attic #201).
- better Exception msg if no Borg is installed on the remote repo server, #56
- create a RepositoryCache implementation that can cope with >2GiB, fixes attic #326.
- fix Traceback when running check –repair, attic #232
- clarify help text, fixes #73.
- add help string for –no-files-cache, fixes #140

Other changes:

- improved docs:
  - added docs/misc directory for misc. writeups that won't be included "as is" into the html docs.
  - document environment variables and return codes (attic #324, attic #52)
  - web site: add related projects, fix web site url, IRC #borgbackup
  - Fedora/Fedora-based install instructions added to docs
  - Cygwin-based install instructions added to docs
  - updated AUTHORS
  - add FAQ entries about redundancy / integrity
  - clarify that borg extract uses the cwd as extraction target
  - update internals doc about chunker params, memory usage and compression
  - added docs about development
  - add some words about resource usage in general
  - document how to backup a raw disk
  - add note about how to run borg from virtual env
  - add solutions for (ll)fuse installation problems
  - document what borg check does, fixes #138
  - reorganize borgbackup.github.io sidebar, prev/next at top
  - deduplicate and refactor the docs / README.rst
- use borg-tmp as prefix for temporary files / directories
- short prune options without "keep-" are deprecated, do not suggest them
- improved tox configuration
- remove usage of unittest.mock, always use mock from pypi
- use entrypoints instead of scripts, for better use of the wheel format and modern installs

---

- add requirements.d/development.txt and modify tox.ini
- use travis-ci for testing based on Linux and (new) OS X
- use coverage.py, pytest-cov and codecov.io for test coverage support

I forgot to list some stuff already implemented in 0.23.0, here they are:

New features:

- efficient archive list from manifest, meaning a big speedup for slow repo connections and "list <repo>", "delete <repo>", "prune" (attic #242, attic #167)
- big speedup for chunks cache sync (esp. for slow repo connections), fixes #18
- hashindex: improve error messages

Other changes:

- explicitly specify binary mode to open binary files
- some easy micro optimizations

Version 0.23.0 (2015-06-11)

Incompatible changes (compared to attic, fork related):

- changed sw name and cli command to "borg", updated docs
- package name (and name in urls) uses "borgbackup" to have less collisions
- changed repo / cache internal magic strings from ATTIC* to BORG*, changed cache location to .cache/borg/ - this means that it currently won't accept attic repos (see issue #21 about improving that)

Bug fixes:

- avoid defect python-msgpack releases, fixes attic #171, fixes attic #185
- fix traceback when trying to do unsupported passphrase change, fixes attic #189
- datetime does not like the year 10.000, fixes attic #139
- fix "info" all archives stats, fixes attic #183
- fix parsing with missing microseconds, fixes attic #282
- fix misleading hint the fuse ImportError handler gave, fixes attic #237
- check unpacked data from RPC for tuple type and correct length, fixes attic #127
- fix Repository._active_txn state when lock upgrade fails
- give specific path to xattr.is_enabled(), disable symlink setattr call that always fails
- fix test setup for 32bit platforms, partial fix for attic #196
- upgraded versioneer, PEP440 compliance, fixes attic #257

New features:

- less memory usage: add global option –no-cache-files
- check –last N (only check the last N archives)
- check: sort archives in reverse time order
- rename repo::oldname newname (rename repository)
- create -v output more informative
- create –progress (backup progress indicator)
- create –timestamp (utc string or reference file/dir)

- create: if "-" is given as path, read binary from stdin

- extract: if –stdout is given, write all extracted binary data to stdout

- extract –sparse (simple sparse file support)

- extra debug information for 'fread failed'

- delete <repo> (deletes whole repo + local cache)

- FUSE: reflect deduplication in allocated blocks

- only allow whitelisted RPC calls in server mode

- normalize source/exclude paths before matching

- use posix_fadvise to not spoil the OS cache, fixes attic #252

- toplevel error handler: show tracebacks for better error analysis

- sigusr1 / sigint handler to print current file infos - attic PR #286

- RPCError: include the exception args we get from remote

Other changes:

- source: misc. cleanups, pep8, style

- docs and faq improvements, fixes, updates

- cleanup crypto.pyx, make it easier to adapt to other AES modes

- do os.fsync like recommended in the python docs

- source: Let chunker optionally work with os-level file descriptor.

- source: Linux: remove duplicate os.fsencode calls

- source: refactor _open_rb code a bit, so it is more consistent / regular

- source: refactor indicator (status) and item processing

- source: use py.test for better testing, flake8 for code style checks

- source: fix tox >=2.0 compatibility (test runner)

- pypi package: add python version classifiers, add FreeBSD to platforms

Attic Changelog

Here you can see the full list of changes between each Attic release until Borg forked from Attic:

Version 0.17

(bugfix release, released on X)

- Fix hashindex ARM memory alignment issue (#309)

- Improve hashindex error messages (#298)

Version 0.16

(bugfix release, released on May 16, 2015)

- Fix typo preventing the security confirmation prompt from working (#303)

- Improve handling of systems with improperly configured file system encoding (#289)

- Fix "All archives" output for attic info. (#183)

- More user friendly error message when repository key file is not found (#236)

- Fix parsing of iso 8601 timestamps with zero microseconds (#282)

Version 0.15

(bugfix release, released on Apr 15, 2015)

- xattr: Be less strict about unknown/unsupported platforms (#239)

- Reduce repository listing memory usage (#163).

- Fix BrokenPipeError for remote repositories (#233)

- Fix incorrect behavior with two character directory names (#265, #268)

- Require approval before accessing relocated/moved repository (#271)

- Require approval before accessing previously unknown unencrypted repositories (#271)

- Fix issue with hash index files larger than 2GB.

- Fix Python 3.2 compatibility issue with noatime open() (#164)

- Include missing pyx files in dist files (#168)

Version 0.14

(feature release, released on Dec 17, 2014)

- Added support for stripping leading path segments (#95) "attic extract –strip-segments X"

- Add workaround for old Linux systems without acl_extended_file_no_follow (#96)

- Add MacPorts' path to the default openssl search path (#101)

- HashIndex improvements, eliminates unnecessary IO on low memory systems.

- Fix "Number of files" output for attic info. (#124)

- limit create file permissions so files aren't read while restoring

- Fix issue with empty xattr values (#106)

Version 0.13

(feature release, released on Jun 29, 2014)

- Fix sporadic "Resource temporarily unavailable" when using remote repositories

- Reduce file cache memory usage (#90)

- Faster AES encryption (utilizing AES-NI when available)

- Experimental Linux, OS X and FreeBSD ACL support (#66)

- Added support for backup and restore of BSDFlags (OSX, FreeBSD) (#56)

- Fix bug where xattrs on symlinks were not correctly restored

- Added cachedir support. CACHEDIR.TAG compatible cache directories can now be excluded using `--exclude-caches` (#74)

- Fix crash on extreme mtime timestamps (year 2400+) (#81)

- Fix Python 3.2 specific lockf issue (EDEADLK)

Version 0.12

(feature release, released on April 7, 2014)

- Python 3.4 support (#62)

- Various documentation improvements a new style

- `attic mount` now supports mounting an entire repository not only individual archives (#59)

- Added option to restrict remote repository access to specific path(s): `attic serve --restrict-to-path X` (#51)

- Include "all archives" size information in "–stats" output. (#54)

- Added `--stats` option to `attic delete` and `attic prune`

- Fixed bug where `attic prune` used UTC instead of the local time zone when determining which archives to keep.

- Switch to SI units (Power of 1000 instead 1024) when printing file sizes

Version 0.11

(feature release, released on March 7, 2014)

- New "check" command for repository consistency checking (#24)

- Documentation improvements

- Fix exception during "attic create" with repeated files (#39)

- New "–exclude-from" option for attic create/extract/verify.

- Improved archive metadata deduplication.

- "attic verify" has been deprecated. Use "attic extract –dry-run" instead.

- "attic prune –hourly|daily|..." has been deprecated. Use "attic prune –keep-hourly|daily|..." instead.

- Ignore xattr errors during "extract" if not supported by the filesystem. (#46)

Version 0.10

(bugfix release, released on Jan 30, 2014)

- Fix deadlock when extracting 0 sized files from remote repositories

- "–exclude" wildcard patterns are now properly applied to the full path not just the file name part (#5).

- Make source code endianness agnostic (#1)

Version 0.9

(feature release, released on Jan 23, 2014)

- Remote repository speed and reliability improvements.

- Fix sorting of segment names to ignore NFS left over files. (#17)

- Fix incorrect display of time (#13)

- Improved error handling / reporting. (#12)

- Use fcntl() instead of flock() when locking repository/cache. (#15)

- Let ssh figure out port/user if not specified so we don't override .ssh/config (#9)

- Improved libcrypto path detection (#23).

Version 0.8.1

(bugfix release, released on Oct 4, 2013)

- Fix segmentation fault issue.

Version 0.8

(feature release, released on Oct 3, 2013)

- Fix xattr issue when backing up sshfs filesystems (#4)
- Fix issue with excessive index file size (#6)
- Support access of read only repositories.
- **New syntax to enable repository encryption:** attic init –encryption="none|passphrase|keyfile".
- Detect and abort if repository is older than the cache.

Version 0.7

(feature release, released on Aug 5, 2013)

- Ported to FreeBSD
- Improved documentation
- Experimental: Archives mountable as FUSE filesystems.
- The "user." prefix is no longer stripped from xattrs on Linux

Version 0.6.1

(bugfix release, released on July 19, 2013)

- Fixed an issue where mtime was not always correctly restored.

Version 0.6

First public release on July 9, 2013

Authors

Borg authors ("The Borg Collective")

- Thomas Waldmann <tw@waldmann-edv.de>
- Antoine Beaupré <anarcat@debian.org>
- Radek Podgorny <radek@podgorny.cz>
- Yuri D'Elia
- Michael Hanselmann <public@hansmi.ch>
- Teemu Toivanen <public@profnetti.fi>
- Marian Beermann <public@enkore.de>
- Martin Hostettler <textshell@uchuujin.de>
- Daniel Reichelt <hacking@nachtgeist.net>
- Lauri Niskanen <ape@ape3000.com>
- Abdel-Rahman A. (Abogical)

Borg is a fork of Attic.

Attic authors

Attic is written and maintained by Jonas Borgström and various contributors:

Attic Development Lead

- Jonas Borgström <jonas@borgstrom.se>

Attic Patches and Suggestions

- Brian Johnson
- Cyril Roussillon
- Dan Christensen
- Jeremy Maitin-Shepard
- Johann Klähn
- Petros Moisiadis
- Thomas Waldmann

BLAKE2

Borg includes BLAKE2: Copyright 2012, Samuel Neves <sneves@dei.uc.pt>, licensed under the terms of the CC0, the OpenSSL Licence, or the Apache Public License 2.0.

Slicing CRC32

Borg includes a fast slice-by-8 implementation of CRC32, Copyright 2011-2015 Stephan Brumme, licensed under the terms of a zlib license. See http://create.stephan-brumme.com/crc32/

Folding CRC32

Borg includes an extremely fast folding implementation of CRC32, Copyright 2013 Intel Corporation, licensed under the terms of the zlib license.

xxHash

XXH64, a fast non-cryptographic hash algorithm. Copyright 2012-2016 Yann Collet, licensed under a BSD 2-clause license.

License

Copyright (C) 2015-2017 The Borg Collective (see AUTHORS file)
Copyright (C) 2010-2014 Jonas Borgström <jonas@borgstrom.se>
All rights reserved.

Redistribution and use in source and binary forms, with or without
modification, are permitted provided that the following conditions
are met:

1. Redistributions of source code must retain the above copyright
   notice, this list of conditions and the following disclaimer.
2. Redistributions in binary form must reproduce the above copyright
   notice, this list of conditions and the following disclaimer in
   the documentation and/or other materials provided with the
   distribution.
3. The name of the author may not be used to endorse or promote
   products derived from this software without specific prior
   written permission.

THIS SOFTWARE IS PROVIDED BY THE COPYRIGHT HOLDERS AND CONTRIBUTORS
"AS IS" AND ANY EXPRESS OR IMPLIED WARRANTIES, INCLUDING, BUT NOT
LIMITED TO, THE IMPLIED WARRANTIES OF MERCHANTABILITY AND FITNESS FOR
A PARTICULAR PURPOSE ARE DISCLAIMED. IN NO EVENT SHALL THE COPYRIGHT
OWNER OR CONTRIBUTORS BE LIABLE FOR ANY DIRECT, INDIRECT, INCIDENTAL,
SPECIAL, EXEMPLARY, OR CONSEQUENTIAL DAMAGES (INCLUDING, BUT NOT
LIMITED TO, PROCUREMENT OF SUBSTITUTE GOODS OR SERVICES; LOSS OF USE,
DATA, OR PROFITS; OR BUSINESS INTERRUPTION) HOWEVER CAUSED AND ON ANY
THEORY OF LIABILITY, WHETHER IN CONTRACT, STRICT LIABILITY, OR TORT
(INCLUDING NEGLIGENCE OR OTHERWISE) ARISING IN ANY WAY OUT OF THE USE
OF THIS SOFTWARE, EVEN IF ADVISED OF THE POSSIBILITY OF SUCH DAMAGE.